Prince and Popular Music

Prince and Popular Music

Critical Perspectives on an Interdisciplinary Life

Edited by
Mike Alleyne and Kirsty Fairclough

BLOOMSBURY ACADEMIC
NEW YORK • LONDON • OXFORD • NEW DELHI • SYDNEY

BLOOMSBURY ACADEMIC
Bloomsbury Publishing Inc
1385 Broadway, New York, NY 10018, USA
50 Bedford Square, London, WC1B 3DP, UK
29 Earlsfort Terrace, Dublin 2, Ireland

BLOOMSBURY, BLOOMSBURY ACADEMIC and the Diana logo are trademarks of Bloomsbury Publishing Plc

First published in the United States of America 2020
This paperback edition published in 2022

Volume Editors' Part of the Work © Mike Alleyne and Kirsty Fairclough, 2020
Each chapter © of Contributor

Cover design: Louise Dugdale
Cover image © Kristin Zschomler, 2020

All rights reserved. No part of this publication may be reproduced or transmitted in any form or by any means, electronic or mechanical, including photocopying, recording, or any information storage or retrieval system, without prior permission in writing from the publishers.

Bloomsbury Publishing Inc does not have any control over, or responsibility for, any third-party websites referred to or in this book. All internet addresses given in this book were correct at the time of going to press. The author and publisher regret any inconvenience caused if addresses have changed or sites have ceased to exist, but can accept no responsibility for any such changes.

Whilst every effort has been made to locate copyright holders the publishers would be grateful to hear from any person(s) not here acknowledged.

Library of Congress Cataloging-in-Publication Data

Names: Alleyne, Mike (Michael Randolph) editor. | Fairclough-Isaacs, Kirsty, editor.
Title: Prince and popular music: critical perspectives on an interdisciplinary life / edited by Mike Alleyne and Kirsty Fairclough.
Description: New York: Bloomsbury Academic, 2020. | Includes bibliographical references and index. | Summary: "A holistic, academic assessment of Prince's life and legacy, exploring his multiple identities and the ways in which they were manifested through his recorded catalogue and audiovisual personae"–Provided by publisher.
Identifiers: LCCN 2019051406 | ISBN 9781501354656 (hardback) | ISBN 9781501354687 (pdf) | ISBN 9781501354663 (epub)
Subjects: LCSH: Prince–Criticism and interpretation. | Popular music–United States–History and criticism.
Classification: LCC ML420.P974 P75 2020 | DDC 782.66092 [B]–dc23
LC record available at https://lccn.loc.gov/2019051406

ISBN: HB: 978-1-5013-5465-6
PB: 978-1-5013-9175-0
ePDF: 978-1-5013-5468-7
eBook: 978-1-5013-5466-3

Typeset by Deanta Global Publishing Services, Chennai, India

To find out more about our authors and books visit www.bloomsbury.com and sign up for our newsletters.

Contents

Acknowledgements vii
Notes on contributors viii

Introduction *Mike Alleyne and Kirsty Fairclough* 1

Part One Sound and vision

1 Baby, I'm a star: Prince's *Purple Rain* *Jason Wood* 9
2 *Under the Cherry Moon*: Prince as his most authentic self *De Angela L. Duff* 15
3 Before the rain, 1979–84: How Prince got 'the look' *Casci Ritchie* 34
4 'Prettyman' in the mirror: Dandyism in Prince's Minneapolis *Karen Turman* 45
5 The sound of purple: Prince and the development of the Minneapolis Sound *Maciej Smółka* 56

Part Two Purple performance and presence

6 Glam slammed: Visual identity in Prince's *Lovesexy* *Mike Alleyne and Kirsty Fairclough* 67
7 For you: The neglected guitar style of Prince *Michael Ugrich* 76
8 To make purple, you need blue: Prince as the embodiment of the postmodern blues aesthetic *Tom Attah* 84
9 'Tears go here': Commemorating the Minneapolis Prince and the international Prince *Suzanne Wint* 102

Part Three Gender

10 Re-imagining masculinity: Prince's impact on millennial attitudes regarding gender expression *Natalie Clifford* 117
11 'We can't hate you, because we love you': A look at Prince, queerness, misogyny and feminism *Leah Stone McDaniel and Shannan Wilson* 129

12 'Flying the Seduction 747': Prince, humour and horizontal erotics
    Annie Potts   137

13 When were you mine?: Prince's legacy in the context of transgender
    history *Joy Ellison*   149

Part Four Politics and race

14 Prince: Introduction of a new breed leader *Kamilah Cummings*   161

15 'Microchip in your neck': Prince's 'War' *Zack Stiegler*   175

16 Prince: Conscious and strategic representations of race *Twila L. Perry*   184

17 It's all about what's in your mind: The origins of Prince's political
    consciousness *Crystal N. Wise*   198

Index   209

Acknowledgements

Mike's Acknowledgements:

Thanks to Leah at Bloomsbury and all who supported this book project, all who assisted with the 2017 Purple Reign conference event, particularly Ken Paulson and Dez Dickerson, and the MTSU Department of Recording Industry.

Kirsty's Acknowledgements:

Thank you to Leah and all at Bloomsbury for the support, the University of Salford for taking a chance on the conference, my son for being my greatest champion and, of course, Prince for bringing together a community of scholars and fans who continue to do the work.

Contributors

Mike Alleyne is Professor in the Department of Recording Industry at Middle Tennessee State University (MTSU), USA. He is the author of *The Essential Hendrix* (2020) and *The Encyclopedia of Reggae* (2012) and the contributing editor of *Rhythm Revolution* (2015). He has lectured internationally, published numerous book chapters and contributed articles to journals such as *Popular Music & Society*, *Rock Music Studies*, *Journal on the Art of Record Production*, the award-winning *Grove Dictionary of American Music*, *Popular Music History*, *Ethnomusicology Forum*, *Journal of Latin American and Caribbean Studies* and *Billboard* magazine, and in the online SAGE Business Case Series in Music Marketing.

Tom Attah is BMus Popular Music Course Leader at Leeds College of Art, UK. His research focusses on the effects of technology on blues music and blues culture. Tom's teaching and blues advocacy includes workshops, seminars, lectures and recitals delivered internationally. As a guitarist and singer, Tom performs solo, with acoustic duos and as leader of an electric band. Tom's media appearances include performances and documentaries for BBC Radio and Sky Corporation. Tom's journalistic writing regularly features in specialist music publications, and his original research papers and book reviews are published in internationally peer-reviewed journals.

Kamilah Cummings is Visiting Senior Professional Lecturer in writing and communications at DePaul University in Chicago, USA. She has presented on Prince at several academic conferences and symposia including *Purple Reign* at the University of Salford, Manchester, and the *Eye No: Prince Lovesexy Symposium* at New York University. Cummings has also published on Prince in the *Howard University Journal of Communications* and developed an interdisciplinary Prince course. A lover of House music, she has presented on House at Harvard University and taught her original course 'The House Chicago Built'. Her research interests include representations of Black identity in popular culture.

Natalie Clifford is an educator who has worked with youth in the fields of theatre, college access and sexual violence prevention. She has facilitated workshops on LGBTQ+ identities, masculinity, consent, healthy relationships, rape culture and teen dating violence with middle and high school students. Currently, she teaches emerging multilingual youth in San Antonio, Texas. She is passionate about using education to challenge injustice and social norms. She proudly came of age in Prince's hometown of Minneapolis, Minnesota. Prince's legacy of social justice provides inspiration for Ms Clifford in guiding young people to develop strong understandings of their purpose.

De Angela L. Duff is Industry Professor in Integrated Digital Media at New York University, USA. She curates music symposia – *BATDANCE: Prince Batman Soundtrack Symposium*, *EYE NO: Prince Lovesexy Symposium* and *Betty Davis – 'They Say I'm Different' Symposium* – speaks about music, design and technology at numerous conferences internationally, including *Black Portraiture[s] II-V* conferences, the *Prince from Minneapolis* symposium in Minneapolis, Minnesota, and the *Purple Reign* conference in Manchester, England, and produces, co-hosts and edits the Prince and Prince-related podcasts on Grown Folks Music's podcast network. You can view her past and present work at http://polishedsolid.com.

Joy Ellison is a PhD candidate in women's, gender, and sexuality studies at Ohio State University, USA. Their forthcoming dissertation documents transgender political movements and communities in the Midwestern United States from the post-Second World War to 2000. They are the author of the blog 'If We Knew Trans History', which seeks to make transgender history accessible to activists. Their academic work, cultural criticism and creative writing are available at www.jmellison.net.

Kirsty Fairclough is Associate Dean Research & Innovation in the School of Arts and Media at the University of Salford, UK. A speaker, author and event curator, Kirsty has published widely on popular culture and is the co-editor of *The Music Documentary: Acid Rock to Electropop* (Routledge), *The Arena Concert: Music, Media and Mass Entertainment* (Bloomsbury) and *Music/Video: Forms, Aesthetics, Media* (Bloomsbury). Kirsty's work has been published in *Senses of Cinema*, *Feminist Media Studies*, *SERIES* and *Celebrity Studies* journals and has been featured in the *Guardian*, *Creative Review* and on the BBC. She is Chair of Manchester Jazz Festival.

Twila L. Perry is Professor of Law and the Alexander P. Waugh Sr. Scholar at Rutgers University School of Law, USA, where she teaches in the areas of torts and family law. Most of her scholarship addresses the intersections of these subjects with issues of race, gender and class. During the past few years, she has also been writing about Prince and about opera.

Annie Potts is Professor, Head of Cultural Studies and Director of the New Zealand Centre for Human-Animal Studies at Te Whare Wānanga o Waitaha/University of Canterbury in Aotearoa, New Zealand. She teaches critical animal studies, critical sexuality studies, intersectionality, horror cinema, true crime and popular criminology. She is the author of *The Science/Fiction of Sex: Feminist Deconstruction and Vocabularies of Heterosex* (2003) and *Chicken* (2012), and co-author of *A New Zealand Book of Beasts: Animals in our Culture, History and Everyday Life* (2013), *Animals in Emergencies* (2014), and editor of *Sex and the Body* (2004) and *Meat Culture* (2016).

Casci Ritchie is an independent fashion historian and life-long fan of His Royal Badness. Having gained a BA Hons in fashion design and MA in fashion bodywear, she most recently completed an MLitt in dress and textile histories at the University of Glasgow. She has continued to develop her passion for twentieth-century fashion from creation to consumption with a particular interest in fashion in film and subcultures and hosts a regular film night focusing on costume design. Currently, she is researching all aspects of Prince's sartorial legacy and has presented her ongoing research all over the UK, Roubaix and Minneapolis.

Maciej Smółka is a scholar affiliated with the Jagiellonian University in Poland and specializes in popular music, popular culture and American studies. A critic, fan and researcher of popular music, his primary research concerns how music is being associated with cities. He published papers on such topics as music localities and identities, the music industry, and relations between culture, music and politics. He is an author of *Say Yes! to Michigan* (2017), a book about Sufjan Stevens's vision of the state of Michigan. He was a visiting researcher at Dickinson College in 2015 and the University of Minnesota in 2018.

Leah Stone McDaniel is a dynamic journalist, independent scholar, international speaker and brand marketing professional focused on emerging marketing mediums. Hailing from Cincinnati, Ohio, Leah attended the Ohio State University graduating with a dual degree in Marketing and International Business and obtained an MBA. from the Regis University. Throughout her brand management career, she has worked with industry leaders like Procter & Gamble and Kao USA Inc. Leah is a frequent contributor to *Atlanta Tribune, The Magazine* and other publications. Recently, her life-long fascination with the artist Prince led to speaking at the first global conference on his legacy.

Zack Stiegler is Associate Professor of communications media at Indiana University of Pennsylvania, USA, where he teaches courses on media theory and culture. His research has appeared in *Communication and the Public, Teaching and Learning in Medicine, Journal of Radio and Audio Media, Journal of Popular Music Studies, Javnost: The Public* and a number of edited volumes. He served as contributor and editor to the collection *Regulating the Web: Network Neutrality and the Fate of the Open Internet* (2012).

Karen Turman is Preceptor of French in the Department of Romance Languages and Literatures at Harvard University, USA. She earned her PhD (2013) in French literature with an emphasis in applied linguistics at the University of California, Santa Barbara, USA. Her interdisciplinary research interests include nineteenth-century Bohemian Paris, music and dance during the Jazz Age, fashion and popular culture studies, and teaching cultural competence to French language learners. Her essay on Prince, Josephine Baker and Claude McKay entitled 'Banana Skirts and Cherry Moons: Utopic French Myths in Prince's *Under the Cherry Moon*' will appear in the upcoming book *Prince and the Minneapolis Sound*.

Michael Ugrich is an active musician and a Minnesota native, currently working towards completion of dual M.M. Music History and M.M. Instrumental Conducting degrees from the University of South Dakota. He graduated with a bachelor's in Classical Guitar Performance from the University of Wisconsin-Superior in 2012. While enrolled, he was the recipient of the 2010 Matinee Musical Scholarship, winner of the 2010 UWS Orchestra and UWS Symphonic Band Concerto Competitions and recipient of the 2012 UWS Certificate in Outstanding Jazz Performance. As a graduate assistant at USD, Michael currently lectures the Rock 'N Roll History section.

Suzanne Wint is an independent ethnomusicologist in St. Paul, Minnesota, USA, who is researching public mourning in Minnesota in the wake of Prince's passing. She has taught at St Olaf College, De Paul University, Reed College and Northwestern University. Her research in Uganda examines the ways in which post-colonial subjects create transnational networks out of institutions founded by colonizers, specifically considering the case of Western classical music. She earned both her PhD in ethnomusicology and her master's in music history and theory from the University of Chicago.

Crystal Wise holds a PhD in literacy, language and culture and a graduate certificate in African American studies at the University of Michigan, USA. She is a postdoctoral research fellow at the University of Michigan, working on an interdisciplinary team to develop a curriculum for and with urban communities. She has published articles on innovative, effective and culturally responsive early literacy instruction and practices. She also studies African Americans' historical and contemporary language and literacy practices as acts of empowerment, resistance and liberation. She is a former public elementary school teacher from Gary, Indiana.

Jason Wood is a film curator and writer, and Artistic Director of HOME (a trading name of Greater Manchester Arts Centre Ltd.). His previous books include works on Mexican cinema, Nick Broomfield and Road Movies. He is currently completing a book on the British musical group Scritti Politti.

Introduction

Mike Alleyne and Kirsty Fairclough

Prince's sudden death on 21 April 2016 under dramatic and obscure circumstances provoked deep grief among his fans and also registered on the consciousness of others less attached to his music and creative personae. For audiences particularly concerned with popular music's histories, contexts and meanings, Prince's passing demanded prompt re-examination of his eclectic and spectacular career and its place(s) within the cultural catalogue of exceptional artistry. As we considered the enormous void created by Prince's absence and the need to facilitate formal recognition of his highly influential career, we began to tentatively discuss the possibility of an academic conference that would also be accessible and appealing to Prince fans. Out of those loosely framed ideas arose Purple Reign, the first such academic conference solely focused on Prince.[1] It took place from 24 to 26 May 2017 at the University of Salford in Manchester, England, bringing together academics and fans alike, thereby reinforcing the scope of his appeal and the extent to which Prince's work invites wide-ranging interpretation. The inclusion of a public-facing keynote by Dez Dickerson, formerly of The Revolution,[2] added a dimension to the event which cemented its integrity and relevance given Dickerson's first-hand knowledge of Prince's creative process and musical output. The event attracted scholars and Prince followers from all over the world, essentially creating a new network which has since reconvened in both small and large units at other conferences, concerts or social gatherings.

The broad scope of conference topics and the thematic and spatial logistics involved in compiling the chapters contained in this book meant that many contributions could not be included. Rather like the process of collating a Prince album, there was much material left in the vault after final selections were made, with choices determined by the premise of creating an appropriately cohesive collection. The anthology of selected papers from the 2017 Purple Reign conference consequently incorporates multiple methodologies.[3] The selections include ethnographic, musicological, sociological, gender studies and cultural studies approaches to analysing Prince's career. Contributors have utilized widely varied approaches, all of which fuse the academic with the actual, the philosophical with fandom, and the conceptual with the textual fabric of Prince's work. Throughout the course of the book we have attempted to provide an assessment of Prince's life and legacy, exploring his multiple identities and the ways in which they were manifested through his recorded catalogue and audiovisual personae through a range of disciplinary lenses.

Prince's position in popular culture has as yet undergone only limited academic scrutiny, and even less so in peer-reviewed print publications since his death in 2016.

Our intention is that the book will become one of the foundational templates for posthumous academic examination of Prince, encompassing the many layers of his cultural and creative impact. With this in mind, the book discusses key components of Prince's identities and the various means whereby he successfully projected them into global public consciousness. It is a holistic assessment of his life and legacy and is structured into four thematic parts – 'Sound and vision', 'Performance and presence', 'Gender' and 'Politics and race' – and features meaningful snapshots of perceptions of Prince's legacy a year after his death, with those perspectives remaining acutely relevant several years later.

Although the lack of critical attention that Prince has received is gradually changing with renewed and widened interest in his career, we hope that this book will become a useful critical resource providing pivotal points of analytical departure. The scope of Prince's output reaches far beyond music and has created significant impact in the fields of fashion, film and visual art, and the collection does not purport to cover Prince's entire impact on the global cultural landscape, but instead aims to draw attention to the inherent complexities of what might seem to be a typical musical career to the casual observer.

Long before his passing, Prince's artistic boldness and refusal to be typecast within genre boundaries had helped establish his legendary status. Although his frequent changes of direction unsettled critics and some audiences, he maintained a high degree of commercial success within and beyond his first decade as a recording artist, film star and image icon. In the immediate aftermath of Prince's death, the recognition of his work and the extent of his posthumous presence were clearly both critical and commercial. Acknowledgement of this duality permeates the chapters and is itself vital to comprehending the scope of the Prince phenomenon. It is this ability to confound critics and primarily make music for himself rather than pandering to momentary musical fads that made him at once impossible to understand as well as deeply intriguing. His career mosaic is further complicated by intermittent business and artistic missteps with, for example, the observation by tour manager Alan Leeds that 'Prince's music in the 90s suffered because, for the first time, he allowed outside trends to influence his work' (Draper 99). The later decades of Prince's work remain the subject of intense, polarizing debate, and there are undoubtedly other interpretations of his attempts to integrate hip hop aesthetics into his work with mixed results. This is also coupled with ambivalent approaches to digital technologies – musical and otherwise – and an overt instinct to exert psychological, creative and even emotional control over both his professional and personal associates. Nonetheless, Prince's ability to supersede such inconsistencies and idiosyncrasies and in so doing to create a rich artistic legacy is at the heart of this anthology.

The immediate posthumous sales impact of Prince's records was directly indicative of the extent to which his music had become embedded within the fabric of listeners' lives. In the week ending 14 May 2016,[4] Prince became 'the first act to concurrently chart five albums in the top 10 of the Billboard 200' album chart. In another first, Prince held the top ten positions on Billboard's Catalog Albums Chart. In the previous chart week, *The Very Best of Prince* held the number one position, immediately followed by the thirteen-times platinum *Purple Rain* soundtrack (Caulfield). The resurrection of his former backing bands The Revolution and the New Power Generation (NPG) as tribute touring acts points to a sustained public hunger for Prince's work (as well as a need for collective mourning and celebration among fans), though it simultaneously raises questions about the validity of concert experiences attempting to simulate the presence of an absent group leader.

The stories of the full historical and musical contexts of Prince's albums are still unfolding as posthumous reissues that began with 2016's *4Ever* and 2017's *Purple Rain Deluxe Edition* and albums of previously unreleased material (2018's *A Piano & A Microphone 1983* and 2019's *Originals*) reach the marketplace through his estate and Warner Records (formerly Warner Bros.).[5] Given the reportedly overwhelming amount of unreleased archival recordings formerly housed in Prince's Paisley Park complex and now relocated to California, other parts of the narrative chronology are certain to be expanded in the coming years. In mid-2019, the Prince estate's vault archivist Michael Howe confirmed that such compilations are underway and that years of work will be involved in digitizing the recorded contents (Sinclair). The seemingly haphazard chronological sequence of the reissues suggests that critical re-examination of Prince's evolution as a recording artist will be a continual process. It is somewhat ironic that Prince's prolific recording output which displeased Warner Bros. while he was under contract to the label is now likely to be mirrored in the volume of material issued through that same outlet and other imprints.[6] In addition, international complexities have arisen, as demonstrated by the 2019 German four-disc Deluxe Edition CD/DVD re-release of the 1987 *Sign 'o' the Times* concert package. Issued only in Germany with video playback limited by region due to licensing restrictions, this is possibly the most comprehensive posthumous document contribution to date, containing hours of extensive additional interview material and a detailed booklet of reproduced memorabilia. However, it can only be accessed by a fraction of the potential global audience, raising the spectre of the limited availability of future items.

At the time of writing, even the very issue of administrative control over Prince's estate remained contentious. The identities of the lawful heirs to the estate were finally confirmed in a Minnesota court a year after Prince's death, but even before this announcement the heirs objected to the manner of the estate's management by Comerica, the banking entity that replaced the Bremer Trust (Rys; Christman; AP). The estate's protective tenacity was first revealed when it blocked the release of the *Deliverance* EP by George Ian Boxill, formerly Prince's recording engineer, claiming that he had violated the terms of his contract. In April 2019, a Minnesota court issued a judgement of $3.96 million against Boxill for copyright infringement of Prince recordings made between 2006 and 2008 (Eggertsen; Savage).[7]

In March 2016, shortly before his death, publication news of Prince's autobiography *The Beautiful Ones* was announced, though the work was ultimately incomplete, consisting of little more than fifty handwritten pages (Cain). Released in October 2019, this volume might either illuminate or obscure the essence of Prince's own life. This autobiographical fragment seems likely to provoke more questions than answers, but given Prince's emphasis on creating an artistic mystique, it may be an ironically appropriate posthumous literary statement.

Prince's music, films and performance aesthetic are presented here in a wide range of chapters which explore his vast and varying output. His work in film from *Purple Rain* (1984), his first and indeed critically and commercially most successful cinematic foray, helped to cement his legendary status. Pursuit of his muse in *Under the Cherry Moon* (1986) bemused most audiences, and the critical and commercial failure of *Graffiti Bridge* (1990) allowed Prince a different outlet for his talent. But none was as iconic as his first attempt at putting himself onto celluloid. Emerging as Prince's record sales finally began to match his prodigious output and his behaviour, *Purple Rain* was the epitome of his musical prowess. Capitalizing on the huge sales of the pre-release album of the same name, which appeared in stores some months prior to the film's release, selling 1.5 million copies in America in its first week alone, *Purple Rain* was a perfect synthesis of rock 'n' roll fable and autobiography.

Prince was lauded critically and commercially for his live shows. Anyone who saw a Prince show was in no doubt that they were in the presence of musical greatness. He was a performer who channelled talent and performance prowess as well as racial and gender subversion in often kinetic ways in the spaces he occupied. Prince often combined an overt expression of sexuality in his performances, an often perceived flamboyance in his costuming and moreover challenged notions of hegemonic masculinity – especially Black masculinity – perpetuated within American society and by his male contemporaries.

Prince's styling has left a subversive mark upon popular culture, one that expands expressions of gender and eroticism for both musical performers and the consumers of his image and music.

As Nancy Holland has argued in her paper 'Prince: Postmodern Icon',

> His music provides the basis for deconstructing the obvious hierarchies of race, gender, and sexuality, but also those of the sacred and the profane, the writer/composer/producer and the performer, and even Self and the Other. He touched the hearts and lives of a far wider audience than any theorist and helped create a new cultural climate without any apparent awareness of academic postmodernism. This opens the possibility for a deconstruction on the meta-level of another traditional hierarchy, the one between reason and intuition, or put differently, between words and music. (Holland, 2017)

Unusually, given the overtly regressive aspects of the music industry at the time Prince emerged and in subsequent years, he achieved huge global commercial and critical success throughout his lifetime, despite his rejection of conventional notions of masculinity present in the music industry throughout his career. One of the primary reasons for this was his unique use of stage presentation, including costume and other aesthetic markers, such as his dance style which subverted traditional understandings of masculinity. Prince emerged as what appeared to be a full-fledged artist in the 1970s and rapidly achieved global recognition through the late 1980s through to his death.

The explicit eroticism of Prince's performance and costuming also played into his defiance of convention and categorization. Specifically, he used choreography to aid his rebellious aesthetic. To see Prince's choreography live was thrilling: he traversed a stage both with grace and style and combined it with unambiguous sexuality. Prince essentially created his own artistic presentation and began to reimagine the possibilities of gender and performance in music and popular culture more broadly. It is these aspects that the 'Performance and presence' and 'Gender' sections of the book interrogate. They are concerned with the ways in which Prince's risk-taking in his own gender expression created space for others to find freedom in exploring expressions of gender nonconformity and how he invented new possibilities within dominant cultural constructions of masculinity.

Prince is one of the few American artists whose career as an established, respected act spans the distasteful conservatism of Ronald Reagan in the 1980s through to the unexpected ascent and progressive perspectives of Barack Obama in the 2000s. Prince lived long enough to witness the materialization of presidential political polar opposites, representing ideals which he either spoke against or supported. One can only theorize as to the likely nature of his social commentary if he had also witnessed the dawn of the anachronistic and prejudice-tainted Trump administration. While many articles in the media have described Prince as an artist who traversed boundaries of genre, politics, gender and race, there has been little in-depth exploration of any of Prince's relationships with these issues, and particularly absent to the issue of race. Indeed, media treatment of Prince has often suggested that race was not important to him or that somehow he had 'transcended' race. In the early years of his fame, the mainstream media often celebrated Prince as a kind of 'post-racial' icon and Prince himself contributed to the confusion about his racial identity – a conscious and strategic response to the racialized and often racist structure of the recording industry of that time.

The chapters herein suggest that race was indeed a factor of central importance throughout Prince's life and career. At important junctures in his life and career, Prince made conscious and strategic choices in his representation of race that reflected issues and dilemmas of both historical and contemporary relevance in the lives of many African Americans.

This book's analysis of Prince as an artist is wide and situates him as one of the most liberated artists of the twentieth century who sits within a musical history of which he is one of the revolutionaries who challenged the dominant classist, racist and sexist systems who attempt to repress the desires of others. It is our hope that the scholarship contained within will help to propel further analysis of his vast output and keep his legacy alive for many more generations to discover.

Notes

1 In January 2017, Yale University held a two-day dual-focused event titled *Blackstar Rising & The Purple Reign: Celebrating the Legacies of David Bowie and Prince*.
2 Dez Dickerson was interviewed by Ken Paulson, Dean of the College of Media & Entertainment at Middle Tennessee State University.

3. One essay written by this book's editors, 'Glam Slammed: Visual Identity in Prince's *Lovesexy*', is adapted from a paper presented at the June 2018 Prince Lovesexy Symposium that took place in New York.
4. *Billboard* noted that the 14 May chart reflected 'activity in the week ending April 28, the first full tracking week following Prince's death'. It is also noted that Prince's posthumous chart dominance was aided by a change in chart rules in 2009 regarding previously separate listings of catalogue and current titles. Artists such as Michael Jackson and The Beatles would have preceded Prince's feat if current chart rules had been in effect during their respective commercial peaks (Caulfield).
5. At the end of May 2019, Warner Bros. Records announced it was rebranding as Warner Records and that it would have a new logo.
6. Not all of the posthumous releases have been issued through one label, as post-Warner releases of 1996's *Emancipation*, 1996's *Chaos and Disorder*, and 1995's previously unreleased *The VERSACE Experience: Prelude to Gold* have all appeared on Sony's Legacy imprint.
7. The BBC reported that the estate was awarded '$3 million for breach of contract with a further $960,000 to cover costs' (Savage).

Works cited

Associated Press. 'Prince Estate Taking over Management of Paisley Park from Graceland Holdings'. *Billboard*, 27 Aug. 2019, https://www.billboard.com/articles/business/8528477/prince-estate-paisley-park-management-graceland.

Cain, Sian. 'Prince's "Deeply Personal" Memoir Announced for October'. *The Guardian*, 22 Apr. 2019, https://www.theguardian.com/books/2019/apr/22/prince-memoir-announced-october-the-beautiful-ones.

Caulfield, Keith. 'Prince Sets Record with Five Albums in Top 10 of Billboard 200 Chart'. *Billboard*, 3 May 2016, https://www.billboard.com/articles/columns/chart-beat/7356812/prince-sets-record-five-albums-top-10-billboard-200.

Christman, Ed. 'Prince Heirs Object to Bank's Request for More Freedom in Managing Estate'. *Billboard*, 15 March 2017, https://www.billboard.com/articles/news/7727830/prince-heirs-object-to-banks-request-for-more-freedom-in-managing-estate.

Draper, Jason. *Prince: Life & Times* (Revised and Updated Edition). New York: Chartwell, 2016.

Eggertsen, Chris. 'Engineer Ordered to Pay $4 Million to Prince's Estate over Unauthorized "Deliverance" EP'. *Billboard*, 8 April 2019, https://www.billboard.com/articles/business/legal-and-management/8506389/prince-engineer-deliverance-ep-4-million-ruling.

Holland, Nancy. 'Prince: Postmodern Icon'. *Journal of African American Studies* 21 (2017): 1–17. 10.1007/s12111-017-9363-7.

Rys, Dan. 'Judge Determines Prince Heirs in Estate Hearing'. *Billboard*, 19 May 2017, https://www.billboard.com/articles/business/7801017/judge-determines-prince-heirs-estate.

Savage, Mark. 'Prince Estate Wins £3m Ruling over Engineer's Unauthorised EP'. *BBC News*, 9 April 2019, https://www.bbc.com/news/entertainment-arts-47866455.

Sinclair, Paul. 'Interview: Prince's Vault Archivist, Michael Howe, Talks to SDE'. *Super Deluxe Edition*, 27 June, 2019, http://www.superdeluxeedition.com/interview/princes-archivist-michael-howe-talks-to-sde/.

Part One

Sound and vision

1

Baby, I'm a star

Prince's *Purple Rain*

Jason Wood

From the relatively early days of cinema, figures from the world of popular music have been cast in acting roles. The reasons are legion and run from a desire to maximize branding to a drive to capitalize on a specific audience, with teenagers being a recurring target demographic, and, on relatively few occasions, to an actual ability to act. Both Harry Belafonte and Frank Sinatra certainly had something of the actor about them.

In the 1950s and 1960s it became relatively commonplace for figures such as Elvis Presley, Cliff Richard, The Dave Clark Five and The Beatles to feature in movies specifically crafted to trade on their tidal waves of popularity. *Head* (Bob Rafelson, 1968[1]) and *Slade in Flame* (Richard Loncraine, 1975[2]) seemed to kill off the pop band star vehicle for good. But then the phoenix rose from the ashes when The Spice Girls were given their own movie.[3] If only, as Cher sang, 'I could turn back time.'[4]

What is relatively clear is that most music performers don't have to struggle to make it as actors, treading the boards and appearing in B-movie-type fare (or worse still, on television – that is, before it became the new cinema); by the time they are in the main cast in motion pictures, they are already famous. The opportunity to appear on screen also usually corresponds with that moment when they are about to transcend stardom. To quote Jean-Luc Godard's *Alphaville* (1965), they 'suffer a fate worse than death', they 'become a legend'. This legendary status turns them into living brands, which presents to music and film executives the potential to make an awful lot of money.

Though he was already a star by the time of *Purple Rain* (1984), his first and, in fact *only*, critically and commercially most successful big screen endeavour, the film helped to cement the legend of Prince Rogers Nelson. Emerging as Prince's record sales finally began to match his prodigious output and with him behaving as if he were already a star (certainly in his reserving the right to dress without regard for convention, and this in the face of a relative lack of airplay for extremely personal LPs such as *Dirty Mind*, 1980, and *Controversy*, 1981), the film was lightning in a bottle. Capitalizing on the huge sales of the pre-release album of the same name, which appeared in stores some months prior to the film's release, shifting 1.5 million copies in America in its first week alone, *Purple Rain* was a perfect synthesis of rock 'n' roll fable and autobiography.

But before returning to *Purple Rain* in more specific detail we need to lay a little more pop star on film groundwork, as a number of more general observations that follow are pertinent in regard to Prince. They also perhaps help to provide some context as to why his parallel big screen stardom burned both brightly and briefly.

As the counterculture began to take hold in the 1960s the casting of pop stars became less about brand and profit, and more about a desire to capture a spirit of rebellion or mystique. Directors sought a certain 'otherness' – that elusive quality that separates stars from mere mortals. One immediately thinks of Marianne Faithful in Jack Cardiff's *The Girl on a Motorcycle* (1968), Mick Jagger in Donald Cammell and Nicolas Roeg's *Performance* (1970), Dennis Wilson and James Taylor in Monte Hellman's *Two-Lane Blacktop* (1971) and Bob Dylan in Sam Peckinpah's *Pat Garrett and Billy the Kid* (1973, also featuring Kris Kristofferson). David Essex impressed in Claude Whatham's *That'll Be the Day* (1973, also featuring Ringo Starr), a role he reprised in Michael Apted's *Stardust* (1974, also featuring Adam Faith). Roeg proved himself perhaps the master of casting alchemy, persuading David Bowie to play an emaciated alien in *The Man Who Fell to Earth* (1976) and then drawing a good performance from Art Garfunkel in *Bad Timing* (1980).[5] John Lydon also got in on the act, proving rather credible as a sneering psychopath who makes crooked New York cop Harvey Keitel his quarry in Roberto Faenza's *Order of Death* (A.K.A *Cop Killer*, 1983). With his refusal to conform and the fusion of black R&B, white guitar rock and overtly sexual lyrics and persona, Prince certainly had one foot in the counterculture camp.

Throughout the 1980s, 1990s and 2000s a relatively select number of pop stars and high-profile musicians went on to achieve successful parallel careers: Tom Waits, Cher, Deborah Harry, Yasmin Bey (aka Mos Def), Will Oldham (who began as an actor, appearing in *Matewan*, 1987, for John Sayles), Iggy Pop and Justin Timberlake. But not Sting, never Sting, though he does appear in *Radio On* (1979), Chris Petit's majestic paean to the road movie genre and the new wave pop music of the early 1980s, a decade about to have Thatcher's stilettoed heel held unceremoniously and callously to its throat.

Other pop figures of the era and the intervening years had acting careers that more or less came and went: Bjork (*The Juniper Tree*, Nietzchka Keene, 1990, and *Dancer in the Dark*, Lars von Trier, 2000, which put her off acting for good), Grace Jones (*Vamp*, Richard Wenk, 1986), Michael Hutchence (*Dogs in Space*, Richard Lowenstein, 1986) and PJ Harvey (*The Book of Life*, Hal Hartley, 2000) to name but four. It's instructive to note that in each instance the aforementioned were playing variations of themselves; one of the prerequisites for casting a pop star is that the star should at least be recognizable to their fans or perform as a thinly veiled version of themselves.

Madonna tried desperately to run a parallel acting career, shining in *Desperately Seeking Susan* (Susan Seidelman, 1985), but then stumbled ever after in under-par fare such as *Body of Evidence* (Uli Edel, 1992), which traded without subtlety on the association with Madonna and sex. Madonna also offers evidence of a popular theory that many pop stars equip themselves well in their first role but then falter thereafter as they move away from roles for which they are tailor-made to those for which they are actually required to act. Five words: Mick Jagger in *Ned Kelly* (Tony Richardson,

1970). Standing in front of a movie camera and attempting to turn on the charisma is not always the same as taking the stage to an audience of screaming and adoring fans. Prince was unable to sustain a film career post his debut in *Purple Rain*, in which he appears as himself, filmed performing actual concerts around which a rather tenuous and hackneyed narrative is spun, though he did have two more stabs at it with the largely lamentable *Under the Cherry Moon* (1986) and the utterly regrettable *Graffiti Bridge* (1990).

Madonna, like Prince, with whom she battled it out for dominance in the MTV era, is a figure whose presence in a film project frequently extends to a vocal performance or theme song. This raises the awareness of the project in question while also appeasing those who follow the artist in order to buy their music. In short, it's another marketing and money-generating opportunity. It doesn't always work out, as was the case with Bowie's aborted (or reportedly rejected) score to *The Man Who Fell to Earth*. However, images from the film did adorn two Bowie albums of the period: *Station to Station* (1976) and *Low* (1977), again maximizing marketing impact. Prince of course wrote all the music for *Purple Rain*, which contained the anthemic *When Doves Cry* and the title track, and of course for his subsequent two movies. He would continue to offer his services as a soundtrack composer for others, perhaps most significantly to Tim Burton's *Batman* (1989) and Spike Lee's *Girl 6* (1996).

The casting of iconic reggae star Jimmy Cliff in *The Harder They Come* (Perry Henzell, 1972) certainly leant the film added authenticity in terms of the social, geographical and political Jamaican landscape it depicted. Described as 'Jamaica's very first feature', the presence of Cliff, who also contributed to the score after enjoying crossover success in America, would also have attracted the reggae fans and Jamaicans to whom the film would have wished to appeal. Following the cycle of exploitation of Black American cinema, the rise of hip hop culture led to a call to depict on screen with more integrity and diversity the lives of young Black Americans experiencing everyday racism, intolerance, deprivation and inequality. Films such as *Boyz n' the Hood* (John Singleton, 1991), *Juice* (Ernest R. Dickerson, 1992) and *Set It Off* (F. Gary Gray 1996) cast, respectively, Ice Cube, Tupac Shakur and Queen Latifah to great effect, utilizing their affinity with their communities, their spokesperson-like status and their rising popularity predominantly but not exclusively among Black consumers of African American film, music and culture.

Purple Rain goes to great lengths to satisfy Prince's Black and White fan bases. He appears as the son of a Black father and a White mother, and it is interesting how the audience at the club that is so central to the drama are almost exclusively mixed couples. Cynthia Rose observed that as 'well as depicting the perpetual conflict between men and women, with the only unity being carnal',[6] another motif of Prince's life and work, the fact that a number of the key relationships and issues at the heart of *Purple Rain* are Black and White in terms of race is recurrence enough that it can but assume clear resonance.

Readers of this chapter will no doubt be more than familiar with the film but in terms of a concise synopsis, it stars Prince as 'The Kid', a Minneapolis musician escaping a tumultuous home life through writing and performing with his band, The

Revolution. Desperate to avoid making the same mistakes as his errant, domineering father, 'The Kid' rises through the Minneapolis club scene and his rocky relationship with the singer, Apollonia. However, though 'The Kid's' incredible writing and performing prowess seems sure to set him on the path to romance, redemption and stardom, another musician is waiting in the wings to capsize his dreams and steal his crown.

The directorial debut of film school graduate Albert Magnoli, who would go on to collaborate with Prince on a number of subsequent pop promos,[7] Magnoli's suitability for the project was displayed in his debut short, *Jazz*, the tale of three Los Angeles jazz musicians. The short came to the attention of Prince's management who hired Magnoli to overhaul a script originally written and conceived by William Blinn. Softening some of the darker and more abrasive elements of the original script, but sadly not the view of women which was regressive even for the time, Magnoli began to develop the project to act as a vehicle to specifically bring to the spotlight Prince's performing talents and to showcase what would be an accompanying new album.

Shot almost exclusively in Prince's Minneapolis hometown and utilizing the legendary First Avenue Nightclub, this self-referential tale with a frankly hackneyed premise also unabashedly fuses Prince's personal and group history. There is an interesting element of 'reality' to the film in that almost all of the central characters are real-life Prince associates and appear under their own names. The rival is named Morris and is played by Morris Day of The Time, the Minneapolis funksters Prince played some part in discovering. One of the very few changes was the replacement of Vanity (lead singer of Vanity 6, original name Denise Matthews), one of Prince's female protégés, after an altercation between the pair. Her replacement was Apollonia Kotero, with the vocal group re-christened Apollonia 6, though Jennifer Beals[8] was apparently considered for the role.

Purple Rain also dramatizes in narrative terms 'The Kid's' rocky relationship with his screen father, Francis L, played by Clarence Williams III, to whom he tearfully dedicates the title track. Prince's real-life relationship with John L. Nelson, a jazz musician, is subject to debate, with a long-running theory, which may or may not carry credence, being that it was strained due to altercation between the pair when Prince was a teenager and was caught in flagrante in his room with a teenage girl. Internet theories abound.

What is clear is that the film, which was distributed by Prince's record label, Warner Bros, was able to compensate for its undoubted flaws and status as pure hagiography by having a genuine dramatic arc and by neatly folding the actual musical performances into the plot. Prince was required to act just little enough to not extinguish the brio and energy of the live concert footage. It also helped, of course, that the songs were first-rate, with *Let's Go Crazy* and *When Doves Cry* being registered as instant classics and topping the *Billboard* singles chart. The soundtrack album, and Prince's first record to feature The Revolution on the cover billing, would go on to sell over 25 million copies. As a film entity *Purple Rain* fed and fed off this success. Made on a budget of approximately $7.2 million, the film would gross $68 million at the US box office and over $80 million worldwide. At the 1985 Academy Awards, *Purple Rain* won Best

Soundtrack, and remains among the biggest selling soundtracks of all time. *Purple Rain* proved that Prince was able to be a star in the music studio, on the performing stage and on the cinema screen.

Having achieved bona-fide megastar status, *Purple Rain* bequeathed Prince another cinematic legacy, the opportunity to make another film. Using the power he now possessed in Hollywood, Prince took the director's reins for the ill-fated and poorly received *Under the Cherry Moon*. Working from a script by Becky Johnston,[9] the film features Prince as a gigolo living on the French Riviera who attempts to seduce a young heiress (Kristin Scott Thomas, making her feature debut) with a considerable trust fund. Shot by master DOP Michael Ballhaus, who would go on to work with Martin Scorsese (and photograph 1988's *Dirty Rotten Scoundrels* for Frank Oz, which in plot terms *Under the Cherry Moon* resembles, but minus the laughs), the film is to at least be admired for steadfastly refusing to repeat the formula that had served Prince on *Purple Rain* so well, though it does regrettably retain the former's objectification of women as sexual objects who are apt to be subject to humiliation.

It certainly looks the part, the black-and-white photography and return-to-the past visuals are sublime, but the performances are uninspired and there is more sexual chemistry between Prince and his cohort in crime (played by Jerome Benton, returning from *Purple Rain*) than there is between Prince, here playing a character named Christopher Tracy, and Kristin Scott Thomas, who is so switched on that she seems to be Mary Sharon.

Certainly confirming that Prince is not an actor in any conventional sense, though he displays some ability with his comic timing, and without the live music performances to compensate (less emphasis is placed on the music in the film, with *Kiss* appearing in the background and Scott Thomas performing a musical number before Prince does), *Under the Cherry Moon* was viewed as a vanity project and suffered critical and commercial failure. The soundtrack, which appeared under the title *Parade*, also features less prominently in the film and failed to match the sales of *Purple Rain*. However, when listened to outside of the context of the film, it remains one of Prince's strongest and most diverse albums.

Following Prince's death in 2016 there have been a few apologists, with writer Peter Sobczynski offering a defence of the film. 'If one applies normal critical standard to *Under the Cherry Moon* it could easily be dismissed ... and yet if you can get post those flaws it proves to be utterly fascinating film due to the multiple contributions on both sides of the camera by Prince.'[10] Whether one agrees or not, Sobczynski's comment that Prince was to be admired for 'pursuing his own distinct personal vision, no matter what the possible commercial repercussion might have been'[11] certainly holds true, a philosophy by which Prince could be said to have applied throughout his career.

Subsequently directing the concert documentary *Sign 'o the Times* (1987), Prince seemed to consign his film career to history. Perhaps unwilling to work in the collaborative manner the film-making process requires, Prince was ultimately coaxed back for *Graffiti Bridge*, a loose sequel to *Purple Rain* that was written, directed and scored by Prince, in which he also reprises his role as 'The Kid', resuming his spat with Morris Day as a pair rival nightclub owners. A contemporary musical drama, the film has frankly very few, if any, saving graces. A work that also corresponded with Prince's relative critical and commercial demise, it displayed unfortunate leanings towards a Messiah complex and lacked vigour even in the music performances. A film that seems immune to critical revisionism, watching it, one is reminded of Bowie's reaction to seeing *Just a Gigolo* (David Hemmings, 1978), which he described as 'my thirty two Elvis Presley movies rolled into one'.

Notes

1. It was a psychedelic movie that just about destroyed the career of the Monkees. The film ends with their suicide.
2. A film, set in Northern Britain, which did almost destroy the career of Slade.
3. Bob Spiers, 1997. One of the true acts of atrocity committed against cinema.
4. 1989. Written by Diane Warren.
5. Described by its distributor as a sick film by a sick person for sick people.
6. Cynthia Rose, *Purple Rain*, *Monthly Film Bulletin*, October 1984.
7. As well as the promos for the tracks taken from the film, which were edited sequences of film footage, Magnoli also directed *Partyman* (1989), *Scandalous* (1989) and *Batdance* (1989).
8. The star of *Flashdance*, Adrian Lyne, 1983.
9. Other credits include *The Prince of Tides*, Barbra Streisand, 1991 and *Seven Years in Tibet* Jean-Jacques Annaud, 1997.
10. Peter Sobczynski, New Position: A Defense of *Under the Cherry Moon* , 4 May 2016, www.rogerebert.com
11. Ibid.

2

Under the Cherry Moon

Prince as his most authentic self

De Angela L. Duff

While *Under the Cherry Moon*, Prince's second feature film and directorial debut, is maligned by most, the film is the ultimate public document of Prince as his most authentic self. While *Purple Rain*, Prince's first film, presents one side of him, the mysterious, aloof artist he exhibited in public from the onset of his career, *Under the Cherry Moon* represents him as he truly was with his close friends and associates: hilariously funny. Early on, Prince's sense of humour could be gleaned from some of the songs that he penned primarily for The Time, the band he constructed as a vehicle for his childhood friend, Morris Day. With the release of *Under the Cherry Moon*, Prince's quick wit was unveiled and showcased at its finest for all to witness and acknowledge. The film also showcases how unapologetically Black Prince truly was, while also displaying his love of the piano, handwritten notes and vintage cars. While exploring Prince's recurring, core themes of love and death, the film could also be viewed as a homage to his father, John L. Nelson. However, the film's ultimate legacy is its testament to Prince's countercultural stance – to always embrace doing the opposite of what is expected. In 2016, Stephanie Zacharek would give *Under the Cherry Moon* its most fitting review, as 'pure Prince'.

Released in the United States on 27 July 1984 and in the UK on 31 August 1984, *Purple Rain*, Prince's first film release, centres around a young, aspiring musician, 'The Kid', struggling to keep his foothold in a local Minneapolis club, while also tackling a tug of war with the leader of his rival band at the same club, Morris Day, over newcomer, Apollonia (PrinceVault). He is also having family troubles at home due to the domestic violence between his father and his mother. In the end, he wins the girl and cements his band's spot as the best performing act in the club.

'Do U Lie?'

Purple Rain is often viewed as being autobiographical or semi-autobiographical. However, beyond most of the characters using their real names and some of the real-life rivalry between Prince and his band and The Time, the film is not as autobiographical as portrayed by the press. In *Purple Rain*, The Kid is presented as being of mixed race. This film role perpetuated the myth that Prince used as a marketing scheme initially to avoid being labelled Black. In the 1985 MTV interview which aired on 13 November 1985 Prince revealed:

> Seriously, I was brought up in a black-and-white world – black and white, night and day, rich and poor. I listened to all kinds of music when I was young, and when I was younger, I always said that one day I would play all kinds of music and not be judged for the color of my skin but the quality of my work, and hopefully that will continue. (MTV)

He explicitly told Lenny Waronker, head of A&R at Warner Bros. at the time, in 1977, 'Don't make me Black!' (Star Tribune Staff), not wanting his music to be relegated to the Black charts. The press latched on to his myth of being half Black and half Italian, which was true of his friend and collaborator Jill Jones (Adler; Peace Bisquit). His lyrics in the song 'Controversy' from the album of the same title questioned his racial identity and continued to perpetuate this mistruth. He wanted to cross over to the mainstream. One of the other main storylines in the film, where The Kid does not want to listen to Wendy and Lisa's music, also presents a falsehood. In an interview for Yahoo! in 2017, Wendy Melvoin, guitarist in The Revolution, emphatically stated that he listened to everything she and Lisa composed back then (Yahoo!). Despite having a residency in the film at the real club where most of the film takes place, First Avenue and 7th St Entry, two music venues housed in the same building in downtown Minneapolis since 1970, Prince only performed at First Avenue ten times as the main act and twice at 7th St Entry (PrinceVault).

Upon the release of *Purple Rain*, many critics thought that The Kid's persona, 'diffident and paranoid – the tormented Romantic genius as a postmodern James Brown', mirrored Prince in real life (Hoberman). If anything, *Purple Rain* simulated Prince's public, not his private, persona at that time, as Neal Karlen would reflect in his second Prince interview for *Rolling Stone* magazine in 1990, 'Prince Talks':

> Not that Prince hadn't shown some signs of unease with his still-new superstardom. Alone, he'd been animated, funny and self-aware. But out in public, even walking into places as hospitable as Minneapolis's First Avenue club, he would palpably stiffen at the first sign of a gawk, his face set in granite, his voice reduced to a mumble. … Many things, however, have stayed the same. Prince is still very funny.

For about a year, Prince had been writing ideas for *Purple Rain* in a Mead spiral notebook (The Last Interview). As he would for *Under the Cherry Moon* with the 'wrecka stow' scene, Prince wrote the dialogue for one of the most memorable and comedic scenes in *Purple Rain*, 'What's the password?' between Morris Day and Jerome Benton, even though the film script is credited to director Albert Magnoli (Dr. Funkenberry). Some people were offended by what they saw as sexism or misogyny in *Purple Rain*. However, when questioned about this in an interview for MTV in 1985, Prince responded,

> I didn't write *Purple Rain*. Someone else did. It was a story, a fictional story, and it should be perceived that way, and nothing else. Um. Violence is something that happens in everyday life, and we were only telling a story and I wished it was looked at that way, but I don't think anything we did was unnecessary. Sometimes for the sake of humour, we may have went overboard and if that was the case, then I'm sorry but it was not the intention.

This quote is important for multiple reasons. First and foremost, Prince himself did not view *Purple Rain* as autobiographical. Secondly, even before *Under the Cherry Moon*, humour was also an important aspect in *Purple Rain*. Thirdly, the violence depicted was not an accurate representation of his parents' relationship. The Kid's parents might have been construed to be modelled after Prince's own family and childhood, due to one of the few in-depth interviews he gave in the early 1980s where he talked about a tormented childhood with parents who fought (Bream 2001: B1). In a 1984 *Star Tribune* interview, Prince's mother, Mattie Shaw, thought she and Prince's father, John L. Nelson, had 'normal disagreements', during their thirteen-year marriage. When asked by Minneapolis' *Star Tribune* if the movie accurately depicted him, Prince's father responded that he never used a gun like the father in *Purple Rain*, played by Clarence Williams III, who was known for the hit TV series *Mod Squad* (Bream 1984: 1C; Bream, 2001: B1; IMDB). Prince further corroborates his father's story in his 1985 interview with Neal Karlen in *Rolling Stone* magazine by sharing, 'That stuff about my dad was part of [director–co-writer] Al Magnoli's story. … We used parts of my past and present to make the story pop more, but it was a story. My dad wouldn't have nothing to do with guns. He never swore, still doesn't, and never drinks.' Again, Prince stresses that *Purple Rain* is a fictional story.

On the heels of the massive success of *Purple Rain*, most artists would have followed up with a sequel, but Prince did not, choosing *Under the Cherry Moon* as his second film instead. Even though *Graffiti Bridge*, Prince's third narrative film, technically serves as a more official sequel to *Purple Rain*, Marie Plasse in her 1996 *Journal of Popular Culture* article argued that both the concert film, *Sign o' the Times* (1987), and *Graffiti Bridge* (1990), both directed by Prince, could be viewed as 'two alternative follow-ups to *Purple Rain*' (58). In comparing the two films, Plasse observes that *Sign o' the Times* 'doesn't literally pursue the narrative thread of *Purple Rain*' but 'operates, in spirit, as a kind of sequel to the earlier film, sustaining and often surpassing *Purple Rain*'s exuberant celebration of Prince as a performer' (58). Ultimately, Prince labelled *Graffiti Bridge* 'a different kind of movie. It's not violent. Nobody gets laid' (Karlen 1990). Reading between the lines, Prince essentially defines *Purple Rain* as a drama and *Under the Cherry Moon* as a romance. The themes of *Graffiti Bridge* are more ambitious than *Purple Rain*'s, exploring art, commerce and spirituality.

Released on 2 July 1986 in the United States and on 19 October 1986 in the United Kingdom, *Under the Cherry Moon* is a daring and artistic, buddy film, shot on location in the French Riviera on the Cote d'Azur and at Studios de la Victorine in Nice, France (PrinceVault). The film broke social norms at the time by turning race (interracial relationships) and same-sex intimacy on their heads. The themes of duality that Prince revisits throughout his entire career persist from start to finish in *Under the Cherry Moon*: life versus death, love versus lust and rich versus poor. However, the most pervasive theme throughout the movie is fun. In fact, Prince's first words in the alternate opening and his final words in the film are exactly the same: 'We had fun. Didn't we?' In the context of Prince's recent passing, these words have never meant more than they do now.

In the film *Under the Cherry Moon*, the character of Christopher Tracy, played by Prince, is an American piano player by day and a gigolo by night on the French Riviera with his best friend and partner in crime, Tricky, performed by Jerome Benton. Having relocated from Miami, Florida, to the French Riviera, they decide to fulfil their childhood dream of becoming rich by seducing an uptight young heiress, Mary Sharon, played by Kristen Scott Thomas in her film debut role. The promotion notes described the film as a 'modern tale – timeless, romantic, a little offbeat, sometimes irreverent – essentially the simple and perennial story of two young people who fall hopelessly in love' (Bream 1986 (2), 1G). As a tribute to the classic romantic comedies of the 1930s and the 1940s, Prince ultimately wanted the film to be in black-and-white and set in an exotic location like Palm Beach, Miami or Capri (PrinceVault). After visiting the French Riviera, Prince decided to shoot the film there (PrinceVault). Considering Prince's Francophilia in his songs up to this date, 'It's Gonna Be Lonely', 'Condition of the Heart' and Sheila E.'s Prince-penned 'The Belle of St. Mark', this is not surprising (Thorne). His publishing company, Parisongs, reflects his fascination with France and the name of his production alias, Joey Coco, could possibly be interpreted as a reference to Coco Chanel, the famous French fashion designer (Bream 1987: 2C).

Under the Cherry Moon was panned widely upon its original release. Gene Siskel of the *Chicago Tribune* called it an 'absurdly bad movie' (Goble). In the *Minneapolis Star and Tribune* of Prince's own hometown, Jeff Strickler offered one of the funnier critiques, suggesting that the film could have been subtitled 'Purple Pain' (Strickler 1986 (2): 19C). However, Paul Attanasio, staff writer for *The Washington Post*, was not so light in his review, declaring the film an 'unconscionable mess of unyielding crassness' and offering that, if you gave an NYU film student ten or twelve million bucks to shoot his thesis 'you'd probably end up with something like *Under the Cherry Moon*. Then again, you might get something a whole lot better' (C2). The most brutal review was most fittingly from Hollywood in the *Los Angeles Times*, as Patrick Goldstein declared the film a 'dismal flop that will probably be Exhibit A for years to come in any debate over the wisdom of letting pop stars make their own vanity Hollywood projects. … it might well be called *Under the Cherry Bomb*' (Goldstein). Coincidentally, with both reviews being released on the same day, Goldstein mirrored Attanasio's observation that 'most of the scenes are so awkward, so hopelessly inept that the whole affair looks like a student film that somehow inherited a multimillion-dollar budget'.

For some African Americans particularly, there was a disconnect with Prince's gigolo character in France (Dean). However, on the Michael Dean podcast in 2016,

Jill Jones did not find the premise of the film far-fetched at all, having met men like that in France. She and Prince would often watch films from the 1930s together, and even though she is not in the film, Jones was in France with Prince while Prince was shooting *Under the Cherry Moon* (Dean).

Despite the poor reception, there were some film critics who genuinely enjoyed the film upon its release. *New York Times* critic Michael Wilmington declared Prince 'a promising first-time director' and wrote that the film revealed Prince 'as someone fascinated with artistic risk' (Olsen). Joe Baltake in the *Philadelphia Daily News* was extremely enthusiastic in his review:

> Actually, it's several movies – part Antonioni, part Howard Hawks, part Andy Warhol, part who knows – all jumbled together and seemingly based on the mental landscape of its kinetic, eccentric, self-consciously lascivious star. I've seen *Under the Cherry Moon*, I enjoyed it enormously, but I haven't quite figured out what it's supposed to be. Still, I like it … . Word leaked out a few weeks ago that *Under the Cherry Moon* was something of a stinker. Horsefeathers! It's unique, by far the boldest film of the summer. (47)

One of the most thoughtful reviews was from J. Hoberman, former film critic for the New York City newsweekly *Village Voice*, in 1986, where he analyses *Purple Rain* as an 'angst-ridden psychodrama' and *Under the Cherry Moon* as 'revisionist Astaire-Rogers; it has the engraved titles and, thanks to cameraman Michael Ballhaus, the elegant black and white cinematography of a Woody Allen film' (56). Later in a 1990 interview, Prince would speak of his admiration of Woody Allen because he appreciated anyone who got the final cut (Karlen 1990).

'I'm my own man, just like Liberace'

While most film critics took stabs at Prince's audacity to direct, Hoberman praised the directorial debut skills of Prince who took over the film's direction from first-time feature director Mary Lambert, best known for directing Madonna's 'Material Girl' video at this point. Lambert bowed out after only sixteen days of shooting. Hoberman observed that 'all things considered, he did an extremely credible job' and described Prince as 'radically subversive' (56).

Prince always played by his own rules. His desire to produce his first album as a mere teen is evidence of this. As a result, directing his own film was only a natural progression. In his 1985 MTV interview, he shared his directing style: 'One of the things I try to do with the things I direct – namely for our acts – is go for the different, the out-of-the-norm, "the avant-purple", so to speak' (MTV). In his *Rolling Stone* interview of the same year, he also shared that what he wanted to do was exactly the 'things somebody else wouldn't do' (Karlen 1985). Sean Doyle in 'Prince Among Men: UTCM' for *Film Comment* acknowledged this as well by observing, 'In the years that followed its release, Prince would go against the grain time and time again, inventing new personas, pursuing strange personal projects and triple albums' (Doyle). Even though test audiences gave it favourable ratings upon seeing the alternate ending where Prince gets the girl in the end, Prince insisted that he die at the end of the film (Thorne). Howard Bloom, Prince's publicist at the time, 'knew exactly why Prince had done what he did and killed off the main character, because in his mind the main character was a scamp – dishonest, defying God and breaking the rules of morality. To become moral, to become faithful to God, he had to kill his previous self off. It was a huge mistake' (Thorne). Prince also demanded that the film be presented in black-and-white. Warner Bros. objected due to fears that it would affect the film's appeal to the audience (Thorne). He also did not want the film to be a musical, even though some critics went so far in 1986 as to coin *Under the Cherry Moon* a failed musical, when clearly the film was not one (Cain P/1). Hoberman surmised that Prince wanted to prove that he could do a film without musical sequences throughout:

> What's truly bizarre is that, given the film's evocation of the '30s musical, Prince restricts himself to two production numbers, one of them (a delirious vision of Christopher's ascension into heaven) thrown away under the final credits. … Perhaps Prince took *Purple Rain*'s reviews too seriously and wanted to show he could hold a film simply with the force of his personality. If so, he's won a pyrrhic victory. (56)

Film critics, the general public and even some diehard Prince fans all wanted a sequel to *Purple Rain*; they didn't want something different. They wanted the mysterious, sulking, brooding Kid, not the chipper Christopher Tracy. They wanted multiple musical performances as *Purple Rain* had, not the single performance of 'Girls and Boys' in the film and 'Mountains' during the end credits, which are both featured on the accompanying album for the film, *Parade* (1986).

Expecting a sequel to *Purple Rain* is perplexing because, in the years before and following its release, Prince would go against the grain time and time again, inventing new sounds, personas and styles as easily as most people change their clothes. *Purple Rain* was nothing like *Around the World in a Day* (1985) which itself was nothing like *Parade*. At this time, Prince did not want to ride the commercial wave. Why would Prince's second feature length be any different? Film critics such as Peter Sobczynski understood this desire for a *Purple Rain 2* upon his re-examination:

> The hell of it is that once one gets past the fact that it does not resemble 'Purple Rain 2' in even the slightest, it reveals itself to be an offbeat gem that may one day go down as the MTV era equivalent of Marcel L'Herbier's infamous 1924 silent epic 'L'inhumaine' – an unabashed vanity project that both revels in and transcends its solipsistic underpinnings in ways that are alternately perplexing and endearing, an endeavor further bolstered by a stunning visual style and a central performance that, for better or worse, you cannot take your eyes off of for a second, not that you ever have a chance to do so.

Some wanted Prince to follow the template that John Waters had established of continually casting his friends in many of his films, but Prince wanted a professional cast and crew instead. Members of the Prince 'kingdom' or 'camp' who are very present in *Purple Rain* were all non-existent during the film except for Jerome Benton. Some of the other members, Wendy Melvoin, Lisa Coleman, Brownmark, Bobby Z, Dr. Fink, Miko Weaver, Eric Leeds, Atlanta Bliss, Wally Safford and Greg Brooks, appear in the film's end credits where the video of 'Mountains' is being played. Originally, Susannah Melvoin, Prince's girlfriend at the time and Wendy Melvoin's twin sister, was originally going to be the romantic lead in the film, but Kristin Scott Thomas was hired instead (Thorne). Even Jill Jones, who played the blonde waitress at First Avenue in *Purple Rain*, auditioned for a role in the film (Dean). Instead, Prince hired an A-list production team, beginning with Michael Ballhaus, a German cinematographer who died a year after Prince, also, in April. He is best known for his work with German director Rainer Werner Fassbinder with whom he made fifteen movies in the late 1960s, with acclaimed American filmmaker Martin Scorsese with whom he worked on *Goodfellas* (1990), *The Age of Innocence* (1993), *Gangs of New York* (2002), *The Last Temptation of Christ* (1988) and *The Departed* (2006), and with Francis Ford Coppola, for whom he was the cinematographer for the 1992 horror classic, *Dracula* (IMDB). *Under the Cherry Moon*'s production designer, Richard Sylbert, worked on *The Graduate* (1967), *Rosemary's Baby (1968)*, *Chinatown* (1974) and *The Cotton Club* (1984), and received an Oscar for 1966's *Who's Afraid of Virginia Woolf?* (IMDB; Bream 1986 (2) 1G). At one point, Prince wanted Scorsese to direct the film, and, at another time, Jean-Baptiste Mondino, the photographer and director who would eventually shoot Prince's 1988 *Lovesexy* album cover and direct his 'I Wish U Heaven' video for the same album, as well as Jill Jones's, Prince-penned *Mia Bocca* video in 1987 (Duff; PrinceVault). He also wanted established actors in the film. Golden Globe and Cannes Film Festival award-winning actor Terence Stamp (*Billy Budd* (1962), *Superman* (1978), and *Superman II* (1980)) was originally hired as Mary Sharon's father but was soon replaced by Steven Berkoff (*A Clockwork Orange* (1971), *Barry Lyndon* (1975), *Octopussy* (1983), and *Beverly Hills Cop* (1984)) when Stamp left the film's production (IMDB; Ro). Alexandra Stewart, who played Mary Sharon's mother, had appeared in many films, including Otto Preminger's *Exodus* (1960), Louis Malle's *The Fire Within* (1963) and *Black Moon* (1975), Arthur Penn's *Mickey One* (1965) with Warren Beatty, and François Truffaut's *The Bride Wore Black* (1968) and *Day For Night* (1973) (IMDB). Francesca Annis, who played Ms. Wellington, had film credits in films such as *Krull* (1983) and *Dune* (1984) (IMDB).

Since Prince's passing, the film has seen positive reappraisals by several journalists. In 2016, Sean Doyle delighted that

> *Under the Cherry Moon*, for all its flaws, is a sterling representation of everything I loved about him. It is, warts and all, quintessentially Prince. A clever, stupid, indulgent, transcendent mess of personal interests, produced with no regard to anyone else's expectations, unleashed on the world with nothing but cool, collected confidence. Prince was the very definition of an artist, endlessly, stubbornly

determined to fly past our opinions of him and follow his own path, wherever it took him.

In 'Prince's Lavish Fantasies Came to Life in Under the Cherry Moon', Blake Goble also praised the film: 'This film's like getting a glimpse at Prince's brain, scattered but at least to a breathtaking degree. His interests seem to be in his poised allure, his love of old fashion, and his unflappable hard-on for true love. As far as debuts go, not many directors would dare to let it all out like this.' Also in 2016, members of the African American Film Critics Association acknowledged that Prince was making a 'bold statement' in *Under the Cherry Moon* by positing:

> How many films set and actually shot in the French Riviera starred a Black man then or even star a Black man now? With 1986's *Under the Cherry Moon*, Prince inserted himself and Black men as a whole in places where society insisted he nor his kind belong. The fact that Prince shot *Under the Cherry Moon* in black and white is no coincidence. In an actual 1930s era film, a Black man dressed like Prince's Christopher Tracy would most likely be a butler or performing usually for whites only. In many ways, he used *Under the Cherry Moon* to correct, or at least, challenge Hollywood's stereotype and that of American society at large of where Black men, in particular, belonged.

'An Honest Man'

Under the Cherry Moon is far more biographical and revealing than *Purple Rain*. It's only fitting that the instrumental of 'An Honest Man' is one of the first songs featured in the film. Through the film and its publicity, Prince begins to reveal the man behind Prince, the performer. In *Under the Cherry Moon*, Prince's authentic self emerges. Certain critics caught glimpses of this in real time. Bruce Dessau in *Blitz* magazine observed, 'Unlike *Purple Rain*, where Prince played, we are led to believe, himself, here he acts, often with considerable charm and humour. Cocky and self-assured, there is none of the misogynistic undertow of *Purple Rain*'(16). J. Hoberman described Prince in *Under the Cherry Moon* as 'the supremely confident high priest of his personal Dionysian cult' (56). The keyword being 'supremely confident'. Prince wasn't always supremely confident. In a lot of his early songs, he was the victim: 'Why You Wanna Treat Me So Bad', 'Gotta Broken Heart Again' and 'It's Gonna Be Lonely' come to mind. However, in *Under the Cherry Moon*, Prince is finally comfortable with being himself on screen.

'Butterscotch. Chocolate. No way!'

As compared to *Purple Rain*, Prince's character in *Under the Cherry Moon* is clearly Black. While the characters in the film never acknowledge Prince's Blackness,

Christopher does throughout the entire film. Most notably, Mary Sharon's father views him as a poor 'peasant' instead. In one scene, Mary Sharon wants to know what he's wearing on his head, as he channels Little Richard. Christopher responds, 'Soul!' This is not the first time we see Prince in a headscarf. He wore one in the 27 October 1985 live performance for the 'America' video filmed at the Théâtre de Verdure in Nice, France, for *Around the World in a Day*, which was released before *Under the Cherry Moon*, but filmed afterwards, and he also wore one during his unforgettable, 4 February 2007 Super Bowl XLI performance (PrinceVault; NFL). In describing Mary Sharon to herself, Christopher Tracy imagines what she would sound like if they had intimate relations, 'And then you get black!' as he mimics how she would vocalize ecstasy and excitement. In real time, J. Hoberman was one of the few critics who acknowledged the Blackness on display in the film, noting that Christopher and Tricky 'revel in black street jive (*Under the Cherry Moon* should make "wrecka stow" a household phrase)' (56).

If one looks close enough, *Under the Cherry Moon* could be viewed as a homage to his father, John L. Nelson, who was a pianist at Twin Cities nightclubs and strip joints (Bream 2018: E3). At the age of twelve or thirteen, Prince would watch his father play at these clubs, but as soon as his father would finish playing, Prince would rush back home so his father wouldn't see him. Perhaps, a young Prince witnessed the lifestyle that he mimics in the film. In the 1950s, billing himself as the 'Fabulous Prince Rogers', Nelson fronted the jazz group Prince Rogers Trio, and Prince's mother, Mattie Shaw, was the singer, but she quit the group after marrying Nelson, who was forty years old and she twenty-three, on 31 August 1957 in Northwood, Iowa (Des Moines Tribune 20). On 7 June 1958, they named their son after the group, Prince Rogers Nelson (Bream 2001: B1). Even the name Christopher Tracy mirrors John Nelson in its formality as opposed to Jerome's name in the film, Tricky, and Prince's in *Purple Rain*, The Kid. However, Prince called Jerome 'Tricky' in real life before the film and had written a song called 'Tricky' on the B-side of The Time's 1984 'Ice Cream Castles' single (Duff).

Patterning after his father, Prince's first instrument was the piano. In a 1984 interview, Prince's mother recalled that when Prince was at the age of three or four 'we'd go to the store, and he'd jump on the radio, the organ, any type of instrument there was. Mostly the piano and organ. And I'd have to hunt for him, and that's where he'd be – in the music department'. At the age of eight, he took his first and only piano lesson with a woman who lived across the street from his parent's house. His mother asked him why and he said, 'Because she wants me to play what she wants me to play and I want to play what I want to play' (Bream 1984: 1C). Prince himself acknowledged that around the time he was eight years old, he 'had a pretty good idea what the piano was all about' (Carr 1D). According to Prince's half-sister, Sharon Nelson, who is eighteen years older than him, Prince's father taught him Duke Ellington chords as a kid (Bream 2018: E3). Prince's dad left home when Prince was about ten, leaving his piano behind (Bream 1984: 1C). In fact, during high school, Prince was known for keyboards instead of guitar (Star Tribune Staff). Coming full circle in 2016, Prince was essentially touring as Christopher Tracy for his *Piano and a Microphone* tour exactly thirty years later. Little did we know that Prince would soon suffer a similar fate as Christopher Tracy.

Prince's father contributed music to the film even though no one knows exactly what his contributions were, but John L. Nelson received co-writing credit for 'Christopher Tracy's Parade' and 'Under the Cherry Moon'. According to Matt Thorne in *Prince: The Man and His Music*, 'It seems likely from what those close to Prince have said that this was in recognition of a progression in the song that echoed something he remembered from his father's piano-playing.' In addition to these two songs, John L. Nelson also received co-writing credit on 'Computer Blue' on *Purple Rain*, due to the motif of 'Father's Song' played within the tune, 'The Ladder' on *Around the World in a Day*, and 'Scandalous' on 1989's *Batman* original motion picture soundtrack (Bream 2001: B1). John L. Nelson also received sole credit for 'Father's Song' in *Purple Rain*, even though the song was most likely co-written by Prince.

'If you wanted to buy a Sam Cooke album, where would you go?'

The biggest reveal of *Under the Cherry Moon* is Prince's true genius for humour. In 1986, Sean Doyle also recognized this, stating, 'Still, the film's broad comedy is absurd and charming, and reveals one more of Prince's many natural gifts: his sense of humor.' However, at the time, many critics did not see this brilliant display of humour. Roy Proctor for the *Richmond Times-Dispatch* in 'So Much for Love, So Much for Drama' laments, 'It's hard to take anything in *Under the Cherry Moon* seriously, even on the fantasy level in which much of it is intended to play, but that doesn't mean the average moviegoer won't find a lot to laugh about. Trouble is, he'll be laughing at the movie, not with it' (25). Therein lies the problem for many of the film's naysayers because *Under the Cherry Moon is* pure fun.

Ultimately, this film revealed to the public that Prince was a human being with an incredible sense of humour. One of the critics who immediately got the film's humour was David Foil, who posited in 1986's 'Humor in Under Is Wicked' for *The Baton Rouge Morning Advocate*:

> And I thought I'd lost the capacity for surprise: I haven't had as much crazy, off-the-wall fun at a film this summer as I had at Prince's Under the Cherry Moon. ... I get the feeling people are taking the film far too seriously. Don't do that. I don't think Prince, who directed it, did ... . He reportedly relied heavily on cinematographer Michael Ballhaus for technical guidance, but the wicked, deadpan sense of fun in the film probably has a great deal to do with him. (11)

By acknowledging Prince's humour during the film's original release – 'Prince's fun is infectious' – Hoberman was able to review the film favourably (56). Jeff Strickler in the *Minneapolis Star and Tribune* also noted that Prince showed 'a remarkable aplomb for light comedy' (Strickler, 1986 (1): 2C).

For evidence of Prince's wicked sense of humour, most fans of the film cite the 'wrecka stow' scene between Christopher Tracy, Tricky and Mary Sharon as being one of, if not the most, memorable scene from *Under the Cherry Moon*. Susannah Melvoin offers that Prince wrote this scene and was very proud of it, saying, 'He couldn't wait to shoot it. I guess some of these things were jokes from when he'd been a kid' (Thorne). Paul Peterson, later re-christened St. Paul by Prince for Prince's 1985 side project, The Family, where Melvoin would be the co-lead, revealed to the *Star Tribune* that Prince made him do the 'wrecka stow' exchange the very first time they met in 1983, years before the filming of *Under the Cherry Moon* (Star Tribune Staff).

In fact, several scenes from Becky Johnston's third and final draft of the script were reorganized, added or removed during the shooting of the film to add to the film's humour. Most of these additions were written by Prince. The scene where Christopher mistakenly climbs into bed with Mary's mother isn't in the script, nor is the café scene where Christopher and Tricky are the first to run out of the establishment after spotting bats in the ceiling (Nilsen 63). In an interview, Jerome Benton revealed that the bat scene was from a real-life incident in a southwest Minneapolis warehouse by the University of Minneapolis where The Time was rehearsing while Prince was watching (Duff). Like with the 'wrecka stow' scene, Prince was borrowing from his real life.

The comedic timing of the banter between Prince and Jerome Benton in this film rivals not only that of Morris Day and Jerome in *Purple Rain* but also that of other great comedic duos such as Laurel and Hardy, Dean Martin and Jerry Lewis, and Chris Tucker and Ice Cube. Benton has the distinction of being one half of two of the most comedic, dynamic duos on film, with Morris Day in *Purple Rain* and with Prince in *Under the Cherry Moon*. J. Hoberman observed that Prince 'gave Morris Day the chance to walk off with *Purple Rain*, and he does the same with Jerome Benton here' and that 'Christopher and Tricky (just the juxtaposition of the names cracks me up) are as de facto desecratory as the Marx Brothers in their Monkey Business prime' (56).

In hindsight, you can see breadcrumbs of Prince's humour. When it was eventually revealed that The Time project was essentially Prince and Morris Day, most assumed that Morris Day was Prince's alter ego and Morris, perhaps, had a sense of humour that Prince didn't possess. Again, Prince was thought to be 'serious'. However, if you revisit lyrics for songs such as 'Tricky', 'Cloreen Bacon Skin', and 'Movie Star', which were all written by Prince, it is very clear that, while Morris Day also possesses sharp, comedic talent – Prince and Morris were essentially two sides of the same coin. The obvious difference being that Morris was expected to be witty and funny, while Prince was not, based on Prince's public persona and perception up until this point. 'It's funny', reminisced Susan Rogers, 'when Prince would do that funny voice – that was him imitating men of his father's generation, you know barber shop guys. "Cloreen Bacon Skin" was the same kind of a voice and same kind of … . He was doing his dad' (Tudahl). Also, Christopher Tracy is essentially Prince in rehearsal, as tour rehearsal documentation reveals he often cracked jokes during the process. Even Prince's ninth-grade algebra teacher, George Headrick, remembered his 'sophisticated sense of humor', and Ronnie Robbins, a songwriter and producer who was in one of Prince's rival bands, Cohesion, during their teens, labelled Prince 'quite the prankster' after sitting on a tack that Prince placed on his chair in a drama-reading class at Central High School (Bream 1984:1C).

One would continually see evidence of Prince, the jokester, throughout his entire career. In 2004, Prince performed in disguise as the opening act for the *Essence Music Festival* in New Orleans. In 1998, Prince was disguised as an old man to present Chris Rock with comedian of the year for GQ's Men of the Year Awards. In 1997, Prince surprised Bryant Gumbel on his last day on *The Today Show* by dressing up as a carbon copy of the TV anchor. Additionally, there were always glimpses of Prince's playful nature which appeared often when he would abruptly run away from people; that running away was notably on display at the premiere of *Under the Cherry Moon* in Sheridan, Wyoming. There are other clips of Prince running away from Japanese paparazzi in an airport on 8 September 1986, as well as from a documentary filmmaker, Steve Purcell, when he gets on an elevator to perform during the Nude tour in 1990. The previously cited bat scene from *Under the Cherry Moon* also consisted of Prince and Jerome Benton being the first to run out of the café after seeing the bats, even though they were not seated by the door.

'Nobody like your body, baby!'

Clearly, Prince had a love of vintage cars and cars in general. Prince showcased this love in *Under the Cherry Moon*. Christopher Tracy drove Prince's own 1964 Buick Wildcat. In the film as he admires Isaac Sharon's Rolls Royce in Ms Wellington's driveway, he strokes the car while saying, 'Nobody like your body, baby!' At the end of the film, Tricky is in Miami, also riding a Rolls Royce. When an inventory of his vehicles was submitted to a probate court in Minnesota upon his death, Prince still owned the Buick, as well as the white 1968 Ford Thunderbird Landau Sedan gifted to him by his father and the customized, deep-purple, metallic 1984 BMW 633CS he gifted to his father for his birthday (State of Minnesota; Karlen 1985). Prince actively drove his father's Thunderbird and also sung about it from the lead single from Lovesexy, 'Alphabet St', incorrectly citing the vehicle's year in doing so (Karlen 1985). In 2004, Bob Cavallo revealed that during tour rehearsals for 1988's *Lovesexy*, Prince would make his entrance onstage in the Thunderbird. However, after reviewing video rehearsal footage, Prince decided 'he was too small in relation to the vehicle' (Star Tribune Staff). As a result, Bob Cavallo was charged with getting a three-quarters version of the car, not only for scale but also for practicality, as it had to be pushed around on stage rails (Star Tribune Staff). The 1985 MTV Prince interview also showcased Prince's humour and love for cars. As Emmanuelle Sallet, the actress who played Katy in *Under the Cherry Moon*, asked Prince if she should retrieve his Cadillac during the interview, Prince laughed and responded, 'Cadillac? Oh no. I don't drive no Cadillac, all right? I used to, but I don't anymore.' However, in Prince's final inventory both a 1985 Cadillac Fleetwood Brougham Stretch Limousine and 2004 Cadillac XLR Roadster were both listed (State of Minnesota). During interviews, many of Prince's associates and even journalists have fond memories of listening to Prince's music in the car while Prince was driving. Prince noted this himself in his 1990 interview with Karlen, 'When I'm getting ready to go out or driving in the car, I listen to my own stuff' (Karlen 1990). So cars were important not only to him personally but also for processing his music.

Handwritten notes played a significant part in Prince's personal life and provide another glimpse into Prince as his most authentic, playful self. Prince once wrote 'written in spit' on the back of an envelope addressed to Jackie Swanson, an actress and friend of Prince who made her professional debut in Prince's 'Raspberry Beret' video from *Around the World in a Day* (Bryant). The importance of the handwritten word was also very present in *Under the Cherry Moon*. Within five minutes of the beginning of this film, we see a handwritten note left by Christopher Tracy in his grotto. During the opening scene of the film, Tricky sends a stream of handwritten notes on napkins to encourage Christopher to seduce and serenade Ms Wellington, performed exquisitely by Francesca Annis.

Prince's core themes of love, God and death are often expressed in his personal handwritten notes. Two of these themes are evoked in *Under the Cherry Moon*. The B-side to the single 'Kiss' from the film's soundtrack, '♥ or $', is at its essence a simple summary of the plot of *Under the Cherry Moon*. One of the aforementioned paper napkin notes that Tricky sends to Christopher during the opening scene has a dollar symbol written on it. Prince's own 1964 Buick Wildcat which Christopher Tracy drives in *Under the Cherry Moon* has the word 'LOVE' on its licence plate. The theme of love, which isn't new to *Under the Cherry Moon*, is carried over to *Sign o' the Times* explicitly with the illustrated iconography of the heart and most notably *Lovesexy* with the title of the album itself and the mirrored heart bracelet Prince wore during the tour of the same name. The theme of God often appeared in his personal handwritten notes, as well. A note to Bruno Mars, 'May your only heroes be God and yourself' is an example of this. *Under the Cherry Moon* ends with the text 'Love God. May u live 2 see the dawn', which he often used before and after this time period, later transitioning the phrase to 'Welcome to the Dawn' (Primeau).

'Sometimes It Snows in April'

However, the theme that ends the film is death. *Under the Cherry Moon* is not the first time he addresses death. In all of his narrative films, death is a key component, even though *Under the Cherry Moon* is the only film where Prince's character dies. The Kid's father attempts to commit suicide in *Purple Rain* and you also see The Kid hanging from a noose for a very brief sequence, showing he is contemplating suicide, too. Jill Jones's character in *Purple Rain* was possibly going to contemplate suicide as well, based on the unreleased song, 'Wednesday', which she was originally set to perform in the film (Tudahl). In an additional scene of *Graffiti Bridge* that did not make the final cut, Prince's character puts a noose around his own neck in a game of real hangman, a word-guessing game, which he is playing with Ingrid Chavez's character, Aura. In the released version, The Kid draws a hangman's noose and four spaces on a heart-shaped notepad and Aura gets hit by a car and dies instead (Thorne). During his acceptance speech for *Purple Rain* as favourite Pop album of the year at the American Music Awards in 1985, Prince shared, 'For all of us, life is death without adventure and adventure only comes to those who are willing to be daring and take chances' (Prince, American Music Awards).

Prince also believed in an afterworld. He was quoted twice in two different interviews in 1985 explicitly saying so: the *Rolling Stone* magazine interview with Neal Karlen and his MTV interview. Prince wrote about the afterworld in both 'Let's Pretend We're Married' and 'Let's Go Crazy'. The phrase, 'May u live 2 see the dawn' could also be interpreted as a reference. The video behind the end credits of *Under the Cherry Moon*, which was also released as a video for the song 'Mountains', essentially illustrates Christopher Tracy floating to the 'upper room' and serves as a visual metaphor for the afterworld.

Prince often wrote about death in his songs. He sang about the grim reaper in 'Let's Go Crazy', and his own death in 'Old Friends 4 Sale'. He also wrote about death in songs he penned for others like Sheila E.'s 'Dear Michaelangelo'. He sings about death in two songs from the film, the title track, 'Under the Cherry Moon', and 'Sometimes It Snows in April', which plays in the background during the final scene of the film. However, the song holds even more meaning now, after Prince's passing on 21 April 2016. The song, which was coincidentally recorded on 21 April 1985, was a centrepiece and poignant part of The Revolution's concert reunion sets after Prince's transition, where Wendy Melvoin and Lisa Coleman, co-writers of the song, perform it alone on stage during the middle of the performances.

In real life, Prince died alone. In the film, Christopher Tracy didn't. Prince was adamant that Christopher Tracy dies in the film, despite this being a point of contention between him and Warner Bros. because they wanted a happy ending instead (Thorne). This scene should not be taken lightly. During the narration in the very first scene of the film, we are informed that Christopher will die for the woman he loves. When he dies, Christopher Tracy is surrounded by love, not only from the woman he loves but also from his best friend who is present just around the corner. Why is this scene important? Because it was important to Prince. He fought to keep Christopher Tracy's death in the film despite a better audience reception during screen tests for the film without it (Thorne). Unlike the released version of the film, which ends with Tricky and his former landlord, Katy, played by Emmanuelle Sallet, moving on with life in Miami, one cut of the film closes with the words 'The End', while an ambulance with Tricky, Mary and Christopher's dead body drives away (Nilsen 63). The film's released ending appears to be a compromise. However, the original ending would have been even more poignant, highlighting Prince's constant recognition of death and emphasizing the finality of death. In his 1990 interview with Neal Karlen, Prince said, 'When I pray to God, I say, "It's your call – when it's time to go, it's time to go. ... But as long as you're going to leave me here" – he slapped his hands – "then I'm going to cause much ruckus!"' Upon Prince's death, Neal Karlen reflected about the numerous conversations that he and Prince had about death. He revealed,

> I just pray Prince wasn't cognizant, even for a mite of a moment, that he was dying alone in a nondescript elevator, in a Wonder Bread suburb of the city that was

one day too late in telling him we loved him as much as he loved Minneapolis. ... Because there's one thing I'm positive I know about Prince. After knowing him in forever alternating cycles of greater, lesser and sometimes not-at-all friendship over the last 31 years: His biggest and perhaps only fear was dying alone. ... Yet he always accepted what was coming, and was trying to prepare, he told me as far back as 1985. (2016)

From Prince's own words, you can surmise he wasn't afraid of death, but from the depiction of Christopher Tracy's death in *Under the Cherry Moon* perhaps he, indeed, did not want to die alone.

However, Prince's main themes of love and death often overshadow his other core theme: fun. Fun is truly the underlying tenet of *Under the Cherry Moon*. The film is not the first time he promotes fun. The opening lines of '1999', as well as 'Let's Pretend We're Married', contain fun. Also, Sheila E.'s Prince-written 'Oliver's House' references fun several times. There are literally thirteen references to fun in the dialogue of *Under the Cherry Moon*. And again, in the unreleased version, the very first and last words that Christopher Tracy speaks in the film are, 'We had fun. Didn't we?' We most certainly did, Prince!

Under the Cherry Moon only got made and released due to the massive success of *Purple Rain* for Warner Bros. *Purple Rain* was the godsend that allowed *Under the Cherry Moon* to be shot and directed as Prince wanted. Prince was very happy and loving during this period of his life. For proof, you only have to watch Prince hug Jerome Benton from the outtakes of the filming of the 'Mountains' video, where he has the widest grin and gives Benton the biggest hug anyone could give. Benton would later reveal that Prince did not give hugs (Duff). This gesture was extremely rare. During this period, Prince was finally able to let his guard down and reveal parts of the real man behind the many curtains of construction.

Prince was complex and multifaceted. Those of us who did not know him will never get to know all sides of Prince. However, he was open enough to reveal more of who he really was to the public in *Under the Cherry Moon*. He exhibited facets of his personality that he hadn't exposed outright up until this point so directly. In his essay, Glen Helfand sums up *Under the Cherry Moon* brilliantly, 'It's so wonderful that it exists, a time capsule ... a vision. For you.' For us. We can always witness Prince as his most authentic self in *Under the Cherry Moon*.

Works cited

AAFCA Members. 'Prince in Cinema Remembered by the African American Film Critics Association'. *African American Film Critics Association*, 3 Oct. 2016, aafca.com/our-blog/2016/10/3/prince-in-cinema-remembered-by-the-african-american-film-critics-association.

Adler, Bill. 'Will the Little Girls Understand?' *Rolling Stone* (#337), 19 Feb. 1981.

America. Directed by Prince. Warner Brothers, 1985.

Attanasio, Paul. 'Movies Prince's Waning "Moon"'. *The Washington Post*, 4 July 1986, p. C2.
Baltake, Joe. 'A Batty Prince on the Riviera'. *Philadelphia Daily News (PA)*, 3 July 1986, 9STAR, FEATURES, p. 47.
Bream, Jon. 'Joey Coco? That's Prince's New Self'. *Star Tribune*, 6 Mar. 1987, p. 2C.
Bream, Jon. 'John Nelson, Well-Known Jazz Musician and Father of Pop Star Prince, Dies at 85'. *Star Tribune*, 28 Aug. 2001, p. B1.
Bream, Jon. 'The Music of Prince's Father'. *Star Tribune*, 11 Mar. 2018, p. E3.
Bream, Jon. '"Parade" Is Marketing Savvy Test'. *Star Tribune*, 31 Mar. 1986, p. 1C.
Bream, Jon. 'Prince Roger Nelson Encountered Sour Notes In Life'. *Minneapolis Star and Tribune*, 23 July 1984, p. 1C.
Bream, Jon. 'Under The Cherry Moon'. *Minneapolis Star and Tribune*, 8 June 1986, p. 1G.
Bryant, Kenzie. 'Prince's Intimate Handwritten Letters Are Up for Auction'. *Vanity Fair*, 13 Feb. 2017, vanityfair.com/style/2017/02/prince-auction-handwritten-letters.
Cain, Scott. 'Prince Proves Pretentious in New "Moon" - Movie Review'. *The Atlanta Journal and The Atlanta Constitution*, 4 July 1986, PREVIEW, p. P/1.
Carr, Tim. 'Prince: A One-Man Band and a Chorus, Too'. *Minneapolis Tribune*, 30 Apr. 1978, p. 1D.
Dean, Michael. 'Jill Jones Interview'. *The Prince Podcast from Podcast Juice*, 23 Oct. 2016, podcastjuice.net/jill-jones-interview.
Des Moines Tribune. 'Iowa Licenses To Wed'. *Des Moines Tribune* [Des Moines, Iowa], 18 Sep. 1957, p. 20.
Dessau, Bruce. 'Under The Cherry Moon'. *BLITZ*. No. 45, Sep. 1986, p. 16.
Doyle, Sean. 'Prince among Men: Under the Cherry Moon'. *Film Comment*, 29 Apr. 2016, filmcomment.com/blog/prince-among-men-cherry-moon.
Dr. Funkenberry, '#48 Jerome Benton'. *The Dr. Funk Podcast*, 13 Apr. 2017, podcasts.apple.com/us/podcast/48-jerome-benton/id1087272594?i=1000384348520.
Duff, De Angela L. 'GFM's behind the Film Podcast – Jerome Benton'. *GFM Podcast Network*, 12 Oct. 2017, podcasts.apple.com/us/podcast/gfms-behind-the-film-podcast-jerome-benton/id1085920009?i=1000393153911.
Foil, David. 'Humor in Under Is wicked'. *The Baton Rouge Morning Advocate*, 11 July 1986, FUN, p. 11.
Goble, Blake. 'Prince's Lavish Fantasies Came to Life in *Under the Cherry Moon*'. *Consequences of Sound*, 2 July 2016, consequenceofsound.net/2016/07/princes-lavish-fantasies-came-to-life-in-under-the-cherry-moon.
Goldstein, Patrick. 'Movie Review: A Misbegotten "Moon" from Prince'. *Los Angeles Times*, 4 July 1986, https://www.latimes.com/archives/la-xpm-1986-07-04-ca-696-story.html.
Graffiti Bridge. Directed by Prince. Paisley Park Films, Warner Bros., 1990.
Helfand, Glen, 'Prince Moments 2: *Under the Cherry Moon*, 1986'. *glen helfand*, 10 June 2016, glenhelfand.com/blog/2016/6/10/prince-moments-2-under-the-cherry-moon-1986.
Hoberman, J. 'Swing Time'. *Village Voice*, 15 July 1986, p. 56.
I Wish U Heaven. Directed by Jean-Baptiste Mondino. Paisley Park Records, 1988.
IMDB. 'Alexandra Stewart'. *IMDB*, imdb.com/name/nm0829155/bio.
IMDB. 'Francesca Annis'. *IMDB*, imdb.com/name/nm0000768.
IMDB. 'Michael Ballhaus'. *IMDB*, imdb.com/name/nm0000841.
IMDB. 'Richard Sylbert'. *IMDB*, imdb.com/name/nm0843129.
IMDB. 'Steven Berkoff'. *IMDB*, imdb.com/name/nm0000925.
IMDB. 'Terence Stamp'. *IMDB*, https://www.imdb.com/name/nm0000654.

Johnson, David, and Julie Shapiro. 'How Prince's *Purple Rain* Totally Dominated 1984'. *Time*, 21 Apr. 2016, time.com/4303815/prince-dead-purple-rain-1984-album.

Karlen, Neal. 'Letters from Prince: A Minneapolis Writer Remembers His Relationship with a Lost Star'. *Star Tribune*, 29 Apr. 2016, startribune.com/letters-from-prince-a-minneapolis-writer-remembers-his-relationship-with-a-lost-star/377555951.

Karlen, Neal. 'Prince Talks'. *Rolling Stone*, 18 Oct. 1990, rollingstone.com/music/music-news/prince-talks-189956.

Karlen, Neal. 'Prince Talks: The Silence Is Broken'. *Rolling Stone*, 12 Sep. 1985, rollingstone.com/music/music-news/prince-talks-the-silence-is-broken-58812.

Mia Bocca. Directed by Jean-Baptiste Mondino. Paisley Park Records, 1987.

Mountains. Directed by Prince. Warner Brothers, 17 Nov. 1986.

MTV. 'MTV Presents Prince'. *MTV*, 13 Nov. 1985, mtv.com/video-clips/ev9cwl/mtv-news-prince-s-debut-tv-interview-from-1985.

NFL. 'Prince Performs "Purple Rain" during Downpour | Super Bowl XLI Halftime Show'. *Youtube*, 12 Feb. 2016, youtube.com/watch?v=7NN3gsSf-Ys.

Nilsen, Per & jooZt Mattheij with the UPTOWN Staff. *The Vault*. Sweden, Uptown, 2004.

Olsen, Mark. 'Film Shows a Door into Prince's World'. *Toronto Star (Canada)*, 29 Apr. 2016.

Peace Bisquit. 'Jill Jones'. *Peace Bisquit*, peacebisquit.com/jill-jones.

Plasse, Marie A. '"Joy in Repetition"?: Prince's "Graffiti Bridge" and "Sign o' the Times" as Sequels to "Purple Rain"'. *Journal of Popular Culture* 30.3 (1996): 57.

Primeau, Jamie. 'Were Prince & Bruno Mars Friends? His Grammys Tribute Is A Perfect Way to Honor the Legend'. *Bustle*, 12 Feb. 2017, bustle.com/p/were-prince-bruno-mars-friends-his-grammys-tribute-is-a-perfect-way-to-honor-the-legend-37603.

Prince. '♥ or $'. *Kiss*, Paisley Park Records, 1986. 12' Vinyl.

Prince. '1999'. *1999*, Warner Brothers, 1992. CD.

Prince. *Around the World in a Day*, Paisley Park Records, 1985. CD.

Prince. 'Cloreen Bacon Skin'. *Crystal Ball*, NPG Records, 1998. CD.

Prince. 'Condition of the Heart'. *Around the World in a Day*, Paisley Park Records, 1985. CD.

Prince. 'Computer Blue'. *Purple Rain*, Warner Bros. Records, 1984. CD.

Prince. 'Father's Song'. *Purple Rain*, Warner Bros. Records, 1984. CD.

Prince. 'Girls and Boys'. *Parade*, Paisley Park Records, 1986. CD.

Prince. 'Gotta Broken Heart Again'. *Dirty Mind*, Warner Bros. Records, 1980. CD.

Prince. 'It's Gonna Be Lonely'. *Prince*, Warner Bros. Records, 1979. CD.

Prince. 'The Ladder'. *Around the World in a Day*, Paisley Park Records, 1985. CD.

Prince. 'Let's Go Crazy'. *Purple Rain*, Warner Bros. Records, 1984. CD.

Prince. 'Let's Pretend We're Married'. *1999*, Warner Bros. Records, 1992. CD.

Prince. *Lovesexy*, Paisley Park Records, 1988. CD.

Prince. 'Movie Star'. *Crystal Ball*, NPG Records, 1998. CD.

Prince. 'Old Friends 4 Sale'. *The Vault … Old Friends 4 Sale*, Warner Bros. Records, 1999. CD.

Prince. *Parade*, Paisley Park Records, 1986. CD.

Prince. 'Prince in Airport'. *Youtube*, uploaded by lemoncrush, 17 Dec. 2016, youtube.com/watch?v=N-08CScLF_0.

Prince. *Purple Rain*, Warner Bros. Records, 1984. CD.

Prince. 'PRINCE Dominates the American Music Awards 1985'. *Youtube*, uploaded by Purplesnowlovem 26 June 2013, youtube.com/watch?v=S8ZQTKlO3kY.

Prince. 'Scandalous'. *Batman*, Paisley Park Records, 1989. CD.
Prince. 'Sometimes It Snows in April'. *Parade*, Paisley Park Records, 1986. CD.
Prince. 'Why You Wanna Treat Me So Bad'. *Prince*, Warner Bros. Records, 1979. CD.
PrinceVault. 'Album: Purple Rain'. *PrinceVault*, princevault.com/index.php?title= Album:_Purple_Rain.
PrinceVault. 'Alphabet St'. *PrinceVault*, princevault.com/index.php?title=Alphabet_St.
PrinceVault. 'First Avenue'. *PrinceVault*, princevault.com/index.php?title=First_Avenue.
PrinceVault. 'One Off Performance: 3 August 1983'. *PrinceVault*, princevault.com/index.php?title=03_August_1983.
PrinceVault. 'Parade'. *PrinceVault*, princevault.com/index.php?title=Album:_Parade.
PrinceVault. 'Purple Rain'. *PrinceVault*, princevault.com/index.php?title=Film:_Purple_Rain.
PrinceVault. 'Sometimes It Snows in April'. *PrinceVault*, princevault.com/index.php?title=Sometimes_It_Snows_In_April.
PrinceVault. 'Under the Cherry Moon'. *PrinceVault*, princevault.com/index.php?title=Film:_Under_The_Cherry_Moon.
PrinceVault. 'Wednesday'. *PrinceVault*, princevault.com/index.php?title=Wednesday.
Proctor, Roy. 'So Much for Love, So Much for Drama'. *Richmond Times-Dispatch*, 3 July 1986, p. 25.
Purcell, Steve. 'Steve Purcell: A Day in the Life 1990'. *Daily Motion*, dailymotion.com/video/x5jg25q.
Purple Rain. Directed by Albert Magnoli. Warner Brothers Pictures, 1984.
Raspberry Beret. Directed by Prince. Warner Brothers, 1985.
Ro, Ronin. *Prince: Inside the Music and the Masks*. Kindle ed., St. Martin's Press, 2016.
Sheila E. 'The Belle of St. Mark'. *The Glamorous Life*, Warner Bros. Records, 1984. CD.
Sheila E. 'Dear Michaelangelo'. *Romance 1600*, Paisley Park Records, 1985. CD.
Sheila E. 'Oliver's House'. *The Glamorous Life*, Warner Bros. Records, 1984. CD.
Sign o' the Times. Directed by Prince. Cineplex Odeon Films, 1987.
Sobczynski, Peter. 'New Position: A Defense of "Under the Cherry Moon"'. *Roger Ebert*, 4 May 2016, rogerebert.com/balder-and-dash/new-position-a-defense-of-under-the-cherry-moon.
Star Tribune Staff. 'Oral History: Prince's Life, as Told by the People Who Knew Him Best'. *Star Tribune*, 7 June 2019, startribune.com/the-life-of-prince-as-told-by-the-people-who-knew-him/376586581.
State Of Minnesota, County of Carver, First Judicial District Court Probate Division. 'Court File No. 10-PR-16-46, Estate of Prince Rogers Nelson, Decedent, Inventory Original'. 4 Jan. 2017, mncourts.gov/mncourtsgov/media/CIOMediaLibrary/Documents/Inventory.pdf.
Strickler, Jeff. 'Cherry Pits'. *Minneapolis Star and Tribune*, 25 July 1986, p. 19C.
Strickler, Jeff. 'Creator-star Shines as Singer, Bombs as Actor'. *Minneapolis Star and Tribune*, 4 July 1986, p. 2C.
Thompson, Austin. 'The 20 Best-Selling Movie Soundtracks of All Time'. *Mental Floss*, 13 Dec. 2018, mentalfloss.com/article/567464/best-selling-movie-soundtracks-of-all-time.
Thorne, Matt. *Prince: The Man and His Music*. Kindle ed., Agate Publishing, 2016.
The Time. 'Tricky'. *Ice Cream Castles*, Warner Brothers, 1984. 7' Vinyl.
Tudahl, Duane. *Prince and the Purple Rain Era Studio Sessions: 1983 and 1984*. Expanded ed., Kindle ed., Rowman & Littlefield Publishers, 2018.

Under the Cherry Moon. Directed by Prince. Warner Brothers Pictures, 1986.
Yahoo! 'Backspin: The Revolution Talk Prince's "Purple Rain"'. *Yahoo!*, 4 May 2017, youtube.com/watch?v=-yCWato9aZ8.
Zacharek, Stephanie. 'The Beautiful One: Prince On-Screen'. *Time*, 21 Apr. 2016, time.com/4303941/prince-dead-movies.

3

Before the rain, 1979–84

How Prince got 'the look'

Casci Ritchie

Since his creative debut in the late 1970s, Prince dressed much like he steered his musical career, to the beat of his own Linn Drum machine. Drummer Michael Bland recalled working with Prince during the 1990s and described the importance of fashion to the performer, stating, 'He was from a tradition in this business where you don't come out with Crocs and a T-shirt. You don't present yourself in a slovenly manner. Anytime you saw Prince, it looked like he was coming to go onstage or was leaving stage' (Browne). A purple chameleon, Prince morphed into varying visual representations of himself as he embarked on each new project. Examples of this sartorial shape-shifting can be found throughout his career, as, for example, the polka dots and graphic texts of *Lovesexy* (1988) and the psychedelic Afrofuturism stylings of *Art Official Age* (2014). Prince took immense pleasure in fashion and it became an extension and expression of himself and his music.

Following his death in 2016 the cultural impact of Prince is increasingly recognized by his dedicated fans worldwide. As news of Prince's passing spread, international landmarks such as the Sydney Opera House were lit up in purple in remembrance. Even NASA posted an intergalactic purple nebula on their official Twitter account in honour of the musician. It is evident that Prince's impact on popular culture has left a lasting impression; however, it can be argued that dress historians have to date underestimated this. This could be viewed as a massive oversight to the influence Prince held on fashion as he continues to be one of the few artists who is instantly recognizable worldwide through the colour purple, the unpronounceable *Love Symbol* and the myriad of iconic clothes he wore throughout his expansive career.

Purple Rain (1984) is widely viewed as Prince's career-defining masterpiece both musically and visually, with the iconic image of 'The Kid' dressed in a purple studded trench coat and ruffles now firmly established in popular culture. The evolution of this look began as far back as 1979, and this chapter will explore the development of Prince's self-created image that helped define the era.

The release of *Dirty Mind* (1980) saw Prince launch a more provocative and shocking image, introducing the world to his band of musical misfits, soon to evolve into The

Revolution. Blurring race, gender and sexuality, Prince strutted onstage in stockings, intimidating and arousing crowds alike as he performed a fusion of funk, new wave, punk, R&B and rock. The fashion choices of Prince and his band during this influential period foreshadowed what we now view as the iconic visual representation of Prince. This chapter will explore Prince's style progression throughout the catalytic era of *Dirty Mind*, focusing on press photographs, album art, live footage and interviews. I hope to pinpoint pivotal moments in the creative journey and explore the origins, development and impact of Prince's iconic style. A compact object study will focus on the trench coat and will begin to explore the garment from the *Dirty Mind* to the *Purple Rain* era.

A prince is born

Prince's interest in fashion was apparent from a young age with the influence of his musician father, John Nelson, being an often cited sartorial point of reference (Ro 8). Prince left a lasting impression on a former classmate of Central High School, Minneapolis, who remembered him strutting down the corridors in 1972 wearing a 'globular afro and wispy moustache … dress shirt with huge collar points, baggy pants, platform shoes and neckbands' (9). Chazz Smith, Prince's cousin and drummer of Grand Central (Prince's first band), recalled the young musician's attitude towards style:

> We didn't want to look like a whole group wearing the same clothes, that was a no, no. So it was up to individuals to go and find their look and then we'd look at each other and style in the mirror and go that works, that doesn't work. Prince would come in looking like Prince, he'd have the scarves, the silky shirts, the big puff sleeves and we'd try to desperately find that stuff or we'd have someone make it for us. I had a girl make clothes for me, so did Prince, we had people making clothes for us after a while cause we just couldn't find anything in store. We'd go to thrift stores where they had, you know, stuff that people didn't want and we put it on. (Smith 2018)

Prince may have been just another follower of mainstream youth fashion at the time but it was evident that his own sense of individuality was developing in these formative years.

Fast forward to 1977, when Prince signed a landmark deal with Warner Bros. Executives began to formulate the image that would help sell Prince and his music, but the young artist had his own ideas. He grew up idolizing performers such as James Brown, Little Richard and Santana. In fact, Prince loved Santana's style so much that both he and Chazz would hunt through the rails of second-hand stores to find fringed vests and boots in the style of the artist (Smith 2018). These performers influenced him in a variety of ways from stage presence to dance moves (Till 73). James Brown's stage costumes from the early 1970s demonstrate a similarity in garment details such as the personalized monograms and flamboyant, risqué catsuits which were two key features that fed into Prince's style in the coming decades for promotional materials, including the albums *Lovesexy* (1988) and *Graffiti Bridge* (1990). Little Richard's eccentric glamour and femininity would influence Prince's personal grooming especially in make-up and hairstyle. Examples of such can be seen in his outlandish pompadour and typhoon hairstyles during *Diamonds and Pearls* (1991), *Love Symbol* (1992) and *Come* (1994). Little Richard's overt sexuality and flamboyant stylings were popular during the 1950s and the 1960s, but in some cases many of his songs found greater success when performed by White artists (Kirby 135). From the beginning, Prince was incredibly focused on appealing to a wider mainstream audience and would use Brown and Richard's suggestive style to help push his own provocative work that was now more socially acceptable in the late 1970s than in White, conservative 1950s America.

When Prince signed his legendary Warner Bros. deal, he showed up in an extremely low-cut leopard print leotard and topped it off with a delicate waist chain. Prince was wearing body-conscious Danskins at this time, a traditional bodywear brand originally created for dancers but popularly adopted by the disco-goers of the later 1970s. This look was to develop throughout the promotion of the *Prince* (1977) album. Prince was essentially mirroring what the youth were wearing down at their local disco, with a particular focus on female attire. Danskin designer Bonnie August described bodywear as 'right for women today because women have developed a whole new attitude about themselves over the last 10 years ... they show off the body as it is' (Mankowski). Prince's self-confidence in both his appearance and talent allowed the Danskin to act as a fluid expression of his music and a visual representation of his attitude towards gendered clothing. Growing up, Prince was often teased when he openly wore female clothing and experimented with make-up (Smith 2018). It would appear that this was not as a political statement but a self-expression of personal style. The 1960s saw the introduction of more unisex items with men wearing more typical feminine styles such as floral patterns and soft flowing fabrics (Costantino 108). Paul Jobling described what historians refer to as the Peacock Revolution, 'the youthquake generation overthrew the conventions of male dress and masculinity by growing their hair long and adopting gender-bending forms of dress. The sculpted constrictions of suits reflected the new body consciousness' (20). Carolyn Heilbrun suggests that 'androgyny seeks to liberate the individual from the confines of the appropriate' (Heilbrun 212). In reflection of this, androgynous dressing could be seen as an outlet of expression for a young Prince, allowing him to break free from society's perceptions of a young Black male musician from Minneapolis.

Prince continued to formulate his image and it was clear he was keen on portraying himself as a non-traditional visual representation of a Black musician. The unreleased music video for 'I Wanna Be Your Lover' (1979) showed a topless Prince wearing 'baggy shorts, leg warmers and shiny boots, his hair long and glossy as he snuggles against Dez Dickerson and strokes Gayle Chapman's face' (Thorne 53). Prince's affinity towards dance wear was evident here and this grew to literally being stripped down to nothing but a bikini brief by the time *Dirty Mind* was released in 1980.

The 1979 live shows for the *Prince* album saw him wearing next to nothing on stage; this look was originally a rebellion against the management. Guitarist Dez Dickerson told the *Minneapolis Star Tribune*, 'We had morphed into the Spandex kids. We were trying to dress as outrageously and outlandishly as we could' (Brewster). He further stated that during a show in the Roxy, Los Angeles, Prince's manager, Bob Cavallo, came backstage and called Prince out for not wearing underwear, claiming it was 'obscene' (Brewster). This amused Prince greatly and he went back on stage in nothing but his underwear. This look was adopted the following year as the iconic representation of *Dirty Mind* and mirrored the punk, confrontational attitude which would influence the album.

Dressing The Revolution

The 1980 release of *Dirty Mind* saw Prince moving away from the mainstream sound of many contemporary Black musicians. The album content was incredibly risqué, discussing oral sex with a wayward bride on her wedding day ('Head') and tales of incest ('Sister'). It seems natural that Prince's look would visually complement the salacious nature of the music. The *Dirty Mind* album cover shows a young Prince standing defiant in front of bedsprings – baring his chest, wearing nothing but a pair of black bikini briefs, a bandana and an embellished trench coat. Photographer Allen Beaulieu worked with Prince during the photo shoot and commented on Prince's creative control and desire to portray himself as unashamedly provocative as possible (Raiss). As a young Black male musician, Prince wanted his music to be appreciated by all audiences and perhaps felt his shock tactics could help gain notoriety and attract a wider fan base.

Prince stares into the camera inviting the viewer to join him in his lewd musical fantasy. The trench coat thrown over his bikini briefs asserts his sexual prowess as well as his dominant position in the band. Prince at this point was cherry-picking visuals from various cultural references, the bandana being a symbol of the 'dandyfied urban cowboy' (Koda and Martin 80). This inclusion of various cultural references, such as the bandana and the Rude Boy pin, allowed Prince to identify with a varied audience and with their identifiable subcultures. During this time Prince and his band were immersed in varying aspects of popular culture such as new wave and punk music. As a musician, he had yet to explore these potential influences and time would tell how these fed into his musical legacy.

Prince stated in the *Minneapolis Star* in February 1980, 'We can't dress in three-piece suits or glitter outfits or raggedy clothes. It's [the outfits are]basically us. I wear what I wear because I don't like clothes, it's what's comfortable' (Bream). The band is photographed for the album dressed in a juxtaposing mix of trench coats, scrubs and suits. Similar to Prince, André Cymone wears a trench, topless, with dog tags and provocatively unbuttoned tight jeans. Dez Dickerson wears a trench over a two-tone outfit of neck tie and trousers. Matt Fink is wearing his newly acquired scrub uniform which he had recently changed from jail stripes during the Rick James tour (1979). Lisa Coleman wears a luxurious tightly belted trench coat. Bobby Z is more formally attired donning a sharp tailored suit and skinny tie, much in line with the new wave style seen in bands like The Cars. Janice Miller discussed the role fashion plays in a group, stating that 'fashion is seen to be as much about belonging as it is about being individual, as such ways of dressing are methods of allying oneself to a group of people with whom one identifies' (Miller 109). The album heralded a coming of age for Prince – the sexually suggestive content was a departure from *Prince* and *For You*, and *Dirty Mind* can be seen as the beginning of the now legendary Prince sound of the 1980s.

Prince the provocateur

Dress historian Shaun Cole argues that 'by the late 1970s the aesthetics of punk had become commercialized and given birth to a whole series of new subcultural groups' (157). As previously discussed, Prince was soaking up musical influences from his band. According to biographers Hahn and Tiebert, 'Various subcultures were percolating underneath the surface of popular music, and Prince was taking their measure. He had learned of developments in punk and new wave through long conversations with Matt Fink and Dez Dickerson' (116). During this period he also accessorized his stage outfits with a mismatch of badges and wore deconstructed T-shirts, further embodying the punk aesthetic seen in bands such as The Clash. In February 1980, Prince stated in the *Minneapolis Star* that it was the kids who 'got him', explaining 'they were ready for change'. He felt older people found it hard to get into the band, referring to himself as 'shock treatment' and claiming older audiences 'thought we were gay or freaks. We're wild and free. It's no holds barred' (Bream). This mentality of rebellious youth culture follows through the *Dirty Mind* album with songs such as *Party Up and Uptown* where Prince urged listeners to open their minds and encouraged radical freethinking. The battle cry of *Uptown* was visually expressed by Prince and his band through a melting pot of subcultures, genre and race. Costantino remarked of the subculture that 'punk took garments that were recognized symbols of the establishment, including business suits that were slashed and stuck together with safety pins' (118). Prince used the trench coat to a similar effect, defacing the military tailoring with studs and fetishizing the garment with stockings and briefs.

With the albums *Controversy* (1981) and *1999* (1982) Prince moved away from some of the overt punk stylings and focused on the New Romantic trend that was popular in Britain during the early 1980s. New Romantic dressing was noted by Costantino to 'create myths about the past to inspire the wearer a sense of glamour and nostalgia' (115). Prince definitely embraced the glamour of the trend by adopting tailoring during *Controversy*; however, he did not appear to hold any nostalgia for a bygone era, choosing instead to create his own genre, destroying traditional menswear through a melange of various stylistic sources.

Although the public had been more frequently exposed to the eroticized male since the 1950s, they had not yet encountered such an upfront display of overt sexuality as displayed by Prince. He was not the typical White 'trim, muscular male' currently used for advertising purposes. Prince's body, though muscular, was softer, less defined and his feminine facial features were all in contrast to the overtly masculine Adonis figure that was socially acceptable at the time (Delis Hill 23). Josh Sims stated that 'the development in the 1960s of the men's bikini brief, therefore marked a significant advance in erotic design,' describing it as 'crotch consciousness' (128). Designs 'became even briefer to fit beneath lowered waistbands of trousers' but Prince was not concealing the underwear – he was fully exposing it (21).

Would wearing nothing but a bikini brief really be the right outfit for such an athletic show? Probably not, but it was clear Prince was a true provocateur at this time and wanted to challenge his audience and create publicity for himself. Hahn and Tiebert discussed how Prince was 'drawn' to the 'idea of visual sensationalism' after his manager at the time, Owen Husney, 'told him how the Beatles shocked a generation by wearing haircuts that touched their ears' (116). This self-creation of 'visual sensationalism' would be something Prince continued to develop throughout his career (see the series of masks and facial adornment used in relation to Prince's dispute with Warner Bros. in the 1990s).

Prince wore clothes with abandon, defying gender preconceptions and mainstream style. We may never know whether Prince chose to do this as a personal representation of his own sexuality or if this was an attempt to sell records and build on his prolific legacy. As discussed earlier, Prince was stylistically inspired by earlier artists, but he pushed the growing mainstream audience to accept a Black, gender-fluid icon. He followed the footsteps of Jimi Hendrix and helped pave the way for male musicians, especially Black musicians, to express themselves through fashion. Frank Ocean was quoted in NME saying, 'He was a straight black man who played his first televised set in bikini bottoms and knee high heeled boots, epic. He made me feel *more* comfortable with how I identify sexually simply by his display of freedom' (NME News Desk). As Prince continued to push the boundaries of gender and performance, his popularity continued to grow.

Revolutionizing the trench coat

The Revolution drummer Bobby Z reflected on the momentum in Prince's career symbolized by the arrival of the iconic purple trench coat: 'For me, the signal was the purple trench coat … we were coming from shopping at used clothing stores and digging through barrels, and then the symbolism of the purple trench coat was, "this is serious business". I knew he was going for it then' (Lasanta 182).

After humble beginnings during the *Dirty Mind* era, the trench coat visually personified Prince and sparked the makings of a twentieth-century popular culture icon. The trench coat was developed for English officers during the First World War (Sims 57). It was traditionally produced in water-resistant cotton khaki and typically double breasted with raglan sleeves, epaulettes, a belt with D-rings, storm flaps and a rear vent with button closure. After the war, the coat was marketed as rainwear and was famously worn by Humphrey Bogart in *Casablanca* (1942). This helped shift the garment from military wear to popular civilian wear (Koda and Martin 96). The functionality and practicality of the trench coat ensured the popularity of the garment with both men and women. Prince, however, wore the coat with aplomb for aesthetic and theatrical effect. He definitely played up the 'flasher' persona by wearing a trench coat. Louis Wells, one of Prince's early costume designers, commented on Prince's fondness for the trench coat, remarking on his love of the drama and mystery the garment can command (Adducci and Karsen 2016). The trench coat can be a symbol of military presence with Prince as an authority figure within the band. Prince drew attention to the trench coat and remarked to Chris Salewicz, a journalist for the NME, that his 'army surplus flasher's mac' was the only coat he had (Salewicz).

As the band's success grew, André Cymone credited his seamstress sister Sylvia as the original creator of what now had become bespoke trench coats for the band (Cymone). Vintage clothing was one of the first breakaway style trends of the 1970s and much like their purple messiah, fans could easily replicate the garment, customize it to their own tastes and join their own Revolution.

The progression of the trench coat can be tracked through three music videos from the period between 1980 and 1982. *Dirty Mind* (1980) is a gritty music video which visually relies on popular punk aesthetics of the time, such as spray paint, two-tone and second-hand clothing. Prince wears a traditional beige-coloured second-hand trench coat (DIY customized with punk metal studs), skimpy black bikini briefs, stockings and heels. His afro is erratically crimped, very much inspired by the punk hairstyle of guitarist Dez Dickerson. In *Controversy* (1981) many of the punk details remain, but the trench coat has now been dyed a deep purple and Prince is no longer topless. Instead he wears an oversized dress shirt with pin tucks and a tight dark waistcoat. The shirt is so long that it reaches his mid-thighs, but as he performs we can see underneath he wears nothing but black stockings. In *Let's Pretend We're Married* (1982) we see a bright purple trench coat, one not dissimilar to the fully realized coat of *Purple Rain* (1984). He now wears the trench coat with full-length tight black trousers with a cinched waist. Prince is presented more seductively, with close-up camera shots of his profile as he seduces the camera. He wears black eyeliner and mauve eyeshadow, and his hair is exquisitely curled. This is a shift from his previous confrontational Rude Boy *Dirty Mind* persona to a more eroticized, sensual New Romantic artist.

Purple Rain coats

Moving towards *Purple Rain*, Prince was creating the look of the film with the same level of attentive care he gave to the music for the project. Lisa Coleman remembers, 'He was obsessively reading music and fashion magazines, tracking anyone or anything that had some heat, sensing which lessons he might absorb' (Light 79). From 1981, Prince worked closely with designers Louis Wells and Vaughn Terry Jelks to create the stage looks for himself and his protégées. With only a few short weeks before the shooting of the movie, costume designer Marie France was hired to assist with The Kid's wardrobe (France 2019). He maintained close creative control over all aspects of his visuals. Archival sketches of stage outfits show detailed annotations by Prince, with reports of Prince drawing designs himself and passing them to the wardrobe team for manufacture (Matos).

With the global success of *Purple Rain* the trench coat was now fully realized as an iconic look for Prince and his band. Prince styled the classic coat with a sense of eroticism and revolutionary flair that made the trench coat truly his own. During the *Purple Rain* era he cropped the length and adopted more motorcycle-jacket stylings in luxe fabrics such as brocade and paisley prints. One of the key additions to Prince's look during the filming was the ruffled shirt which was one of the first designs France drew for Prince:

> I actually on the spot made a sketch of the ruffle shirt 'cause one thing I had noticed in his music videos was that he was wearing one of those kind of tacky tux shirts and I said you need something much better than that. You need something you know, more Prince like, literally. So I thought of the romanticism of the 18th-century ruffled shirts and I made some quick sketches. (France 2019)

The basic trench coat silhouette and high-waisted trousers were already established from previous music videos; however, France altered the trench coat fabric, investing in a high-quality silk that worked better on screen (2019). The upper collar was altered so that it mimicked a mandarin collar with an abundance of ruffles spilling from his jabot. He embellished with punk rock silver studs, rhinestones and altered the traditional functional fabric to lace, lamé, satins and so on. The masculine tailored lines were off-shot with feminine ruffs of lace and chiffon and his tiny waist was accentuated with skintight trousers adorned with opposing coloured buttons. Louis Walsh recalled introducing lace fabric to Prince, 'right away he caught onto [lace], it was a mixture of romanticism and punk, encompassing multiple genres, just like his music' (Adducci and Karsen 2016). The look was now fully realized. Journalist John Mendelsohn summed up Prince's contribution to pop culture by stating, 'Prince's False-Eyelashes Flasher in Fuchsia Lamé (as in la-me) may be the most wonderful new physical image in American pop since Bob Dylan's Electric-haired Troubadour in Winklepickers period of the mid-'60s' (Mehdelsohn).

Prince's former wife and dancer Mayte Garcia remembered the impact the fashion of the film had on her teenage years: 'The style – even an elementary school kid couldn't miss it. I mean look at the fashion in the film! Prince's ruffles, the motorcycle studs' (Garcia 4). It was not just Prince that influenced what people were wearing. The lingerie as outerwear trend of the decade was epitomized by Prince's girl group, Apollonia 6, with sales of stockings increasing 10 per cent during 1984 (Farrell 81).

As Prince's popularity grew, his music was made increasingly accessible by MTV. Judy McGrath, MTV's creative director commented that the channel was an 'ongoing almost subliminal fashion show' (Cunningham, Manginess and Reilly 216). With the advent of MTV and the hyper-popularization of the music video Prince was finally reaching the mainstream audience he had set his sights upon since the late 1970s. It can be argued that as Prince's mainstream popularity increased there was a move away from the confrontational provocateur to a more polished and palatable visual for the masses. Other influences including his developing religious faith were instrumental in Prince's departure from some of the more controversial and overtly sexual aspects of his work and fashion.

Preserving purple

Prince's legacy is only now beginning to be fully acknowledged by dress historians and there is a wealth of primary sources to be accessed at Paisley Park. Head curator Angela Marchese states that the archive holds over 7,000 costumes, with over 200 just for the *Lovesexy* tour (Matos). The Paisley Park archival team has begun to catalogue this monumental resource and it now constitutes a fascinating array of primary sources that will enable researchers to develop further insight into Prince's impact on fashion and popular culture.

To conclude, Prince Rogers Nelson carved his own way through mainstream style – cherry-picking and adapting from a smorgasbord of influences offered to him by some of his predecessors, band members and peers alike. His perception of gender and sexual awareness allowed him to experiment in both male and female fashion with an unwavering sense of defiance and confidence. By borrowing from various subcultures, he was widening his fan base, but also creatively expressing himself through fashion. Prince's controversial looks at the beginning of his career may be attributed to his desire to create headlines and sell records or to his desire as a young Black musician to explore the boundaries of his sexuality, gender and race. He used specific garments such as the trench coat, bikini briefs and stockings as a vehicle through which to explore this process and develop his image as performer. His true intentions remain elusive since Prince himself was often reluctant to share details of a personal nature and came to create a veil of mystery around himself as a man and as a performer.

Works cited

Adducci, Shannon, and Shira Karsen. 'Purple Rain Exclusive: The Stories and the Sketches Behind the Movie's Groundbreaking Style'. *Billboard.com*, 28 Apr. 2016, http://www.billboard.com/articles/news/magazine-feature/7348550/purple-rain-style-stories-sketches-exclusive-interview.

'Andre Cymone Interview'. *The Prince Podcast*, 2014, http://podcastjuice.net/the-prince-podcast-andre-cymone/.

Bream, Jon. 'World of Music Gets a Sexy Prince'. *The Minneapolis Star*, 6 Feb. 1980, https://sites.google.com/site/prninterviews/home/the-minneapolis-star-6-february-1980.

Brewster, David, ed. 'Oral History: Prince's Life, as Told by the People Who Knew Him Best'. *Minneapolis Star Tribune*, 29 Apr. 2016, http://www.startribune.com/the-life-of-prince-as-told-by-the-people-who-knew-him/376586581/#1.

Browne, David. 'Prince in the Nineties: An Oral History'. *Rolling Stone*, 5 May 2016, http://www.rollingstone.com/music/news/prince-in-the-nineties-an-oral-history-20160505.

Cole, Shaun. *'Don We Now Our Gay Apparel' Gay Men's Dress in the Twentieth Century*, Oxford: Berg, 2000.
Controversy. Directed by Bruce Gowers. Warner Bros., 1981. Music Video.
Costantino, Maria. *Men's Fashion in the Twentieth Century: From Frock Coats to Intelligent Fabrics*. B. T. Batsford Limited, Hillary Weiss, 1997.
Cunningham, Patricia A., and Linda Welters, eds. *Twentieth-Century American Fashion*. Oxford: Berg, 2005.
Diamonds and Pearls. Directed by Rebecca Blake. Paisley Park/Warner Bros., 1991. Music Video.
Dirty Mind. Directed by Unknown. Warner Bros., 1980. Music Video.
Farrell, Jeremy. *Socks and Stockings*. London: Batsford, 1992.
France, Marie. Personal Interview. 25 Apr. 2019.
Garcia, Mayte. *My Life with Prince: The Most Beautiful*. London: Trapeze, 2017.
Graffiti Bridge. Directed by Prince. Paisley Park/Warner Bros., 1990. Film.
Hahn, Alex, and Laura Tiebert. *The Rise of Prince: 1958–1988*. Mad Cat Press, 2017.
Heilbrun, Carolyn. *Toward a Recognition of Androgyny*. New York: W. W. Norton & Company, 1993.
Hill, Daniel Delis. 'Men in Briefs'. *The Gay and Lesbian Review*, 1 Nov. 2011, http://www.glreview.org/article/men-in-briefs/.
I Wanna Be Your Lover. Directed by Unknown. Warner Bros., 1979. Music Video.
Jobling, Paul. *Man Appeal: Advertising, Modernism and Menswear*. London: Berg, 2005.
Kirby, David. *Little Richard: The Birth of Rock 'n' Roll*. New York: Continuum International Publishing Group, 2011.
Koda, Harold, and Richard Martin. *Jocks and Nerds: Men's Style in the Twentieth Century*. New York: Rizzoli, 1989.
Let's Pretend We're Married. Directed by Bruce Gowers. Warner Bros., 1983. Music Video.
Light, Alan. *Let's Go Crazy: Prince and the Making of Purple Rain*. New York: Atria Paperback, 2014.
Mankowski, Diana. 'That's the Way They Liked It: Disco Fashion'. *The Ultimate History Project. Unknown*. http://ultimatehistoryproject.com/disco-fashion.html.
Matos, Michaelangelo. 'Inside Prince's Paisley Park Archives: 7,000 Artifacts Cataloged, Many More to Go'. *NYtimes.com*, 20 Apr. 2017, https://www.nytimes.com/2017/04/20/arts/music/prince-paisley-park-archives.html.
Mehdelsohn, John. 'Eleganza: The Best-Dressed List'. *Creem*, Sept. 1983, https://www.rocksbackpages.com/Library/Publication/creem.
Miller, Janice. *Fashion and Music*. Oxford: Berg, 2011.
NME News Desk. 'Frank Ocean Shares Poignant Tribute to Prince'. *Nme.com*, 20 Apr. 2016, http://www.nme.com/news/music/prince-95-1205140.
'Purple Coats and Bondage Fantasy'. Prince: Before *The Rain*, by Eloy Lasanta, Minnesota Historical Society Press, 2018: 182.
Purple Rain. Directed by Albert Magnoli. Warner Bros., 1984. Film.
Raiss, Liz. 'The Stories Behind Some of Prince's Iconic early Album Cover Photos'. *The Fader*, 21 Apr. 2016, http://www.thefader.com/2016/04/21/prince-dirty-mind-album-cover-photographer-story.
Ro, Ronin. *Prince: Inside the Music and the Masks*. London: Aurum Press Ltd., 2012.
Salewicz, Chris. 'Half a Million Dirty Minds Can't Be Wrong about This Man'. *New Musical Express*, 20 June 1981, https://sites.google.com/site/prninterviews/home/new-musical-express-nme-6-june-1981.

Sims, Josh. *Icons of Men's Style*. London: Laurence King Publishing Ltd, 2011.
Smith, Chazz. Personal Interview. 21 Mar. 2018.
Thorne, Matt. *Prince*. London: Faber & Faber, 2012.
Till, Rupert. 'Pop Stars and Idolatry: An Investigation of the Worship of Popular Music Icons, and the Music and Cult of Prince'. *Journal of Beliefs & Values* 31.1 (2010): 69–80. *T&F*, doi: 10.1080/13617671003666761.
Walser, Robert. 'Prince as Queer Poststructuralist'. *Popular Music and Society* 18.2: 79–89. *T&F*. doi: 10.1080/03007769408591556.

4

'Prettyman' in the mirror

Dandyism in Prince's Minneapolis

Karen Turman

In an interview with Dorian Lynskey, Prince remembers the first time he realized he was famous, around 1979: 'It happened very fast. I had some old clothes on because I was going to help a friend move house and some girls came by and one went: "Ohmigod, Prince!" And the other girl went, he pulls a face, "That ain't Prince." I didn't come out of the house raggedy after that.' From this moment on, Prince fully embodied a carefully designed rock star image, even at home or, allegedly, during pick-up basketball games as regaled by Charlie Murphy and Dave Chappelle (*Chappelle's Show*). Fast-forward twenty years to the track 'Prettyman' in which Prince states that he feels so nice in the morning that when he looks in the mirror he kisses it twice. Nineteenth-century French poet and art critic Charles Baudelaire writes, 'The Dandy must aspire to be sublime without interruption; he must live and sleep before a mirror' (my translation). A 'prettyman' in front of a mirror, the quintessential Baudelairean dandy aspired to the total sublimation of his existence through a constantly deliberate and self-conscious alignment of style, artistic production and social rebellion. The dandy's life constituted a spectacle on display – he was performing at all times, even for himself, as echoed by Prince in 'Prettyman' in which people can't help but stop and stare at his pretty hair.

In George Kalogerakis's article in *Vogue* from 1992, he labels Prince a 'pop dandy' as he describes the style centre[1] within Paisley Park:

> Tailors design and fit the looks that are as rigorous and refined as those of that Regency dandy Beau Brummell – chalk stripes and lace, the high-waisted pants of gros point de Venise, the bolero jackets, and the sleek one-piece jumpsuits with elastic stirrups that fit snugly under his Cuban heels to accentuate the inimitable Prince body line … . He is a pop dandy.

What is a dandy, exactly? While popular media like *Vogue*[2] celebrate Prince's legacy as a 'pop dandy', their definition of the term *dandy* remains one-dimensional, lacking the philosophical underpinnings revealed in its historical context. The *Oxford English Dictionary* summarizes the dandy as '[one] who studies above everything to dress elegantly and fashionably; a beau, fop, exquisite'. In the 2013 Rhode Island School of Design exhibition on modern dandyism, *Artist/ Rebel/ Dandy: Men of Fashion*, curator Kate Irvin explains the project's goal of promoting the image of the dandy as 'an artistic, rebellious figure who employs profound thought and imagination in his sartorial and personal presentation, forging a unique path to self-discovery and self-expression' (1). She also observes that in spite of persistent criticism, the 'elusive figure … has continuously risen above the fray to distinguish himself by conflating art, life, the body, and its accoutrements into a unified concern' (25).

The term's enigmatic opacity, rooted in the dandy's dramatic evolution over two centuries, led me to consider it as an obvious compliment to Prince's own mercurial and nebulous celebrity. I understand the dandy as a person embodying elegant yet socially rebellious style through their art, lifestyle and sartorial expression. Prince's fashion outwardly manifested his radical and provocative nature, akin to that of the original dandies. The theorizing of the dandy figure dates back to England's first 'celebrity', George 'Beau' Brummell, credited for popularizing the modern men's suit at the turn of the nineteenth century. Brummell, a social rebel preoccupied with the intricate details of his look, always projected an air of casualness: he wore the clothes, they didn't wear him.

Dandyism eventually crossed the English Channel and adapted to French society where Balzac's *Treatise on Elegant Living* from 1830 explained the merging of art and the dandy as a figure who 'captures the potential of authority built into his wardrobe while setting himself apart as a productive and creative agitator' (32). While Balzac was better at philosophizing dandyism than embodying it himself, author and self-proclaimed dandy Jules Amédée Barbey D'Aurevilly eventually both analysed and exemplified the cultural phenomenon in his 1845 essay, *Of Dandyism and of George Brummell*. Ellen Moers describes Barbey's dandy as a 'carefully exotic' artist intellectual, 'an alien phenomenon' rebelling against the capitalistic bourgeois establishment (264). A variety of countercultural artistic groups emerged in nineteenth-century Paris, in particular the bohemian artists who were immortalized in Henry Murger's *Scenes of Bohemian Life* (1851) and Puccini's operatic adaptation, *La Bohème* (1895). Primarily members of the bourgeoisie against which they rebelled, the bohemian artists drew inspiration from the Roma culture and working classes in Paris while the dandies rather aspired to emulate aristocratic artifice. Too fastidious to truly espouse the slovenly hirsute bohemian counterculture, Charles Baudelaire, art critic, father of modern poetry and precursor of the symbolism art movement, further explored the depths of the theoretical dandy in the wake of Barbey's essay. In his 1863 collection of essays on modernity entitled *The Painter of Modern Life*, Baudelaire defines the dandy through an analysis of the underestimated artist Constantin Guys. Throughout his essays, he treats the figure of the dandy as spiritual and stoical in his attention to detail regarding his all-encompassing sartorial style and way of life: a hero amid decadence, both glorious and melancholic, and cultivating his life as a work of art itself. Baudelaire exemplified the Second Empire Parisian Dandy: a misunderstood artist suffocating in *ennui* as the *Vieux Paris* dissolved around him leaving an industrialized landscape for the urban poor and a Haussmannian capitalistic playground for the ruling bourgeois class. Mediocrity was the enemy and Baudelaire avoided it at all costs through art, poetry, escapism and controversy.

Baudelaire's choice of dress reflected this sentiment as much as his work: he intentionally prescribed a carefully controlled funereal aesthetic, reflecting his rebellion of mourning – *Le Vieux Paris [qui] n'est plus!* ('The Old Paris is no more!') – symbolized by his sombre choice of hue. His austere aesthetic opposed the colourful and ornate slaves-to-fashion 'fops' of pre-revolutionary France, while standing out against the uniformity of the bourgeois men's fashions. Moers explains that his 'clothes were then cut according to his own minute instructions, and in a manner slightly different from the prevailing fashion: trousers slim and buttoned under his shoes, coat unusually long and straight.' He wore almost entirely black, and as a young man, he would add a pop of colour such as a red cravat or 'pale rose gloves' (272). According to Roland Barthes, French literary theorist, semiotician and fashion critic, these subtle details distinguished the dandy from mainstream men's fashion on a social level because 'it was the *detail* ... which started to play the distinguishing role in clothing'. In his essay 'Le Dandysme et la mode', Barthes cites 'the knot on a cravat, the material of a shirt, the buttons on a waistcoat', and 'the buckle on a shoe' as illustrating social differences and class hierarchy, all pointing to the new ambiguous values of 'taste' and 'distinction' (62).

As pronounced in his 1987 ballad, 'Adore', Prince loved to demonstrate that he was 'a man of exquisite taste', often exemplified in the details of his ensembles that constituted complete works of art from the accessories to the boots. For example, the suit worn during the 'Raspberry Beret' video is constructed of sky-blue silk with hand-painted clouds, which also covers his iconic three-inch-heel booties. This matching of suit and boot material appears in many of his other ensembles such as the red-and-black pinstripe suit worn during the all-star homage to George Harrison at the Rock and Roll Hall of Fame induction ceremony in 2004. This look also echoes the zoot suit aesthetic of the swing era, but with a unique asymmetrical jacket and more closely fitted pants. Due to the exaggerated oversized cut and wide pant leg that consumed an exorbitant amount of material during the Great Depression and the rationing era of the Second World War, wearing a zoot suit became a form of social rebellion for minority groups such as African Americans in Harlem in the 1930s and Mexican Americans in Los Angeles during the 1940s. In *Subculture: The Meaning of Style*, Dick Hebdige uses Barthes's semiological framework to theorize subversive sartorial expression through various subcultures in the UK throughout the twentieth century. He states that 'the challenge to hegemony which subcultures represent is not issued directly by them. Rather it is expressed obliquely, in style. The objections are lodged, the contradictions displayed ... at the profoundly superficial level of appearances: that is, at the level of signs' (17). In the same vein as dandies and zoot suiters, the outward style of subcultures in the UK, such as Hebdige's teddy boys, mods, punks and skinheads, represents a distinctively subversive statement against hegemonic society, a language in and of itself comprised of subtle details and bold statements.

During the Third Republic of France, in the age of decadence at the turn of the century, masculinity was deemed under threat and dandyism was associated with the ostensible degeneration of society. Because of their perceived femininity in gesture, physicality and attention to dress, dandies were often associated with queer culture at this time, with figures such as Oscar Wilde defining dandyism almost a century after Beau Brummell. Prince's inversion and appropriation of women's fashion, while peacocking hyper-masculinity, exemplifies his dandy-like questioning of gender norms but in a decidedly more flamboyant manner than his nineteenth-century French predecessors. Barbey pointed out the androgyny and multiplicity of dandyism, interpreting the sexual ambiguity of the dandy figure as strength rather than weakness. 'Twofold and multiple natures, of an undecidedly intellectual sex, their Grace is heightened by their Power, their Power by their Grace; they are the hermaphrodites of History, not of Fable' (78). This closing statement in his text on dandyism references the plurality of the figure – difficult to define and challenging to frame within a set of guidelines, gendered or otherwise. This 'undecidedly intellectual sex' signifies the dandy's transcendence of gender binaries and definitions, to which Prince was no stranger. Sarah Niblock and Stan Hawkins remind us that 'many considered Prince the gayest and queerest performer ever to hit mainstream pop' due to 'his blurring of binary distinctions throughout all his work' (26). Prince first confounded the public by refusing to adhere to any societally imposed definitions of gender representations. Much in the same way, the dandy embodied this social fear of degeneration in *fin de siècle* France in that he espoused masculine and feminine qualities, avoided domesticity, and thus played with the gender categories as defined by the morally stifling bourgeois society.

The association of queerness with dandyism became further pronounced within the Black community of New York City during the Harlem Renaissance in the late 1920s. Elisa Glick underscores the necessity to recognize 'the dandy's hypermasculinity (and anti-feminism) in order to privilege his effeminacy as a form of gender rebellion' (438). The pronouncement and evolution of the dandy's queer aesthetic in the early twentieth century is further outlined in Monica Miller's work on Black dandyism. Examining issues of race and the associated social rebellion through dandyism addresses one of the main distinctions between Baudelaire's and Prince's dandyisms. Indeed, there is evidence of dandified dress among African Americans in colonial-era festivals, minstrel shows, cakewalk dance performances and later during the Harlem Renaissance. Black dandyism has been present on a global scale for centuries, particularly in Africa and the Caribbean, and remains a niche subculture today as exemplified by the Congolese *Sapeurs*.

The rebellion of the Black dandy represents an act of taking possession over a curated look as a profound statement of power and assertion of agency within a socially oppressed group. Miller acknowledges the urgency of this distinction while highlighting influential Black dandies from the twentieth century, including Cab Calloway, Little Richard, Fonzworth Bentley and André 3000:

> For black people, clothing has long been one of the most important ways of communicating self-possession, self-respect, and a knowingness about the semiotic power of clothing and adornment. Black dandyism, as a mode of creative appropriation, has been not just a strategy of social critique but, as we have seen, a mode of survival.
>
> ('Fresh-Dressed' 153)

Miller's reference to semiotics reminds us of Barthes's work on fashion as a series of signs and symbols that express social meaning. Prince's dandyism is born of a long tradition of Black entertainers who emphasized their corporeal agency through clothing, asserting a certain level of personal and social independence through the intersection of gender, race and class identifiers. Behind Prince's sartorial flamboyance lies the need for Black entertainers to possess artistic and personal freedom. His choice of clothing, however risqué and outlandish, constituted an outward declaration of his personal, artistic and spiritual freedom to engage with the world in his own way, on his own terms.

In light of this cultural and historical context of the practical and theoretical evolution of dandyism, the question remains as to how Prince became an iconic dandy figure. In her 2017 book, *Got to Be Something Here: The Rise of the Minneapolis Sound*, Andrea Swensson addresses the issue exemplified in Dick Clark's famously awkward statement to Prince during his first television interview in 1979: 'This isn't the kind of music that comes out of Minneapolis!' Scholars such as geographer Rashad Shabazz have been aptly deconstructing the myth that Prince materialized through a cultureless vacuum in the northern tundra. Swensson addresses this gap in the discourse of the Minneapolis Sound through her research on urban development in Minneapolis and Saint Paul, highlighting the construction of I-94, 394 and the Olson Memorial Highway as affecting the Black communities with the demolition of Black-owned nightclubs and the quarantine of the Black population that in turn ignited tight-knit creative communities in North Minneapolis, where Prince was raised. During this time period from the 1960s to the 1970s, Prince's potential early style influences can be observed in Charles Chamblis's photographs of the Black community in Minneapolis from the recent exhibition *Sights, Sounds, Soul: The Twin Cities through the Lens of Charles Chamblis*, at the Minnesota Historical Society. Many of the photos of local musicians featured in this catalogue, including images of a teenaged Prince himself, simultaneously appear in Swensson's book, such as Free System, the Valdons and Maurice McKinnies. The latter's tailored pinstriped leisure suits, coupled with elaborate gold costume jewellery, an excessively wide-collared yellow blouse and astutely coiffed pompadour shed light on potential local fashion influences in the context of a charismatic soul performance. The Valdons' matching three-piece powder-blue leisure suits and white loafers rival any televised Motown group ensemble Prince may have witnessed. And while Free System's black-and-white striped bodysuits and purple ruffled blouses may have registered in Prince's subconscious during the 1970s, Chamblis's photography also includes many anonymous musical acts clad in a rainbow of inspirational dandified imagery ranging from buttercup-yellow leisure suits paired with printed blouses, matching feathered fedoras, and white wingtips to teal bell-bottoms, coordinating midriff-baring V-necked tops and Cuban ruffled sleeves in white and magenta. As Prince's cousin and band member from high school, Charles 'Chazz' Smith, pertinently pronounced during the opening plenary session of the Prince Symposium at the University of Minnesota: 'Those cats taught us how to dress' (17 April 2017).

Whereas Prince's early formative fashion influences in the Black community may be easily recognized and inferred through Chamblis's work, the origins of his penchant for androgynous looks, or presenting as femme, may be equally addressed through research into the local queer community. In his seminal 2012 book, *Land of 10,000 Loves: A History of Queer Minnesota*, Stewart Van Cleve highlights the visibility of the gay community in Minneapolis in the 1970s as a direct result of the growing number of openly gay bars in downtown Minneapolis:

> In the early 1970s, local laws that prevented men from dancing together met an unpublicized end; this change forced the straight owners of gay bars to build dance floors (however small) or to reinvent themselves as discos. Key legal battles, such as *Baker v. Nelson* or the adoption of gay rights protections in the Twin Cities, established a sense of self-respect that led many to come out and join the bar scene. (123)

Along with the increase in gay-owned establishments and the bourgeoning visibility of the queer community in the Twin Cities, drag culture was growing during this time. Van Cleve cites the Minneapolis Warehouse District as a fertile ground for androgynous fashion and sartorial creativity as he quotes 'partier' Connie Harlan: 'Everyone dressed in drag. We'd go to shops where you rented suits, tuxedos, fancy men's clothes. ... We'd look forward to it for weeks. It was fun to dress up, and some people spent hundreds' (132). Drag shows became more prevalent in downtown Minneapolis through establishments such as The Sandbox, the Club, the Roaring 20s and the Club Cabaret. Van Cleve defines drag as 'at once a campy celebration of life's absurdities and a dangerous act of retaliation against deeply held convictions. Attacking the very foundation of human identity, drag queens mimicked the socially constructed roles that gender dictated, and the audience loved it' (139–40). The philosophy behind drag culture's notion of inventing a gender-defying performative identity is not inconsistent with the socially rebellious yet elegant conflation of lifestyle and artistic wearable expression espoused through dandyism. While the creative take on the classic men's suit remains the basis of the dandy's image, Prince's early looks in the late 1970s and early 1980s appear more reminiscent of men in drag or presenting as femme. Joy Ellison reminds us that his zebra-print onesie, thigh-high stockings, and long flowing hair called to the trans community in particular, a progressive movement gaining momentum in Minneapolis at that time:

> In fact, the trans movement was particularly fierce in Prince's hometown Minneapolis. In 1975, Minneapolis passed one of the first trans-inclusive non-discrimination ordinances in the United States. The law banned discrimination based on 'having or projecting a self-image not associated with one's biological maleness or one's biological femaleness'. Prince was most assuredly a beneficiary of this landmark civil rights measure. (Ellison)

The increasingly out-and-proud queer community in Minneapolis during the 1970s may have provided aesthetic and performative inspiration to Prince, whose statement of consistently wearing eyeliner as a straight Black man did not go unnoticed and eventually contributed to his establishment as a pop music icon for the LGBTQ+ community.

Although Prince's aggressively feminine looks in 1979 may not have aligned visually with the subversive take on the classic men's suit until his New Romantic ensembles during the *Purple Rain* era, examining his pre-1984 fashion evolution reveals certain key elements regarding his unique dandyism. During the *Dirty Mind* era (1980) his women's leotards dwindled down to a scanty pair of black bikini briefs and a classic red bandana decorating his neck, all beneath a studded beige trench coat. Fashion historian Casci Ritchie explains that the trench, a stylish fashion basic today, was first developed during the First World War for British officers. The utilitarian coat quickly became a cultural icon for both men and women through exposure in Hollywood and eventually proved an egalitarian garment thanks to its accessibility to all classes through army surplus stores. Prince's exploitation of this classic piece combined with his radically subversive feminine undergarments signified a break from any conventional modes of dress for pop musicians in the early 1980s and reflected his uncategorical, new sound and controversially hypersexual lyrics.[3]

The 1981 *Controversy* album cover exhibited Prince's subsequent fashion phase, revealing a slightly more refined look: the now famous trench coat became purple and the bandana gave way to a tuxedo shirt, simple bowtie and halter vest. While this look might appear to resemble more classic menswear, waist down Prince still sported the bikini briefs, thigh-highs and 3" heeled boots. This distinct subversion of the men's suit, hardly noticeable while his guitar blocked the view of the briefs and the trench coat draped over his body, fully revealed a rebellious (pants-less!) take on the three-piece suit the moment Prince let loose on stage with his dance moves.

Prince's trench eventually evolved into a custom-made sparkly purple coat during the *1999* era and the bikini briefs and thigh-highs ceded to his signature high-waisted pants with asymmetrical button fly and matching buttons marching down both legs. This would ultimately develop into his *Purple Rain* uniform: the iconic purple trench coat, white ruffled blouse and black high-waisted pants with the asymmetrical button fly remain his most recognizable ensemble and exemplified the androgynous New Romanticism style worn by his band, The Revolution. The radically diverse collection of musicians in The Revolution was also known to dress androgynously. Joni Todd points out that Nancy Bundt's 1985 promotional photo of Prince and The Revolution acutely exemplifies this phenomenon as each member, regardless of race, gender or sexual orientation, has more or less identical permed hairstyles and all are sporting the eighteenth-century inspired brocade and velvet suits complemented by ruffled high-neck blouses and lace cuffs (with the exception of Matt Fink in his signature doctor's scrubs). This androgynous image circa *Purple Rain* was entirely intentional: Prince's own gender expression, interpreted as iconic for the queer community and the transgender community by Francesca Royster and Ellison, respectively, was transferred onto his band during the *Purple Rain* era. Bundt's photo is an extreme example of this phenomenon, but androgyny and dandyism can be found throughout the film.

Whether on or off the stage at First Avenue – the concert venue in downtown Minneapolis that provides the centralized setting of the film – inside or outside of the club, or in the urban centre of Minneapolis or in the imagined rustic countryside surrounding a mythologized 'Lake Minnetonka', the glamorously androgynous 1980s fashion and the philosophy of dandyism pervades *Purple Rain*. This homage to the Minneapolis Sound through Prince's highly fictionalized biopic showcases both local musical talent and fashionable extras from the area. In line with Baudelaire's idea that 'the Dandy must aspire to be sublime without interruption; he must live and sleep before a mirror', the majority of the cast remains in dandified dress no matter the context throughout the film. The audience members are showcased in full androgynous allure in the club, men and women equally displaying Ziggy Stardust-inspired make-up and asymmetrical hairstyles, lace gloves and leather. Throughout the film the bands themselves, notably The Revolution and The Time, sport the same clothing whether performing or not. Prince's The Kid wears various versions of his iconic *Purple Rain* uniform during band rehearsals, shopping downtown and driving out to 'Lake Minnetonka' on his motorcycle with his love interest, Apollonia. In fact, during the dressed-down scenes in his basement bedroom Prince's signature eyeliner and high heels remain firmly in place. Director Albert Magnoli even includes several pensive shots in the dressing room as Prince contemplates his dandified self in the mirror.

While Prince's highly androgynous New Romantic dandy figure prevails throughout the film, Morris Day's foil presents a quintessential caricature of the essential dandy. Unlike Prince/ The Kid, whom we never see out of his dandified trappings, the opening montage reveals the first glimpse of Day in preparation for his night out, vacuuming in boxers, an undershirt and a do-rag, and therefore indicating the level of work entailed to fully embrace dandyism. After this scene, Day is never spotted without his impeccable zoot suit, Stacy Adams wingtips and various dapper accessories, including canes, scarves, silk handkerchiefs and even a handy mirror that materializes with the ever-present and delightful Jerome Benton, who might be himself considered the ultimate accessory to Day's dandy. Even Day's authentic comedic persona, complete with mockingly aristocratic voice register, turns of phrase and subtle gesture, reflects his devotion to the role of exemplary dandy par excellence, and ultimately allows him to steal the spotlight as the film's loveable and outrageously entertaining villain.

With their duelling approaches to dandyism, Prince and Day's *Purple Rain* characters are rooted in a long-standing practice for men of colour. As Miller outlines in her work, dandyism among men of colour has existed for centuries and continues to thrive today. In addition, Black men's fashion in the Twin Cities is a current topic of interest as exemplified by ongoing 'The Dandies Project' since 2014, in which the dandy is defined as 'a gentleman who places particular importance upon physical aesthetics, refined in language and enjoys leisured hobbies. His life is pursued with the importance of individuality while having a driven purpose of self-awareness' (2). The exhibition's mission is to 'highlight the positive influence and impact that men of color have in their community' (1). In this light, we can see the positive impact that Prince's style has had on both African American communities and queer communities as his ever-evolving sartorial expressions continuously addressed the importance of representation and have inspired progressive movements for decades, intentionally or not. A distinct continuation of the legacy of dandyism, popularized by the British, theorized by the French and embraced by Black and queer communities, Prince's personal style reflected his profound cultural influence as manifested in the ways in which he redefined limits, questioning the social assumptions categorizing race, class, sex, fashion, gender and history itself.[4]

Notes

1. Stacia Lang served as head of Prince's design department at the time of this interview. Her exquisite work includes the many specialized suits from the *Diamonds and Pearls* era through the *Love Symbol* album, and most notably the infamous backless yellow lace pantsuit worn during the 1991 MTV Video Music Awards.
2. In her 1998 book, *Rising Star: Dandyism, Gender, and Performance in the Fin de Siècle*, Rhonda Garelick deftly analyses the *Esquire* piece showcasing Prince as a dandy in 1995, complete with photographs and paper-doll cut-out images suggesting he is at once 'an imposing rock star and diminutive dress-up doll, a living human being and a mere template for the ephemera of *la mode*, an artist and a plaything'. Garelick asserts that the editors do indeed comprehend dandyism beyond the superficial definition (155).
3. Ritchie, Casci. 'Before the Rain 1980 to 1984: How Prince Got "The Look".' *The Costume Society.* 19 April 2018. http://costumesociety.org.uk/blog/post/before-the-rain-1980-to-1984-how-prince-got-the-look
4. 'This essay was written before the release of Prince's memoirs, *The Beautiful Ones* (2019), but it bears mentioning in a study of his style that one of the first memories he includes concerns observing his parents dressing up for a night out (80). He pays homage to their sense of style but focuses specifically on his father's sharkskin suit and arrowhead tie and the sharpness with which he accessorized, admiring how his father seemed to surpass his mother in elegance. In Prince's first wife, Mayte Garcia's, 2016 memoirs, *The Most Beautiful*, she includes a passage on Prince's immaculate dress and the ways in which he would never allow jeans, sweatpants, or sneakers around Paisley Park, unless it was for basketball (122). She describes how he taught her the importance of maintaining style at all times, even at home, and admits that he would often draw inspiration for his own fashions from her wardrobe, thus echoing the sartorial dynamics he observed in his own father and mother as a child and exemplifying Dandyism in married life.'

Works cited

de Balzac, Honoré. *Treatise on Elegant Living.* Trans. Napoleon Jeffries, Wakefield Press, 2010.
Barthes, Roland. 'Le Dandysme et la mode'. *Language and Fashion.* Trans. Andy Stafford. Ed. Andy Stafford and Michael Carter. Bloomsbury, 2013. 60–4.
Baudelaire, Charles. 'Journaux Intimes'. *Œuvres complètes.* Bibliothèque de la Pléiade, Gallimard, 1961. 1247–316.
Baudelaire, Charles. 'Le peintre de la vie moderne'. *Œuvres complètes.* Bibliothèque de la Pléiade, Gallimard, 1961. 1152–92.

Baudelaire, Charles. 'Les Fleurs du mal et autres poésies'. *Œuvres complètes*. Bibliothèque de la Pléiade, Gallimard, 1961. 3–228.

'Charlie Murphy's True Hollywood Stories--Prince'. *Chappelle's Show*, written by Neal Brennan, directed by Neal Brennan and Scott Vincent, Comedy Central, 2004.

d'Aurevilly, Barbey, and Jules Amédée. *Dandyism*. Trans. Douglas Ainslie, PAJ Publications, 1988.

'Dandy'. *The Oxford English Dictionary*. Oxford University Press, 2017, oed.com. Web. 10 May 2017.

Dick Clark Productions. 'American Bandstand'. *ABC Network*, Los Angeles. 26 Jan. 1980.

Ellison, Joy. 'When Were You Mine? Prince's Legacy in the Context of Transgender History'. Conference presentation. *Purple Reign: An Interdisciplinary Conference on the Life and Legacy of Prince*. University of Salford, Manchester, UK. 26 May 2017.

Garcia, Mayte. *The Most Beautiful*. Hachette Books, 2016.

Garelick, Rhonda K. *Rising Star: Dandyism, Gender, and Performance in the Fin de Siècle*. Princeton University Press, 1998.

Glick, Elisa F. 'Harlem's Queer Dandy: African-American Modernism and the Artifice of Blackness'. *MFS Modern Fiction Studies, Volume 49, Number 3*, Johns Hopkins University Press, Fall 2003. 414–42.

Hawkins, Stan and Sarah Niblock. *Prince: The Making of a Pop Music Phenomenon*. Burlington, VT: Ashgate, 2011.

Hebdige, Dick. *Subculture: The Meaning of Style*. Routledge, 1979.

Irvin, Kate. 'Fabricating a Dream: Two Centuries of Sketching and Defining the Dandy'. *Artist/ Rebel/ Dandy: Men of Fashion*. Ed. Kate Irvin and Laurie Anne Brewer. Museum of Art, Rhode Island School of Design, Yale University Press, 2013.

Kalogerakis, George. 'Prince in Vogue: Portraits of an Icon'. *Vogue*, 21 Apr. 2016. Web. 1 May 2017. www.vogue.com/article/prince-from-the-archives.

Lynskey, Dorian. 'Prince: I Am a Musician, and I Am Music'. *The Guardian*, 23 June 2011. Web. 2 May 2017. www.theguardian.com/music/2011/jun/23/prince-interview-adele-internet.

Magnoli, Albert, dir. *Purple Rain*. 1984; USA: Warner Bros, 2007. DVD.

Miller, Monica L. 'Fresh-Dressed Like a Million Bucks: Black Dandyism and Hip-Hop'. *Artist/ Rebel/ Dandy: Men of Fashion*. Ed. Kate Irvin and Laurie Anne Brewer. Museum of Art, Rhode Island School of Design, Yale University Press, 2013.

Miller, Monica L. *Slaves to Fashion: Black Dandyism and the Styling of Black Diasporic Identity*. Duke University Press, 2009.

Moers, Ellen. *The Dandy: Brummell to Beerbohm*. University of Nebraska Press, 1978.

Moody, Richard. *The Dandies Project*. Gallop Studios, 2014.

Murger, Henry. *Scènes de la vie de bohème*. Gallimard, 1988.

Nelson, Prince Rogers. 'Adore'. Released March 1987. Track 16 on *Sign o' the Times*. Warner Bros. Compact Disc.

Nelson, Prince Rogers. *The Beautiful Ones*. Spiegel & Grau: 2019.

Nelson, Prince Rogers. 'Prettyman'. Released November 1999. Hidden track on *Rave Un2 the Joy Fantastic*. NPG Arista. Compact Disc.

Puccini, Giacomo. *La Bohème*. 1896.

Ritchie, Casci. 'Before the Rain 1980 to 1984: How Prince Got "The Look"'. *The Costume Society*. 19 Apr. 2018. http://costumesociety.org.uk/blog/post/before-the-rain-1980-to-1984-how-prince-got-the-look.

Seru, Davu (author) and Charles Chamblis (photographs). *Sights, Sounds, Soul: The Twin Cities through the Lens of Charles Chamblis*. Minnesota Historical Society Press, 2017.

Smith, Charles 'Chazz'. Plenary session at the Prince Symposium at the University of Minnesota, 17 Apr. 2017.

Swensson, Andrea. *Got to Be Something Here: The Rise of the Minneapolis Sound*. University of Minnesota Press, 2017.

Todd, Joni. 'I'll Paint a Beard on the Mona Lisa Even Though It's My Favorite Jaw: The Revolutionary Careers of Prince and Marcel Duchamp'. Conference presentation. *Purple Reign: An Interdisciplinary Conference on the Life and Legacy of Prince*. University of Salford, Manchester, UK. 25 May 2017.

Van Cleve, Stewart. *Land of 10,000 Loves: A History of Queer Minnesota*. University of Minnesota Press, 2012.

5

The sound of purple

Prince and the development of the Minneapolis Sound

Maciej Smółka

Introduction

When we think of a local-music scene, there are always certain people responsible for its establishment. They do not create it out of thin air; rather, it is a product of specific combinations of factors intertwined in a web of regional specificity. When these characteristics are explicitly connected with an urban space, we can speak of the creation of the city's distinctive music scene (Becker 2004: 17). If we accept this reasoning, an obvious yet extremely important fact becomes even clearer: music always comes from a place. It is created by certain people, in certain places, in certain cultural and historical contexts, in certain economic, geographical and social backgrounds (Leyshon et al. 1998: 4–5). One may even say that a culture, in a very broad sense, is a factor that determines an art created in a specific place. This was the case in Minneapolis, where Prince played a crucial role in the development of the phenomenon which connected local specificity and the city itself, resulting in the Minneapolis Sound – music now associated with the local space, Prince, his signature purple colour, people living in the Minneapolis and its culture.

Sometimes it seems that a character of the space from which an art originates is being described by it. We may speak of a strong, unambiguous connection between Joy Division and Manchester, The Beatles and Liverpool, San Francisco and Jefferson Airplane, Detroit and Kevin Saunderson and so on. The place reminds us of the act, and the act reminds us of the place. This association becomes even more powerful when a local scene develops its own specific musical style or, as I will call it in this chapter, sound. Then, in a large number of cases, the art is merged with the place in the most visible, representative way possible – through its name.

The history of American music provides numerous examples of such phenomena. We could speak of New Orleans Jazz, Chicago Blues, the Bakersfield Sound, the San Francisco Sound, the Memphis Sound, Detroit Techno and so on. Each of these examples shows an important correlation between a space and an art, which is created in a broader context. This may lead to an assumption that in academic analyses an understanding of a sound cannot go without an understanding of a place and its context. One has to have in mind the notion of how we consider the city to be the music, and the music to be the city (Pecknold 2014: 20–1). A number of academics analysed such issues, trying and succeeding in taking the approach of cultural studies, sociology, human geography and others in order to understand correlation between the place and the music (Lashua et al. 2014: 3–5).

The Minneapolis Sound can and has to be analysed in such fashion, given the fact that the specific subgenre was and still is submerged in local structures of its specific culture and history in a broad sense. The figure who one must focus on in order to fully comprehend a character of this subgenre is, obviously, Prince, who played a crucial role in shaping the sound now associated not only with his persona but also with the city itself.

In this chapter I will analyse the role Prince played in the development of the Minneapolis Sound in its most recognizable fashion, as well as his influence and input as the main mentor of a group of musicians that shared his artistic vision. The discussion will also consider the genesis of this phenomenon – the cultural context of the city with its social structure in the forefront. In order to fully comprehend the specificity of the Minneapolis Sound, and the significance of Prince in this local-music scene, the linkage between the place and the art that happened on various levels has to be taken into account. So, in this case, the question of the relation between the artist, the city and the local scene has to be asked. Moreover, the issue of how and why these relationships have shaped and have been shaping the phenomenon we associate with Minneapolis so strongly to this day is to be studied.

My study shows that Prince was indeed a mentor and a preceptor of the Minneapolis Sound, and that he developed its most famous form after the release of his 1980 album *Dirty Mind*. However, it has to be mentioned that there was a musical scene in the city before that event, and that he drew from a culture specific to Minneapolis even prior to his biggest successes. This leads to an assumption that he did not invent the Minneapolis Sound per se but redefined, modified, developed, popularized, promoted, cherished, recorded and shared it, thereby becoming a person who indisputably has to be associated with this phenomenon. Moreover, Minneapolis as a living space, put in a distinct cultural context, played a significant role in this process, conveying its messages through Prince, making him the signature artist and the ambassador of the Minneapolis Sound.

The starting point of my discussion will be an overview of the concept of the sound of a city based on a few examples. With knowledge of such a background, one would be able to understand the significance of local specificity in studying music scenes. Afterwards, I will research the social background of the Minneapolis Sound that eventually lead to Prince becoming a significant figure in the city's artistic landscape, and to the release of *Dirty Mind* in 1980. By doing so, I wish to make clear how crucial cultural context is to the proper perception of works of Prince and his key role in developing the sound which is Minneapolis' musical signature mark.

The sound of a city

The first thing that strikes us when hearing about the Minneapolis Sound is probably the connection between the name of the city and the idea that this particular city can actually possess a particular sound. This may bring to mind specific elements that construct an urban sonic landscape, such as the sound of traffic from cars or trains, that of nature from the lakeshore or from birds, and so on. However, this chapter's understanding of this phrase links to another category of sound, similar to the one provided by urban geographers Ola Johansson and Thomas L. Bell, who understand that 'popular music ... is a cultural form that actively produces geographic discourses and can be used to understand broader social relations and trends, including identity, ethnicity, attachment to place, cultural economies, social activism, and politics' (2009: 2).

Therefore, the sound of the city itself can be treated as a work of the local-music scene, which is so characteristic and strongly merged with the urban tissue of the city. Taking this into consideration, one may think of the sound of a particular city as a subgenre of music, distinctly associated with a local-music scene or with a music played within this city, understood more as a cultural region than as an administrative one. Moreover, we may consider this a local phenomenon, which is associated only with just one location, which is the reason why a particular sound is signified with a particular place. This is the reason cities' sounds are much more than just a musical style, subgenre or a local artistic scene. It is a combination of regional culture, art, history and people that create works uniquely and unambiguously connected to a particular place. Hence, the usage of the phrase 'phenomenon' in describing sounds may be the best one – not limiting academics' views to one feature (e.g. strictly musical, sociological or historical) but broadening analyses to a wide range of point of views that ultimately makes it so distinctive.

Popular music, especially in the United States, provided us with numerous examples of such occurrences, some of them having a significant impact on national and global arts industry. A few of them are worth mentioning in order to put Minneapolis' music scene into a broader context. Among others, the San Francisco Sound may be considered as one of the most important city sounds in the history of American music, keeping in mind that it was an essential part of hippies' counterculture in 1960s. The ideology behind this movement was significantly popularized by such bands as Jefferson Airplane, Quicksilver Messenger Service and Grateful Dead. This variation of psychedelic rock created and promoted by groups residing in the Bay Area became one of the first noteworthy subgenres of rock (Smółka 2015: 44–6). Another sound worth mentioning is the one that originated in Seattle, which is now commonly known as grunge, and associated groups like Nirvana, Soundgarden and Pearl Jam, to name just few. The local specificity, economy, geography and rising alternative music record labels, most notably Sub Pop, created a subgenre of rock music that eventually became an international phenomenon transgressing into a world of celebrities, fashion, a rebellious style of life (Grohl 2014: ep. 7). The Palm Desert Sound on the other hand was developed mostly by the impact of natural geography. Group of friends located in Palm Desert, California, and other nearby cities started playing in wide-open spaces in desert areas, creating their variation of rock music, now called as desert rock. Kyuss was the first band to become significantly popular, but the one that still is recording and constantly promoting its variations of the phenomenon is Queens of the Stone Age – one of the most popular contemporary rock acts (Smółka 2016: 130–2, 136–8). Other examples of such sounds include New Orleans Jazz, Chicago Blues, Bakersfield Sound (or broader California Sound), Philadelphia Soul, Nashville Sound, Memphis Sound, Detroit Techno, Denver Sound and so on.

By acknowledging this number of specific local-music scenes, one may wonder if there are any characteristics connecting all of them. I would like to suggest that there are four main aspects that can be applied to most of these phenomena. First of all, (a) there has to be a cooperating group of musicians that eventually create a music scene, who (b) share a common artistic idea about an art they are creating. Moreover, (c) a leader – whether a person or an organization, such as a record company or a studio – is also an important factor. Last but not least, a city is an incontestably key factor, which makes the sound from a city a city sound. Because of that, (d) a specificity of a city – social reality, economy, natural environment, infrastructure or demographics – is an element that cannot be overvalued.

The Minneapolis Sound is, of course, one of the best examples of city sounds, the development of which by a leader – Prince – played a significant, if not a crucial, role. Therefore, I would like to suggest that his figure was a base on which the modern Minneapolis Sound was established, and that this phenomenon also meets the other conditions mentioned above. In order to do so, one has to study each of the elements that eventually construct a city sound – a city and a sound.

The kind and the from

My main inspiration for this chapter came from an unexpected source. On 26 January 1980, Prince took the stage of *American Bandstand*, an extremely popular national television show hosted by the legendary Dick Clark, who at that time, being an extremely influential figure in the music industry, could make an artist a star or end their career. Prince, then a young, 21-year-old musician took a chance and created an enigmatic persona, and through a terribly awkward interview created a performance that became one of the most memorable in the history of the show. However, the fragment that interested me the most was one of the first sentences that Dick Clark said right at the beginning of that interview – 'This is not the kind of music that comes from Minneapolis, Minnesota.' The fact that a few months later Prince introduced to the world the phenomenon later named as the Minneapolis Sound with his album *Dirty Mind* makes Clark's comment seem extremely interesting to investigate what makes a specific sound become a signature mark of a city.

There are two keywords in the sentence in question: 'kind' and 'from'. The television host emphasizes the fact that there is a particular music that can sound as if it is coming from a particular place in the United States. Moreover, it can be concluded that in this statement Clark had done the tremendous work of a cultural studies or a human geography scholar claiming that the cultural context of a place defines what kind of music comes from it. He even highlighted that there is an anticipation of a particular kind of music when a viewer knows where an artist is from. We, as an audience, expect that we will receive a product from a particular brand – in this case from a city with all its heritage and culture.

Dick Clark's 'kind' and 'from' are keywords that may become steps in the process of reconstructing what the Minneapolis Sound is, how it was created and why we associate a particular music with a particular place. Therefore, the beliefs on which Clark based his presumptions would have to be examined. In this case, it would be a cultural reality of Minneapolis prior to 1980 with a focus on a possible background of the Minneapolis Sound.

The element that ought to be at the centre of an academic's attention is the social background of a music scene in the city, especially in communities in which Prince grew up. Therefore, demographics could be the starting point of such an analysis. Data provided in a graph by Minnesota Compass in *Persons of Color as a Percent of Total Population* (2017) shows that their number in Twin Cities area reached approximately 27,447 in 1960, which is a 1.8 per cent of the total population. In 1970, it was respectively 50,067 (2.7 per cent) and 112,603 (5.7 per cent) in 1980. However, a second graph, entitled *Black Population by Regional Counties*, shows that, among those people, Black population was only 20,711 (1.4 per cent of the whole of Twin Cities' population) in 1960, 32,140 (1.7 per cent) in 1970 and 49,183 (2.5 per cent) in 1980. Obviously, these statistics show that the African American population was strikingly low. Because of that, it can be assumed that Minneapolis was not a perfect place from which a mainstream R&B act might have emerged, justifying Clark's reaction.

Dylan Hicks in his insightful article *How Minneapolis Made Prince* (2017) on the website Slate studies and describes the indisputable relation between the cultural context of Prince's environment and the sound later popularized by him. As Hicks writes, until 1976 there was only one radio station regularly playing R&B – KUXL, which ended its broadcast each day after dark. Moreover, the infrastructure for musical entertainment that accepted the Black community was limited due to racism. Successes of local African American acts were just a few exceptions. They were forced to limit their activities mostly to community centres like The Way in northern Minneapolis, while major clubs in downtown Minneapolis which accepted Black audiences were potential targets of police raids. 'Despite all this,' he adds, 'Prince emerged into a small but vibrant, competitive yet nurturing scene of musicians. ... Mind & Matter, Cohesion, Flyte Tyme, and 94 East were among [R&B groups of the period].' It is important to mention that this era was captured on two music label-curated compilations: *Twin Cities Funk & Soul* (2012) by Secret Stash Records and *Purple Snow* (2013) by Numero Group. Both albums are important exemplifications of the both Saint Paul's and Minneapolis' small and mostly forgotten, but at that time – from 1960s to 1970s – thriving African American music scenes (Gonzales 2014; Kellman 2013).

It has to be highlighted that all of these bands brought up by Hicks were active in a similar environment, under similar influences, in the similar social, economic and historical context in comparison to Prince. Because of that, the scene exemplified on the two albums mentioned earlier represents the time in Minneapolis' music history that I would like to consider an aesthetic core – the protoplast on which Prince based his later endeavours, modernizing it and developing the sound now associated with the city.

The sound of purple

Having all of this in mind, a particular image of Minneapolis, which was Prince's reality, becomes visible. Lack of opportunities to get acquainted with R&B acts caused a specific mixture of influences to emerge in the region, to which, I believe, Prince must have been exposed to, and which eventually resulted in *Dirty Mind*'s sound. The artist at that time would listen to top-hits rock stations and build his aesthetics on this ground. Hicks (2016) points out such influences as Santana, Fleetwood Mac, Joni Mitchell, Grand Funk Railroad, and adds Sly Stone, James Brown, The Stylistics and others as acts that Prince studied on his own. Thus, both R&B music and top rock radio hits should be considered as key influences for what would later become the Minneapolis Sound.

There is another fact that cannot be omitted in an analysis of Prince's involvement in reshaping Minneapolis' local-music scene – a complete power over his art, being in control of almost every aspect of it. He was a leader, which eventually turned out to be an effect of his own personal vision. Therefore, what a Prince scholar should be studying in connection with the Minneapolis Sound is the elements that built his vision.

The third aspect that I would like to suggest is Minneapolis' own music scene. It has to be remembered that the city was a place where at the same time as Prince was starting his career, such bands as Hüsker Dü or The Replacements were also playing their first shows and releasing their first albums, which suggests the vibrancy of notable music life in the region, especially in terms of new wave and punk.

Prince's 1980 album *Dirty Mind* has to be treated as a milestone – not only in his career but also in the perception of what is Minneapolitan music. Jeremy Ohmes in his *PopMatters*' article simply titled 'The Minneapolis Sound' (2009) described the LP's sound as 'a visionary, wildly ambitious amalgam of funk, punk, new wave, R&B, pop and experimental rock, laced with sexually explicit lyrics and over-the-top shock'. He also adds,

> From the title track's robotic funk to the synth pop of 'When You Were Mine' to the hyper-drive punk of 'Sister' to the straight-up dance party jams, 'Uptown' and 'Partyup', Prince experiments with everything on *Dirty Mind* and fuses black and white musical styles with little regard for established genres. ... More importantly though, Prince's audacious third album set the style and tone for much of the innovative urban music the Twin Cities would soon be known for.

These few sentences sum up what became a general idea behind the sound of the city of Minneapolis – to merge contrasting influences from different cultural circles, adding the specificity of the region in order to generate a new quality that would epitomize the vision of an artist. *Dirty Mind*, now considered a textbook example of the Minneapolis Sound, presented synthesizers at the forefront, fast tempo, processed drums, and an unmistakable mixture of influences ranging from R&B, through funk, disco and new wave to punk. And the most important aspect of all these observations is the recognition of the fact that this did not come from nothing – it came from a cultural context of the city of Minneapolis, which became a reason to call it a 'Minneapolis Sound'.

Prince wrote each of the songs on the album with an exception of 'Dirty Mind' (co-written with Doctor Fink), 'Uptown' (co-written with André Cymone) and 'Partyup' (co-written with Morris Day). Moreover, the second and the third were originally credited solely to Prince, which highlights the fact that the album should be considered a one-man endeavour. There were only three minor guest appearances: 'Head' (vocals by Lisa Coleman, synthesizer by Doctor Fink) and 'Dirty Mind' (synthesizers by Doctor Fink). Everything else was written, performed and produced by Prince, which makes it rather unquestionably a one-man band's artistic vision. This line of reasoning leads to very specific and strong conclusions about the genesis of the post-1980 Minneapolis Sound – Prince wrote the songs and presented his ideas, which started a movement; he was the one responsible.

However, if we stop at this moment, the story would not be told in its entirety. In order to do so, an example from the *Purple Rain* film could be helpful, but not in terms of the storyline, the signature clothes and scenography, the acting or the legendary album of the same title, but rather in the filmed performances. The movie includes such acts as Prince and The Revolution, The Time, Dez Dickerson and the Modernaires, and Apollonia 6, playing a total of fourteen songs, all of which were written or co-written, and produced by Prince, often under an alias. The truth is that Prince, in fact, was The Time, which he created as a specific side project that he officially was not part of but provided all of the artistic material for. The same goes for many other bands involved in Minneapolis' scene, such as the aforementioned Apollonia 6 or Vanity 6 (Carcieri 2004: 11–17, 27–8).

Prince was not only behind the development of the new sound of Minneapolis but was also a mentor (if not a leader or a commander) of other bands he created in order to promote his idea about the music. His web of artistic acts created a distinct phenomenon that played a characteristic subgenre, which later became associated with the city of its origin. Promotion of his music led to the promotion of artists themselves, and eventually to the promotion of his idea and vision. Consequently, one may as well call Prince the constructor of the Minneapolis Sound, which was built by his own music, but also by the hands of other acts that have taken the city by storm.

The Minneapolis Sound

When Prince is put right in the centre of the Minneapolis Sound, continuing earlier reasoning and stating that he was a key figure, leader and mentor, one may feel tempted to abandon Minneapolis and call this phenomenon 'the Prince Sound' instead. In fact, why should not we do this, considering the fact that he almost single-handedly realized his artistic vision and spread it through a wide web of groups and their albums? The answer to this question is rather simple, but extremely important to understanding the idea behind cities' sounds. This exclusion would lead to a denial of the role of the city, its culture and history that eventually influenced and led Prince to the development of the Minneapolis Sound.

This brings us back to what we discussed in the beginning of this chapter: that music always comes from a certain place, which can influence the art created within. The role of Prince was undeniably crucial in the development of the modern Minneapolis Sound, but so was that of Minneapolis. Its culture, society, demographics, infrastructure and history – each of these elements as well as other specificities of urban life became factors that had this musical phenomenon built.

When compared to characteristics of other cities' sounds I have mentioned before, the Minneapolis Sound without any doubt fits these terms. There was (a) a significant group of musicians working together (b) towards a common artistic vision, (c) led and mastered by Prince (d) in a specific location that considerably influenced his idea about music he wanted to be played under his own guidance.

It could be said that the third one – (c) the leadership of Prince – would be the most important, treating him as the pivotal figure, the catalyst and forerunner in the transformation of local-music scene into something more. There is no doubt that he brought all of the cultural influences, modified the musical environment in which he grew up and then developed a characteristic style, which he popularized and promoted not only by his own music but also with the bands he controlled. All of this led to the beginning, popularity and success of the best-known variation of the local sound, the Minneapolis Sound.

Nevertheless, in the proper understanding of the idea of cities' sounds, the place is the starting point, which may or may not turn out to be the most important factor but should be the base upon which everything else is built. No matter whether we look at the examples of the San Francisco Sound, the Nashville Sound, the Seattle Sound, the Minneapolis Sound or any other, the idea of the place of origin is primary, which is represented by a name of a phenomenon – a combination of place's name and the word 'sound'. There is no city sound without a city, just as there is no art without people who make it. These people are always submerged in the characteristics of a place, all of this being embodied in the final product of their work – the music we all listen to.

Works cited

'Black Population by Regional Counties'. *Minnesota Compass*, http://www.mncompass.org/demographics/race#7-5086-d.

Becker, Howard. 'Jazz Places'. *Music Scenes. Local, Translocal, and Virtual*. Ed. Andy Bennett and Richard A. Peterson, Vanderbilt University Press, 2004. 17–27.

Carcieri, Matt. *Prince: A Life in Music*, iUniverse, 2004.

Gonzales, Michael A. 'Prince Ain't the Only Minneapolis Sound'. *EBONY*, Ebony Media Operations, 18 Apr. 2014, www.ebony.com/entertainment-culture/purple-snow-explores-the-minneapolis-sound-444.

Hicks, Dylan. 'How Minneapolis Made Prince'. *Slate, The Slate Group*, 22 Apr. 2016, www.slate.com/articles/arts/metropolis/2016/04/prince_s_sound_taste_and_drive_were_forged_by_minneapolis.html.

Hicks, Dylan. 'Nowhere But Here'. *Mpls.St.Paul Magazine*, Key Enterprises, 25 June 2014, http://mspmag.com/arts-and-culture/prince/.

Johansson, O., and Thomas L. Bell. 'Introduction'. *Sound, Society and the Geography of Popular Music*. Ed. Ola Johansson and Thomas L. Bell, Ashgate Publishing, 2009. 1–6.

Kellman, Andy. 'Purple Snow: Forecasting the Minneapolis Sound. Allmusic Review'. *Allmusic.com*, RhythmOne, 3 Dec. 2013, http://www.allmusic.com/album/purple-snow-forecasting-the-minneapolis-sound-mw0002587996.

Lashua, Brett et al. 'Introduction: Sounds and the City'. *Sounds and the City: Popular Music, Place, and Globalization*. Ed. Brett Lashua et al., The Guilford Press, 2014. 1–15.

Leyshon, Andrew et al. 'Introduction: Music, Space, and the Production of Place'. *The Place of Music*. Ed. Andrew Leyshon et al., The Guilford Press, 1998. 1–30.

Ohmes, Jeremy. 'The Minneapolis Sound'. *PopMatters*, PopMatters, 3 June 2009, www.popmatters.com/feature/94060-the-minneapolis-sound/.

Pecknold, Diane. 'Heart of the Country? The Construction of Nashville as the Capital of Country Music'. *Sounds and the City. Popular Music, Place, and Globalization*. Ed. Brett Lashua et al., Palgrave Macmillan, 2014. 19–37.

'Persons of Color as a Percent of Total Population'. *Minnesota Compass*, http://www.mncompass.org/demographics/race#7-5081-d.

Smółka, Maciej, 'Jak brzmi pustynia: kulturowa analiza desert rocka jako istoty brzmienia miasta Palm Desert'. *Kultura Rocka 2. Słowo – dźwięk – performance, vol. 1*. Ed. Jakub Osiński et al., Prolog, 2016. 128–40.

Smółka, Maciej. 'San Francisco Sound. Charakterystyka i znaczenie'. *Eyes on America II*. Ed. Radosław Rybkowski, AT Wydawnictwo, 2015. 33–47.

Sonic Highways. Directed by Dave Grohl, HBO, 2014.

Part Two

Purple performance and presence

6

Glam slammed

Visual identity in Prince's *Lovesexy*

Mike Alleyne and Kirsty Fairclough

If *Sign o' the Times* signalled the beginning of a period in which Prince began to wrestle with moral and spiritual questions – good versus evil, God versus Satan, pleasure versus virtue – the release of 1988's *Lovesexy* marked its full arrival.

The central tenet of the album, the battle between God (good) and the Devil (evil, personified on the album as 'Spooky Electric'), which largely seems to be an internalized moral struggle, is introduced early in the album. 'Lovesexy' as a conceptual framework is never made fully clear, but it seems to consist of a state of spiritual contentment that fuses a love of God and a connection with humanity via sexuality. *Lovesexy* presented this set of themes as a postmodern challenge to grand narratives – the look and feel of the album operates to explore these themes in a pop culture package that is brimming with creativity, boldness, colour and energy.

This chapter will explore how the visual identity of the album chimes with the sociocultural tenets of the late 1980s and assess the controversies surrounding the *Lovesexy* album cover. It references the historical roles and functions of the album cover, Prince's status as a visual icon on his cover art and comparative perspectives on his nine preceding album covers. Moreover, the following analysis incorporates the mainstream cover norms at the time of *Lovesexy*'s release, photographer Jean-Baptiste Mondino's collaborative approach to the project with Prince and ways in which negative critical response to the resulting art contributed to its relative commercial failure. The assessment interrogates multiple possible readings of the cover and its implications for Prince's visual presentation on later releases. In order to examine *Lovesexy* as a cultural product, we must first turn to the cultural context in which it was produced.

Postmodernism had emerged as a cultural movement in the mid-to-late twentieth century and by the 1980s, it is not too far a step to suggest that it had reached deeply into popular culture. In cinema, music, art and architecture, its influence could be recognized in the increasingly self-conscious mix of styles and conventions and a general distrust of monolithic art forms. Yet it remained notoriously difficult to define and this difficulty stems from its wide usage in a very wide range of cultural and critical movements since the 1970s onwards. Postmodernism describes not only a period but also a set of ideas, and can only be understood in relation to another equally complex term – that of modernism. Modernism was a diverse art and cultural movement in the late nineteenth and early twentieth centuries whose common thread was a break with tradition, epitomized by poet Ezra Pound's injunction to 'make it new!'. The 'post' in postmodern of course suggests 'after' and postmodernism is best understood as a questioning of the ideas and values associated with a form of modernism that believes in progress and innovation. Modernism insists on a clear divide between art and popular culture. But like modernism, postmodernism does not designate any one 'correct' style of art or culture. It is actually often associated with pluralism and an abandonment of conventional ideas of originality and authorship in favour of a pastiche of 'dead' styles.

Theorists associated with postmodernism often used the term to mark a new cultural epoch in the West. For philosopher Jean-Francois Lyotard, the postmodern condition was defined as 'incredulity towards metanarratives' – that is, a loss of faith in science and other emancipatory projects within modernity, such as Marxism. Postmodernism can also be a *critical* project, revealing the cultural constructions designated as truth and opening up a variety of repressed other histories of modernity, such as those of women, homosexuals and the colonized. The modernist canon itself is revealed as patriarchal and racist, dominated by White heterosexual men. As a result, one of the most common themes addressed within postmodernism relates to cultural identity.

How then did this complex set of ideas find its way into Prince's work in such an overt way?

Prince and postmodernism

Prince's connection to postmodernism is clear in a number of elements of his work, and as Nancy Holland has argued in her paper 'Prince: Postmodern Icon',

> His music provides the basis for deconstructing the obvious hierarchies of race, gender, and sexuality, but also those of the sacred and the profane, the writer/composer/producer and the performer, and even Self and the Other. He touched the hearts and lives of a far wider audience than any theorist and helped create a new cultural climate without any apparent awareness of academic postmodernism. This opens the possibility for a deconstruction on the meta-level of another traditional hierarchy, the one between reason and intuition, or put differently, between words and music. (Holland 2017)

The primary tenet of the postmodern is the deconstruction of hierarchical oppositions (God/mortal, good/evil, male/female, man/nature, mind/body, etc.). These questions have dominated mainstream Western discourse, and it is these very questions of identity, difference and intersectionality that Prince interrogated and unpacked throughout his career. His work appears to lie at the heart of these ideas.

One of the reasons for the persistence of postmodernism as a concept is related to its deconstruction of hierarchical oppositions as measurable paradigms. In an aesthetic context, the modernist logic of linear progress is replaced by conceptions of plurality, both keywords of postmodernist thinking. The notion of innovation and transgression is important to postmodernism. They are crucial to interpretations of varying artistic endeavours in the second half of twentieth century. The tendency towards asynchronism, plurality of approaches and the re-utilization of older media concepts in new contexts to form a kind of bricolage is key to grasping postmodernism and its influence in art. Prince, as a multifaceted artist, can act as a prime example of postmodernism in the context of popular music. His music plays with a crossover of styles, often mixing approaches and breaking rules. In a postmodern sense, Prince plays with not only artistic styles but even constructions of ethnicity, gender and sexuality throughout his work, throwing off such categorizations for a freedom and eclecticism that tends towards excess in its many manifestations. This is no more evident than on the *Lovesexy* album.

Lovesexy and postmodernism

The *Lovesexy* concept both visually and aurally illustrates Prince's relationship to postmodernism. It represents the myriad and varied presentations of images, words and music that Prince was grappling with at that point in his career. This was evident on *Sign o' the Times* which signalled the beginning of a period in which Prince wrestled with such questions and the release of 1988's *Lovesexy* allowed his responses to come to the fore. *Lovesexy* addresses such grand narratives as the battle between God (good) and the Devil (evil, in Prince's world, 'Spooky Electric'), which is depicted as an internal moral struggle. 'Lovesexy' as a conceptual framework is never made fully clear, but it seems to be a state of spiritual contentment that fuses a love of God and a connection with humanity via sexuality. Prince interrogated these dualities, not out of a need to embrace postmodernism directly, but because his own creative output allowed the power of those binaries to be challenged and not to limit, control and contain his own diversity and creativity.

As is well known, *The Black Album* was created in response to music critics and fans who had begun to say that Prince's music was too 'pop-oriented' and that he had abandoned his Black audience. But it was also his way of grappling with the dichotomies of good and evil that presided over this period and his apparent belief that the Black album was evil, and powered by 'Spooky Electric' (the Devil) – an idea which may or may not have been drug induced.

The look and feel of the *Lovesexy* album is light and exudes a sense of emerging from darkness to reach the state of 'Lovesexy', which is seemingly a union of spirituality and sexuality. The album cover, which will be discussed in the latter part of this chapter, provides a moment which exemplifies the relationship between Prince and postmodernism, which is not one of reason versus emotion, or even reason versus intuition, but one of images and music, of a search for truth revealed through an interweaving that provides structure and greater meaning to both. In essence, Prince seems to be presenting a journey of grappling with a duality, a saying no to the Devil, and at the same time, knowing the way to a God which is never fully articulated, its essence unreachable. It is the closest thing to a concept album Prince has ever created.

This is the essence of postmodernism: the idea that there is no essence, that humanity is simply moving through a world of signs, where everything has been seen and done before and is lying around as cultural wreckage, waiting to be reused, combined in new and unusual ways. In postmodernism, nothing is direct, nothing is new. Everything is already mediated. *Lovesexy* at once both conforms to and challenges these ideas and in terms of Prince's personal *mythology* this period was one in which he wrestled with grand narratives and spiritual questions, and in this context, *Lovesexy* remains a key moment where this set of themes worked as an entire piece.

Lovesexy, then, can conceptually be presented as a postmodern exploration of grand narratives. The accompanying aesthetic of the album operates to explore these themes in a shiny, 1980s pop cultural package that is thick with creativity and exuberance.

The visual presentation of such complex postmodern themes warrants an analysis of the album cover, music videos and art direction as part of the evolution of Prince's visual identity. *Lovesexy*'s visual style is essentially Prince's personal *mythos*. It is one of Prince's career highs, a landmark album that displays an artist at the peak of his creative powers using philosophical constructs both visually and aurally in a way rarely seen in the mainstream.

This analysis targets a more holistic understanding of the *Lovesexy* cover and its contexts, synthesizing critical responses, industry circumstances and music press reports around the time of the album's 1988 release, as well as the perspectives of the cover's photographer and Prince himself. Prince's visual representation on the *Lovesexy* album is preceded by nine covers which are both provocative and enigmatic. Although there is no obviously linear visual evolution, there is certainly an image eclecticism that accurately mirrors the musical dynamics of each release and a focused resistance to fixity, with each cover projecting a different version of Prince's persona or artistic vision as preludes to *Lovesexy*'s physical and emotional nakedness. Notably, most cover photos of Prince up to this point (with the exception of 1987's *Sign o' the Times*) feature him looking directly at the camera, while his glance on *Lovesexy* is decidedly averted. The relocation of his gaze arguably prefaces the peculiarity of the creative realm into which he ventures on the record, while seemingly contemplating his degree of exposure on its cover.

Hawkins and Niblock (39) reference the comparative darkness shrouding the cover of Prince's 1978 debut *For You*, accented by what they describe as a 'halo effect' in which radiant backlighting creates a visual aura reflecting depictions of Christian religious figures (68). It may not be certain whether at that stage of his musical omnipotence Prince viewed himself in supernatural terms; however, the partial blurring of his headshot image on that debut cover distinctly foreshadows manifestation of his innately amorphous nature throughout successive releases. The respective covers of *Prince* (1979), *Dirty Mind* (1980) and *Controversy* (1981) all feature Prince looking directly at the camera but also become progressively more provocative, particularly with the latter two records challenging sexual, moral, political and religious norms through either racy clothing or manufactured newspaper headlines. Prince's subversiveness is more subtly embedded in the illustrations adorning *1999* (1982), whereas he is unambiguously astride a purple motorbike on *Purple Rain*, metaphorically riding towards a predestined superstardom. The creative left turn on 1985's *Around the World in a Day*, resisting any temptation to create a stereotypically safe follow-up to a multiplatinum album, is accompanied by suitably esoteric graphics. The imagery created by artist Doug Henders literally places audiences in another world, a proto-fictional realm far removed from the character of Prince's previous covers. Prince is mysteriously depicted in a significantly aged guise in a landscape recalling 1960s psychedelia (Ro 121), and possibly even referencing The Beatles' landmark 1967 release *Sgt. Pepper's Lonely Hearts Club Band*. It's also the first of his album covers – and indeed the only one (front and/or gatefold back panel) – to be populated by so many characters. Interestingly, it's the figures on the back panel that re-emerge on the covers of the singles that excerpt parts of the back cover art. It remains open to interpretation whether the cover represents a visual utopia, a thinly disguised dystopia or a perplexing combination of both. However, there is little doubt that Prince achieved his desired creative distancing from the shadow of *Purple Rain* with both the music and the cover art of *Around the World in a Day*.

Given the critical parallels made between *Around the World in a Day* and The Beatles *Sgt. Pepper* album, it's interesting that there is also a broad visual similarity between the respective follow-up albums;[1] the utter vacancy of The Beatles' 1968 release – loosely referred to as *The White Album* – isn't fully reflected on Prince's black-and-white *Parade*, but the distinct contrast with the festival of colour on each of the preceding sleeves is no less pronounced. There is not an entirely holistic audiovisual relationship here, but the striking sequential parallel demands attention. As the musical accompaniment to the critically reviled film *Under the Cherry Moon* (1986) starring Prince, *Parade* also obliquely echoes The Beatles' own varied adventures with cinematic features and music videos. Their *Magical Mystery Tour* broadcast in Britain in December 1967 was widely considered the group's first major artistic misstep in the same ways that *Under the Cherry Moon* was later condemned to the scrapheap by its apparent artistic self-indulgence.

In conjunction with its cover, the *Lovesexy* album represented the end of a phase in Prince's creative history – one in which the grand narrative of his initial passage from relative oblivion to mainstream global superstardom had practically run its course, ending a series of commercial and artistic successes that constitute the core of his recording legacy for most listeners outside of his diehard constituency (Hahn and Tiebert 9).

Despite some supportive reviews, there was a generally pessimistic critical response to the record, although those same critics reemphasized Prince's creative uniqueness, and also suggested that a narrative of spiritual and artistic regeneration was being audiovisually articulated.

The dream world of the music video for 'I Wish U Heaven', directed by the album cover's photographer Jean-Baptiste Mondino, achieves an interrelationship with the cover's surrealism, extending its implied narratives of innocence, sin and spiritual aspiration. The cover itself is perhaps an agent of transition between those states, symbolizing a realm within which they are all infinitely and inextricably interwoven.

According to acclaimed Hipgnosis cover art designers Storm Thorgerson and Aubrey Powell, cover designs 'are the visual signposts, the flags, symbols, the awning, the camouflage, the 'skin' of these much loved records ... . A cover design is the icon that identifies – and is invariably associated with – the music it represents' (9). This idea of the cover functioning as the record's skin literally assumes naked significance with *Lovesexy* as Prince bares his philosophical body and soul, expanding on visual directions at which he had only previously hinted to varying degrees on *Prince* (1979), *Dirty Mind* (1980) and *Parade* (1986). It was certainly rare for a male superstar to appear virtually naked on his album cover, with previous decades decidedly dominated by exposure of the female body.

The response of many critics on both sides of the Atlantic to the album suggested that the vulnerability displayed on the cover was not only spiritual but also creative, as the record was widely – though not universally – perceived as an artistic miscalculation. It's arguable that no other Prince album cover (*Dirty Mind* included) has attracted quite as much attention and controversy as the *Lovesexy* graphics. Indeed, the album's reviewers typically commented on Prince's nakedness on the cover, often suggesting that the visual content underscored his preoccupation with fantasies and realities associated with the human flesh, and the seemingly paradoxical intersection of theology and biology. Fundamentally, however, the cover created a distraction from the music instead of becoming a seamless complement.

Perhaps it is also more than coincidental that apart from 1980's *Dirty Mind*, *Lovesexy* is the only Prince album from that decade that did not attain platinum certification for sales of over one million copies in America (Whitburn 967). This possibly suggests some interrelationship between the outrageous boldness of the covers as well as the musical content. *Lovesexy*'s European chart performance was more positive than it was in America, but the magnitude of this album cover issue cannot be underestimated. *Billboard* magazine's front-page headline in May 1988 underscored the relationship between revealing cover graphics and their impact on access to retail. The story '"Lovesexy" Too Sexy for Some' referred to 'the singer's provocative pose' and according to a Walmart representative, the chain refused to stock the record because of 'the album cover itself. We find it offensive ... . We choose not to carry in our stores something with graphics of that nature. Our customers, we feel, would find it offensive' ('Lovesexy' 77). It should be noted that by this time Walmart had already rejected releases by rock bands with controversial covers, as well as removing numerous rock publications from its shelves as early as 1986 ('Lovesexy' 77). Nonetheless, the resistance to the cover was reflected among other distributors and retailers nationwide, including some in Prince's home state of Minnesota (Radio & Records 1989). Given the distracting impact of the cover art, it's not surprising that Warner Bros. print ads for the album and singles avoided replication of the full-flesh display, opting to excerpt segments either from the cover or from music video sources. Notably, however, Warner Bros. promptly rebuffed media queries about possible changes to the cover ('Lovesexy' 1).

Although markets beyond Europe and America assumed less commercial significance, it is nonetheless striking that in Malaysia Warner exercised self-censorship by refusing to release the album there, anticipating a level of controversial response likely to contravene the country's strict laws and moral codes (Christie 6). Elsewhere internationally, the cover was also subjected to a variety of inconsistently placed stickers, leading some audiences and at least one British record reviewer to speculate on the potentially salacious nature of the hidden content (Mathur). In other instances (in both Saudi Arabia and Indonesia), the album was re-titled, and Prince's nakedness was circumvented by the artificial superimposition of clothing.

Artist and photographer Steve Parke who joined the Prince entourage in 1988 recalls that the band had been featured on the original artwork, and the members were disappointed to learn of their exclusion from the cover, displaced by flowers (Azhar 56). Conversely, Jean-Baptiste Mondino describes the released version as 'a religious image par excellence' (Denis, 'Mondino'). Perhaps oddly, the finished product was not the result of a grandiose artistic collaboration but instead evolved from a series of lost opportunities to discuss ideas between Mondino and Prince. Prince hired Mondino to shoot the cover while he was working on a video project at Paisley Park (Thorgerson and Powell 97), perhaps sensing a shared iconoclastic streak in their creative personalities. Plans were made to shoot the photos in Los Angeles, but the collaborative aspect was undermined when Prince and Mondino could not be seated together on the same plane, and then could not subsequently converse at a night club (Thorgerson and Powell 97; Denis 'Mondino'). Literally left to his own devices, overnight Mondino created a rough drawing inspired by his perception of Prince's perspectives on spirituality and sexuality, and which Prince apparently described as 'perfect' (Denis 'Mondino'). After shots were taken with a single roll of Kodak Ektachrome film, Mondino retouched the material in Paris where he was later met by Prince who selected one shot and promptly destroyed the rest of the contact sheets (Thorgerson and Powell 97; Q 18).

Prince's physical presence had never previously announced itself on his album covers as it did on *Lovesexy*, and actually never would again. In fact, on 1987's *Sign o' the Times*, Prince's gaze and movement out of the frame seemed to imply his absence from his next sleeve altogether – which might well have been true if *The Black Album* had been the next official release. Furthermore, there were also instances of *Lovesexy* copies being sold in an opaque black plastic bag, lending stronger validity to this reading of potential absence. How then do we rationalize Prince's degree of exposure in an age of clothed and posed pop personae and rising hip hop machismo? To help comprehend the extent of visual contrast that the *Lovesexy* album cover represents, we should consider the covers of several top ten albums in America from 1988, reinforcing the imagery norms for a hit release during the Reagan era of conservative Republican politics. With the possible exception of the Poison album *Open Up and Say … Ahh!*, which, like *Lovesexy*, was also removed from Walmart's shelves, other bestsellers that year by Sade, Run DMC, Tracy Chapman, Kenny G and U2, among other examples, usually did little to challenge the imagination despite arguably representing the artists appropriately. The George Michael album on which songs such as the title track 'Faith' and 'I Want

Your Sex' coexisted with massive commercial success (eventually exceeding ten million copies in America alone) was sharply contrasted by the cool reception to Prince's own musings on pop's perennial polarities of spirituality and sensuality. The differing album cover approach was one of many factors separating the two releases and career trajectories: constraint and calculated concealment on one hand versus multiple levels of physical and metaphorical exposure on the other.

It may well be that there is little actual decoding of this cover to be done, certainly compared to the image-laden *Sign o' the Times* album that immediately preceded it or the earlier *Around the World in a Day*. By 1988, our collective and individual perceptions of Prince were supported by a decade of aural contextualization of the cover images, informing our encounter with *Lovesexy* and its graphics. However, Prince seemed frustrated by the resistance to, and misinterpretation of, the cover, suggesting that perception of the 'rebirth image', as he described it, was essentially a reflection of the individual observer (Draper 86). A wider musical context for the record and its visual representation suggests that Prince was experiencing a phase of creative insecurity, partially indicated by the abrupt withdrawal of *The Black Album* before it was replaced by *Lovesexy*. Tour manager Alan Leeds suggested that Prince was suffering from depression and felt his position on music's cutting edge was under threat from younger acts (Dodds 88). The process of rapidly making *Lovesexy* as a spiritually positive substitute album for a record Prince had begun to perceive as evil is perhaps the polarity manifested on the album's cover as the artist virtually turned himself inside out.

For Prince, the *Lovesexy* album cover may have represented an unequivocally bold artistic statement which, in conjunction with the music, sought to set him apart not only from his competition but also from aspects of his own recorded past. Nonetheless, the description of Prince on the cover of *Musician* magazine in November 1988 as 'an artist at war with himself' seems fully appropriate. His internal conflict, seemingly polarizing segments of his soul, definitely undermined his commercial momentum, potentially fragmenting the artistic respect and critical affirmation that *Sign o' the Times* had earned him. While Prince's creativity is rarely called into question in his prolific career, *Lovesexy* suggests that his artistic impulse may have overruled his business sense and aesthetic pragmatism, discarding lessons to have been learned from the visual representations previously accompanying *Dirty Mind* and *Parade*.

Note

1 While The Beatles' *Magical Mystery Tour* followed the *Sgt. Pepper* album in late 1967, it was originally released in Britain as a two-disc EP, while Capitol Records in America chose to issue the material as an album instead with additional material from other sources. It was first issued in the UK in album form in 1976 (https://www.thebeatles.com/album/magical-mystery-tour). In addition, the colourful graphics were an extension (perhaps unconscious) of the palette employed on the *Sgt. Pepper* album cover.

Works cited

Alleyne, Mike. 'After the Storm: Hipgnosis, Storm Thorgerson, and the Rock Album Cover'. *Rock Music Studies* 1.3 (2014): 251–67.

Azhar, Mobeen. *Prince: Chapter and Verse – A Life in Photographs*. New York: Sterling, 2016.

Christie, Leo. 'Censorship Fears Dethrone Prince Disk in Malaysia'. *Billboard (Archive: 1963-2000)* 100.27 (2 July 1988): 6–6, 84. ProQuest. https://ezproxy.mtsu.edu:3443/login?url=https://search.proquest.com/docview/1438669264?accountid=4886.

Denis, Jacques, 'Jean-Baptiste Mondino: "I Was Completely Under His Spell"'. ID Vice. 28 Sept. 2016. https://i-d.vice.com/en_uk/article/3kqg9k/jean-baptiste-mondino-on-prince-i-was-completely-under-his-spell.

Denis, Jacques. 'Maker of Stars: Jean-Baptiste Mondino'. *Total Records: Photography and the Art of the Album Cover*. Eds. Antoine de Beaupré, Serge Vincendet, and Sam Stourdzé. Aperture, 2016. 158–69.

Dodds, Dan. 'Change of Heart'. *Wax Poetics* 67 (Spring 2018): 87–97.

Draper, Jason. *Prince: Life & Times* (Revised and Updated Edition). New York: Chartwell, 2016.

Hahn, Alex, and Laura Tiebert. *The Rise of Prince: 1958–1988*. New York: Mad Cat Press, 2017.

Hawkins, Stan, and Sarah Niblock. *Prince: The Making of a Pop Phenomenon*. Burlington, VT: Ashgate, 2011.

Holland, Nancy. 'Prince: Postmodern Icon'. *Journal of African American Studies* 21 (2017): 1–17. 10.1007/s12111-017-9363-7.

Inglis, Ian. '"Nothing You Can See That Isn't Shown": The Album Covers of the Beatles'. *Popular Music* 20.1 (2001): 83–97. ProQuest. Web. 4 June 2014.

'"Lovesexy" Too Sexy for Some'. *Billboard (Archive: 1963-2000)* 100.21 (21 May 1988): 1–1, 77. ProQuest, https://ezproxy.mtsu.edu:3443/login?url=https://search.proquest.com/docview/1438679061?accountid=4886.

Lyotard, Jean-François. *La condition postmoderne: rapport sur le savoir*. Paris: Minuit, 1979.

Mathur, Paul. Review. 'Prince: Lovesexy'. *Melody Maker*, 14 May 1988. http://www.rocksbackpages.com/Library/Article/prince-ilovesexyi-paisley-park.

O'Hagan, Sean. Review. 'Prince: Lovesexy'. *New Musical Express*, 14 May 1988. http://www.rocksbackpages.com/Library/Article/prince-lovesexy-paisley-park.

Perry, Steve. 'Prince: The Purple Decade'. *Musician (Archive: 1982-1999)* 121 (1 Nov. 1988): 82–8, 90, 93, 95, 99. ProQuest, https://ezproxy.mtsu.edu:3443/login?url=https://search.proquest.com/docview/964141166?accountid=4886.

Pitcher, Susan K. *Billboard* (Archive: 1963-2000); Cincinnati 100.28 (9 July 1988): 9.

Pound, E. *Make It New*. New Haven, CT: Yale University Pres, 1935.

Ro, Ronin. *Prince: Inside the Music and the Masks*. New York: St. Martin's Griffin, 2016.

Thorgerson, Storm, and Aubrey Powell. *100 Best Album Covers: The Stories Behind the Sleeves*. New York: Dorling Kindersley, 1999.

Whitburn, Joel, *Top 10 Albums 1955–2011*. Wisconsin: Record Research, 2011.

Whitburn, Joel. *Top Pop Albums 1955–2016*. Wisconsin: Record Research, 2018.

7

For you

The neglected guitar style of Prince

Michael Ugrich

Prince Rogers Nelson was many things throughout his lifetime: an actor, producer, performer, artist, composer, humanitarian and so on and so forth. He excelled in all the categories mentioned, but when an individual excels at many different things in life, it is hard to stay focused on any specific element that makes that person great. This can be said about Prince's musicianship, specifically his guitar playing, which is often overshadowed by other aspects of his life. Prince was a monumental guitarist, but this ability often went unnoticed throughout his career. Rolling Stone ranked Prince at number 33, five spots behind Johnny Ramone, on its list of 100 greatest guitarists (100 Greatest Guitarists 2015). *Guitar World* magazine ranks 'Little Red Corvette' at number 64, far behind Kurt Cobain's solo for 'Smells Like Teen Spirit', a guitar solo that merely mimics the melody of Cobain's vocals during the chorus, at number 26 on its list of 100 greatest solos (100 Greatest Guitar Solos 2001, 35–53). Prince did not even play the solo on that song, further demonstrating the disconnection of critics with Prince's guitar abilities. What is not realized by the general public is that Prince was perhaps one of the greatest electric guitarists of the twentieth century. This study will seek to observe the complexity of Prince's guitar style throughout his career and legitimize him as an elite guitarist.

The term 'prodigy' can be defined as an impressive or outstanding example of a particular quality. If Prince were to be analysed from a musical standpoint, he would fit this description. Despite the lack of formal instruction, he excelled on various instruments at a young age: bass, drums, guitar, piano and vocals. His father, John Nelson, was a gifted jazz pianist who gigged around the metro of Minneapolis and his mother, Mattie Della Shaw, was a former singer in the Billie Holiday style. John encouraged his son to learn the piano, and at a very young age Prince began composing music with a melody that he titled 'Funk Machine'.

After the separation of his parents, Prince's mother disapproved of his interest in music, fearing that her son would fall into the same trap that his father had: chasing musical stardom and coming up short. The reinforcement of that disapproval by his stepfather drove a young Prince to run away from home and to seek asylum with his father. This reopened Prince's pursuit of music. Eventually, the two would have a falling out and John would send his son to live with his aunt Olivia in her piano-less house. Taking pity on him since he was no longer able to play the piano, John bought the young twelve-year-old Prince a cheap electric guitar and looked on in astonishment as the boy taught himself to play virtually overnight (Wall, ch. 2).

The transition from playing keyboard to playing guitar, without ever having played one before, is a huge challenge. It takes a considerable amount of time to know and memorize the tuning system, gain muscle memory to be able to instantly grab a certain chord shape and know the fingerings for scales and arpeggios. On top of that, there is a plethora of guitar techniques that are achievable on guitar to consider – for example, palm muting, note bending, vibrato, hammer-ons and pull-offs. To say that Prince was able to learn the guitar overnight may be an overstatement to say the least, but it is entirely possible to gain a large amount of ground in a short time period. It is important to have a good instructor for this to be possible, and for Prince to gain the amount of ground as he did in a short time frame without an instructor is nothing short of remarkable. Prince's childhood friend Jimmy Nelson remarked, 'At twelve years old he knew note for note the whole solo in "Make me Smile" by the band Chicago, and that is a really intricate solo. I was just blown away! He was brilliant even at that age' (Wall ch. 2).

By the age of seventeen, Prince had honed his skills as a musician and was pursuing a record contract, eventually landing one with Warner Bros. The *For You* LP (1978) has a more reserved approach to the way Prince plays guitar on his debut album. No instruments are present in the opening track, 'For You', and 'In Love' is heavily immersed with a synthesized tone. 'Soft and Wet', the only track not completely masterminded by Prince, followed the same instrumentation as the previous track. The next track, 'Crazy You', finally features guitar with a bossa nova-like chord progression, | GMaj7 | F#7(#5, #9) |Bm7 | Am9 D9 |, played on a steel stringed acoustic with a harmonized melody played on electric with a clean tone. Prince improvises subtle guitar swells and licks between the lyrics. While not revolutionary to the way the guitar is approached, 'Crazy You' showcases Prince's ability to stray from the beaten path and implies an out-of-the-box mentality. The chordal structure alone is challenging to execute and demonstrates Prince's influence of jazz and Latin guitar styles. The melody is simple enough, but he complicated it further by harmonizing it at the octave, which gave it a certain dimension and added depth to the overall feel.

Prince lets loose a bit with the guitar on 'My Love Is Forever'. Right away, Prince's tight, syncopated rhythm guitar can be heard comping over the chordal structure in an ostinato-like pattern, an element not present in the previous tracks. This guitar style would become a reoccurring theme in the Prince albums that follow. He also broke out a guitar solo with a distorted tone at around the three-minute mark instead of an onslaught of licks and phrases, which would be typical for an immature guitarist trying to prove him/herself. It is a calculated and melodic solo that demonstrates Prince's ability to attend to detail. He adds further dimension towards the end by harmonizing at the fifth. Guitar harmonization was a rather new trend at the time, perhaps reaching its pinnacle two years prior when Eagles guitarists Joe Walsh and Don Felder recorded

'Hotel California'. It was impressive for the young Prince to execute such an intricate guitar solo such as 'My Love Is Forever' at such an early stage in his career, even more remarkable is that it he recorded them all by himself.

The last track on *For You*, 'I'm Yours', is less conventional in comparison to the other tracks. This demonstrates that Prince also has an aggressive side to contrast the other moods shown on the album. The song opens with a four-bar groove of polyrhythmic drums and a flurry of complex bass slapping, giving the impression that it will launch into some type of funk-driven tune but deceivingly launches into a heavy metal-esque section containing sustained power chords and bass underneath a repeating distorted riff. Prince also adds drum fills towards the end of the bars, giving it a dramatic effect. This foreshadows a section in Iron Maiden's 'Hallowed Be Thy Name', right down to the tempo, the sustained power chords on scale degrees I to VI and the drum fills. The curious thing about the comparison is that it predates Maiden's tune by some four years. Prince also unleashes a raw, unrestrained guitar solo at the end of the track with an added bass/guitar duel, showing off his capabilities as a bassist as well. 'I'm Yours' is unique in that it branches into a new territory of blending heavy metal with funk with the implication of the sexually charged lyrical content. Prince's guitar playing on this particular track is an early example of him as a musical prodigy.

While *For You* did not capture the full potential of Prince as a guitarist or musician, it offered a glimpse of his capability and left the listener yearning for more. Prince would further demonstrate his musicianship and songwriting abilities with his next three albums: *Prince* (1979), *Dirty Mind* (1980) and *Controversy* (1981). *Prince* has some notable guitar work on it with the eye-catching, metal-like track, 'Bambi'. According to Joshua Rothkopf, '"Bambi" is both sleazier and harder than any Kiss song ever recorded. The riff, adorned with full-neck skids and double-stop screeches, gets more powerful with each repetition. Prince's soling, meanwhile, a drooling construction of escalating bends and lusty vibrato come-ons, would make him MVP in any rock outfit' (58).

The disco drenched first hit for Prince, 'I Wanna Be Your Lover' (1979), places the guitar in an accompaniment role. Offering multiple layers with one guitar playing double-stop octave downbeats and the other playing syncopated chord shifts that are in unison with keyboard rhythm, Prince shows off his ability to grab the audience's attention with a catchy hook. The track that follows, 'Why You Wanna Treat Me So Bad?', makes one wonder in which direction the album is heading with its stark contrast from its poppy precursor. The guitar is ever-present with a gritty tone, and a technical/chaotic guitar solo at the end returns to the harmonization technique explored in 'I'm Yours'. Overall, Prince utilizes his guitar skills to a much-increased degree on his sophomore album, displaying a host of different guitar styles ranging from tight syncopated chicken-scratch in 'Sexy Dancer', the belligerent 'Bambi', and the slow ballad 'When We're Dancing Close and Slow'.

In contrast to his second album, *Dirty Mind* hardly contains any heavy use of guitar on any of its eight tracks; not a single guitar solo is present. The album itself is a departure from the disco-like direction of *Prince* that feels like it belongs in the 1980s with its incredibly explicit lyrical content, clearly not marketed for singles, and experimental synthesizer tones. The presence of Prince's funk roots can be observed on half of the album: 'Do It All Night', 'Uptown', 'Head' and 'Partyup'. 'When You Were Mine' channels a new wave vibe with a simple, stripped back guitar tone, playing reserved accompaniment and arpeggiated chords during the chorus.

Released the following year, Prince's fourth album, *Controversy*, returns to his funk guitar roots as evidenced on the title track, 'Controversy'. The chord built on a major second interval is chicken-scratched in an array of variations throughout the track, demonstrating Prince's selective string accuracy and syncopation (Rothkopf 50). If there is a track that could benefit from more guitar on the album, it would be 'Let's Work'. Somehow, the mildly distorted power chords in the intro and chorus were successful in staying out of the way of the extraordinary bass line that followed. Perhaps Prince realized how infectious that groove was and knew that adding a guitar later in the song could offer more shrewdness to the track, adding further dimension to what had at that point become repetitive – a powerful trick to essentially bring the listener back in after drifting off in thought. In the politically charged 'Annie Christian', Prince lays down a nasty solo underneath the mix over some unique chord changes that is consistent throughout the entirety of the track, giving it an uneasy feeling that is relevant to the lyrical content.

Released in the fall of 1982, the double album *1999* contains two of Prince's most beloved songs: the title track '1999' and 'Little Red Corvette'. The album would also project Prince as an international star with the aid of the newly launched MTV. While not an album known for Prince's guitar work, it does offer the establishment of a consistent Minneapolis Sound: heavy synthesized tones, electronic rhythms and vigorous guitar playing (Rothkopf 50). Prince's explosive distorted guitar soloing, as evidenced in the first two albums, is showcased about six minutes into the eight-minute epic 'Lady Cab Driver'. This album is also significant in Prince's discography thus far in that he had relinquished absolute control over his compositions and accepted input from various members of his backing band, The Revolution. The guitar solo for 'Little Red Corvette' was actually recorded by Dez Dickerson. Backing vocals can also be heard from Dickerson, Lisa Coleman and Jill Jones throughout the album, most notably on the track '1999'. This willingness to concede control marked a stage in Prince's evolution as an artist, in which he essentially stopped being a solo artist and started being the leader of a band, setting the stage for his next album, which was also his most successful one.

The album *Purple Rain* (1984) is an absolute masterpiece for rock guitar blended with pop, a first and last in his career. Beginning with its opening track, 'Let's Go Crazy', Prince recorded an engaging power chord/blues riff combo with an incredibly fat tone during the verses. He launched into a flashy solo mid-song with a surplus of guitar techniques: whole note bends, sustained vibrato and triplet pull-offs. Prince then unleashed something sinister with his unprecedented guitar cadenza at the end of the track, adding a wah-wah pedal for a higher end tone to achieve more sustain and feedback.

Conceivably, the crowning jewel of Prince's recorded material in reference to his guitar ability could be 'Computer Blue'. Opening with a bass drum beat and spoken dialogue between Lisa and Wendy, the guitar and keyboards come in with a unique unison riff while a screeching guitar plays under the mix, as if it is off in the distance. After sixteen bars, the band is firing on all cylinders, establishing a groove with some raunchy guitar provided by Prince. The chorus provides a standard rock progression of | VI | VII | I |. He then initiates a spasm of extremely difficult chromatic sixteenth notes for the next twelve bars. The section comes to a dramatic close at the two-minute mark, giving the impression that the song has ended. He then introduces a new section complete with a key change and a different feel from the wild first section. Prince's perplexing guitar work is evidenced by a well-conceived solo, with the melodic material credited to Prince's father, John Nelson (Wall, ch. 2).

In a rare interview with *Guitar Player* in 2004, Prince describes how one should approach the guitar:

> Kids don't learn to play the right way anymore. When the Jackson 5 came up, they had to go through Smokey Robinson and the Funk Brothers, and that's how they got it down. I want to be able to teach that stuff, because kids need to learn these things, and nobody is teaching them the basics. See, a lot of cats don't work on their rhythm enough, and if you don't have rhythm, you might as well take up needlepoint or something. I can't stress it enough. The next thing is pitch. That's universal. You're either in tune or you ain't. When you get these things down, then you can learn how to solo. (Gress 92)

It is possible where Prince shines the best on guitar is not on the recorded material from the LPs but with his live performances. When he performed live, it was almost as if the guitar was an extension of his body and witnessing a performance would leave a concertgoer or viewer amazed and captivated by the showmanship and the sheer accuracy of his playing. It is no easy feat to play either rhythm or lead guitar with the amount of motion that Prince generated on stage, but he did it with the greatest ease. Like many aspects in his life, he made it into an art form. From the synchronized dance moves, to throwing his guitar up into the air, to leaning backwards into the waiting hands of a stagehand, Prince made it a spectacle to watch.

Prince was an exceptional improviser. He rarely played poorly or made mistakes at his live shows. He could improvise in different styles fluidly. According to 3rdeyegirl guitarist Donna Grantis, 'The expectation from Prince, as well as ourselves, was for each and every performance to be perfect – flawless' (Rothfopf 50). He could be reserved and technical, executing intricate harmonies in the spirit of Joe Satriani or Steve Vai and he could unleash absolute fury that would make any metal shredder envious. Perhaps one of his finest moments on stage was during the 2004 Rock N' Roll Hall of Fame Ceremony in which the all-star line-up of Tom Petty, Jeff Lynne, Steve Winwood and Prince performed 'While My Guitar Gently Weeps' to honour the late Beatles guitarist George Harrison, who was being inducted for his solo career.

The performance with Prince almost never happened, with Harrison's widow, Olivia, preferring the performance to be exclusive to people that knew Harrison. Even though Prince had virtually no contact with Harrison and had never even heard the song prior to the performance, the organizers eventually convinced her to let Prince play. The performance also included Mark Mann, guitarist for Jeff Lynne and ELO. Joel Gallen, the show's producer, asked Prince to perform both the middle and the last solo, but in rehearsals Mann took over, playing a note-for-note recreation of Clapton's iconic solo. 'And we get to the big end solo,' Gallen stated, 'and Prince again steps forward to go into the solo, and this guy starts playing that solo too!' With time running short, Prince told Gallen to let Mann take the middle solo and he would take the end solo. According to Gallen, 'They never rehearsed it, really. Never really showed us what he was going to do, and he left, basically telling me, the producer of the show, not to worry' (Greene 2016).

From the beginning of the song, Prince is almost in the shadows to the right of the stage, chugging along on distorted power chords. Petty and Lynne trade between verse and chorus while Mann nails his solo licks and middle guitar solo. Also, present on stage is Harrison's son Dhani playing acoustic guitar. Caught up in the performance, you almost would have forgotten that Prince is on stage, but at about the 3:24 mark of the song, he finally steps forward to take the extended outro solo. What happens next is debatably one of the greatest live guitar solos ever filmed. Prince begins with an iconic unison bend to start his solo. He nearly always starts his guitar solos with a sustained unison bend.

He plays some reserved licks and bends for the next thirty seconds and around the four-minute mark he really starts to turn up the heat with some slides and rapid single string tremolo picking. He adds another series of ascending string bends; it looks like he is really digging down deep for them. At this point, Prince is absolutely tearing it up on stage with his shred and stage antics. Around the 4:45 mark, he leans back into the waiting hands of a stagehand in the pit off stage, right in front of the young Harrison. You can see the look of joy and admiration on his face as he looks on to what we are all witnessing: Prince simply being Prince. After a little over a minute of some blistering licks and runs, the song comes to a close with Prince tossing his guitar up in the air and casually walking off stage like what just took place was no big deal. Still no word on if the guitar has come down yet, as no visual evidence of that exists (Ralston 2016).

Since Prince's untimely death, there has been a void in the guitar community. There is no denying that Prince was a monumental force and inspiration to guitarists around the world. In an interview, Chris Granley, a University of Wisconsin-Superior graduate and jazz guitarist, is quoted as saying,

> I believe there to be large group of people that see him as a gimmick. They see the outfits, weird music, the hair and have a hard time getting past it. I think people see him and make the criticism that music is more of a business transaction than a work of art. The reality is that it was a was a bit of both; he was cognizant of the business side of his music, but stood up against any guitar player, he more than holds his own.

He further explains,

> He has a style of playing even rhythm guitar that you can pick out within about four bars. You say, 'That is either Prince or somebody doing a damn good impression.' There are style differences, but the point that I am trying to make is that people consume guitar gods in a specific way. I don't think a lot of them consider Prince as one of them because he wasn't packaged in that way. I also don't think Prince set

out to be a guitar god, he set out to be a great musician; guitar god just happened because he was that much better. Also, his albums didn't necessarily feature him on guitar as much. He was really big on live performances and wanted people to come see him live for that. (Granley 2017)

In an article written by Joshua Rothkopf for *Guitar World* in 2016, Rothkopf explains, 'Possessed of flash, funk, finesse and fury, Prince takes his rightful place as one of the greatest guitarists of his generation. And if you're not ready to hear that, it's time to open your ears.' World-renowned classical guitarist Ana Vidovic was 'surprised' by his virtuosity with all the live footage of him surfacing on YouTube following his death (Vidovic 2017). In a *Rolling Stone* article by Daniel Kreps, Pearl Jam frontman Eddie Vedder addresses a concert crowd on the day of Prince's passing, 'People know him from the ways he looked, and the different ways he looked, and different things he said – a lot of incredible things to remember him by, but I gotta tell you, Prince was probably the greatest guitar player we've ever seen' (Kreps 2016).

When Prince performed music, the guitar strapped to his shoulder was not just a prop. It was an extension of who he was: a guitar player. He had stamina; he could play a three- to four-hour concert in a stadium and show up at a nightclub after the show to play another two- to three-hour set. He was flawless on stage, executing demanding solos with perfection. He was a master of the syncopated guitar. He was a recording genius. He was able to segue from one style of playing to another with the greatest of ease. Perhaps that is the reason Prince is not taken as seriously as he should be, because he was not limited to any particular style to compare and contrast with others. Perhaps that is why he is unranked on the 100 greatest guitar solos list, or ranked behind Johnny Ramone and Neil Young on the 100 greatest guitarists list. He was simply in a league of his own. There are people who do a lot of a little and people who do a little of a lot. Renowned classical guitarist Ana Vidovic is one of the top guitarists in her field; however, she admittedly cannot play an electric guitar (Vidovic 2017). Chris Granley confessed that he can play many different styles of guitar; however, he is only proficient in maybe one or two of them (Granley 2017). Prince is the rare exception of somebody who did a lot of a lot when it came to guitar. The phrase 'jack of all trades and a master of none' certainly does not apply to him. He was capable of out-shredding the best of them. He could compose incredibly complex solos as well as improvise something on the spot that would make any jazz player envious. This in turn made him an incredibly formidable guitarist but unfortunately weakened that perception in the eye of the public. However, Prince's recordings and live performances unquestionably prove he was among the best in terms of how a guitarist is judged.

Works cited

'100 Greatest Guitar Solos'. *Guitar World Magazine*, Guitar Legends Issue, 2001: 35–53.
'100 Greatest Guitarists'. *Rolling Stone*, 18 December 2015. Web. May 2017. http://www.rollingstone.com/music/lists/100-greatest-guitarists-20111123/carlos-santana-20111122.

Granley, Christopher. Interviewed by author. Vermillion, SD. 2017.
Green, Andy. 'Watch Prince's Incredible "While My Guitar Gently Weeps" Solo'. *Rolling Stone*, 21 April 2016. Web. May 2017. http://www.rollingstone.com/music/news/watch-princes-incredible-my-guitar-gently-weeps-solo-20160421.
Gress, Jesse. '10 Ways to Play Guitar Like Prince'. *Guitar Player Magazine* 45.2 (2011): 90–100.
Kreps, Daniel. 'Pearl Jam on Prince: "Greatest Guitar Player We've Ever Seen"'. *Rolling Stone*, 22 April 2016. Web. May 2017. http://www.rollingstone.com/music/news/pearl-jam-on-prince-greatest-guitar-player-wevE-ever-seen-20160422.
Ralston, Daniel. 'Breaking Down Prince's Epic Guitar Solo at the Rock and Roll Hall of Fame'. *Time Magazine*, 2 May 2016. Web. May 2017. http://time.com/4314151/prince-rock-and-roll-hall-of-fame/.
Rothkopf, Joshua. 'Prince: Purple Reign'. *Guitar World Magazine* (August 2016): 46–61.
Vidovic, Ana. Interviewed by author. Madison, WI. 2017.
Wall, Mick. *Prince: Purple Reign*. Great Britain: Orion Books, 2016.

8

To make purple, you need blue

Prince as the embodiment of the postmodern blues aesthetic

Tom Attah

Introduction

As part of his groundbreaking work as a stylistic provocateur during the 1980s and 1990s, blues music and blues culture provided a fundamental element of Prince's composition, production and live performance practice. This chapter constructs a continuum of blues music performance, including those of Muddy Waters, B. B. King and Jimi Hendrix, positioning Prince as a performer in full command of the aesthetic qualities that characterize African American music-making with specific reference to the stylistic gestures particular to the blues.

This chapter does not attempt to delimit and collapse Prince's activity into a single style or genre of practice, or to disregard his wider contribution to popular music. Neither is this an attempt to claim Prince purely as a bluesman – although the figure of the bluesman is one of great complexity in cultural studies. This is not a reductive polemic. The intention is to deconstruct several key performances and rehabilitate the artist's practice as part of the ongoing continuum of the blues aesthetic.

With this in mind, the chapter will discuss definitions of the blues aesthetic, blues music and blues performers. The chapter will look at several musical examples in pursuit of musical and stylistic analysis before the presentation of conclusions. Specifically, the chapter will discuss a live performance of 'Blues in C (If I Had a Harem)', additionally recordings of *Zannalee* and *The Truth* offer a comparative analysis between Prince's *5 Women* and B. B. King's *The Thrill Is Gone*; Prince's *The Ride* and Jimi Hendrix's *Hear My Train A-Comin'*, and finally Prince's *Purple House* compared to Jimi Hendrix's *Red House*. There will be additional reference to other Prince songs which contain strongly indicative blues material such as *The Question of U*.

Definitions of the blues

In recent years, scholars have sought to define blues in various ways, offering contrasting and sometimes conflicting revivalist and revisionist narratives (Adelt, *Blues Music in the Sixties: A Story in Black and White*; Marybeth Hamilton; Wald). In the most persistent early narratives from the 1950s onward, the blues is characterized as a musical style derived from the oral tradition and field hollers of slavery which journeyed from areas of rural poverty into the recording studios of the early twentieth century (Charters; Oliver). In this narrative, the blues is a style predominantly performed and owned by men, and represents the primal, essential, un-commercialized and unmediated cri de cœur of a displaced and emerging nation (Gellert and Siegmeister; Lomax; Palmer). While this is not necessarily false, it is equally true that the blues was named and established by educated African Americans and initially performed by professional singers in an established performance milieu as part of an existing Black performance continuum (Jones; Lacava; Oakley). From this alternate perspective, the blues are a style that is written down and performed principally by women backed by trained musical ensembles through vaudeville by the 'Blues Queens', including Mamie Smith, Ma Rainey, Bessie Smith and other professional entertainers firmly entrenched in a Western-European styled theatre- and stage-performance tradition (Davis; Harrison; Lieb). Concern has also been raised that definitions of the blues have focused around a hegemony formed by White, middle-class intellectuals which limits the role and autonomy of African Americans, and which also shifts focus away from the poiesis,[1] vitality and catharsis of performance in context and towards the representation of gesture through the materiality of recorded media such as record collecting and re-enactment (Adelt, *Blues Music in the Sixties : A Story in Black and White*; Marybeth Hamilton; King; Petrusich; Ryan; Titon).

Additionally, the blues has been defined in a number of different ways by many music producers, consumers and cultural workers. Debates concerning what constitutes 'real' blues have surfaced in print and through social media, with some of the most heated debates concerning whether or not non-African-American performers have either the ability or the moral right to sing or play the blues (Garon; Grazian; Harris; Hoffman; Keil). In these cases, arguments about the blues play towards problematic notions of authenticity in popular music performance as embodied by the performer, rather than the perceived content or form of the music (Mack; Moore, 'Authenticity as Authentication'; Rudinow).

Strictly musicological definitions of blues music typically make reference to an A-A-B lyric structure, the number of bars in each verse of a blues song, harmonic choice of I IV and V chords typically voiced as dominant sevenths, melodic choices of 'blue' notes in the form of flattened third and seventh scale tones, the use of pentatonic scales, lyrical and musical improvisation, and the use of melisma. While not strictly incorrect, these definitions exclude almost as many compositions and artists as they embrace. Further, from a post-industrial capitalist perspective, 'blues' can also be described as 'a broad range of popular music primarily created by and for black Americans ... thus it is more a trade category than a genre' (Ripani 6). In other words, while it is relatively straightforward for many listeners to recognize a blues influence in a piece of music or artistic performance, it is less easy to agree an absolute definition for what constitutes the style.

'If I Had a Harem'

For example – the Prince song 'Blues in C (If I Had a Harem)' neatly fits a simple musicological definition of the blues. Quite aside from the genre sign-posting of the title, the lyrics follow an A-A-B structure and each verse follows a twelve-bar cycle through I-IV-V chords in the key of C. In the performance of this song, Prince pokes fun at the hypersexual Mandingo[2]-style persona created for him by the printed press represented in the song as 'the papers', while implying in the early part of the song that if he *did* in fact have a harem, he would still be able to satisfy an extra partner – particularly the one to whom the song is addressed.

With specific reference to a live performance of the song in Westfallenhalle, Dortmund, West Germany, on the European leg of the 1988 *Lovesexy* tour, Prince presents the song with a definite blues sensibility. In this specific performance, the lighting is primarily blue, and the song opens with a swung guitar vamp build around chord I which sets the stylistic scene for a blues performance. Counted in from the fourth bar of his vamp by Prince, the band play the first cycle of twelve bars with the horn section delivering a swaggering, direct quotation of Mercer Ellington's 'Things Ain't What They Used to Be' – itself a slow blues written in 1942. As the band reaches a crescendo into the twelfth bar, Prince calls a caesura, halting the music in its tracks, dropping the colourful, pulsing and brass-led texture to a near-silence, the harmonic structure carried now only by the gospel tones of an organ playing the pad chords of the twelve-bar cycle. The lighting has now faded almost to black, punctuated solely by a white spotlight on the artist, and a low blue relief on the band and his interpretive dancer for the tour, Cat Glover. The interaction between Prince and Cat during this song is a critical part of the realization of this particular performance. Prince motions for the audience to quieten down as the band cycles through the second twelve bars, promoting an atmosphere of intimacy and ceremony in the auditorium. This moment of control – over both the band and the audience – might be seen as the beginning of the ritual of the blues: the moment at which the artist takes on a priestly air in the tradition of the gospel church, and the audience assumes its antiphonal role as both witnesses and participants (Keil 164; Lacava 129). Prince then sings the first two verses with a growing sense of sexual urgency, assuring the song's addressee that he would happily give up spending time with the nine members of his fictional harem to take care of this new object of his affections. The fourth cycle continues with the organ carrying the harmony as the brass gently quotes Charlie Parker's 'Billie's Bounce' while Prince appears to mime pleadingly at Cat across the stage. As the band starts the fifth pass through the cycle, still at low level, Prince brings his guitar across his body to the playing position and on the fourth beat of the first bar plays a single, loud and clean C note in the highest register of his telecaster-style instrument, piercing the silence and reverence of the musical texture – at which cue, Cat Glover collapses to the ground! This suggests the potency of Prince's masculinity: with one note he can strike an adult woman down. As the cycle continues, Prince continues to mime concern at the power of his guitar. On the second beat of the fifth bar, he plays the high C again and jumps across the stage, again miming surprise at the physical effect of his instrument. Again, on the second beat of the ninth bar of the cycle he plays the same note – and this time is seemingly thrown bodily across the stage by the might of the instrument's kick. Recovering his composure in the twelfth bar, Prince swaggers across the stage, picking out a T-Bone Walker-style melodic phrase on the guitar to an understated backing from the band. By the fourth bar of the cycle, he is sitting cross-legged on the edge of the stage, in command of the instrument and playing lyrical, conversational lines. Cat has come back to life and is writhing sensually on all fours across the stage from Prince, in time to the music. Prince completes these twelve bars by scraping his pick slowly up the guitar strings, producing a rasping, gasping slide. The next twelve-bar cycle opens with a blistering flurry of semi-chromatic bebop style phrases from the guitar for the first four bars, demonstrating that Prince has the instrument under control and is able to play masterfully. Cat is now back on her feet swaying sensually in time to the music. The audience is now shouting in time to the music, as Prince fires off one last high C, carrying him back across the stage and up to his microphone position for the vocal on the final verse. These last twelve bars are delivered in stop-time[3] – a favourite musical device of blues composer Willie Dixon. In this last vocal verse, Prince describes the command he has over his harem – having four of them to wash his body, his hair, and focusing on different parts of his anatomy. The punchline is that in the final instance, he would then command the harem to make love to the person at whom the song is directed.

While this type of bragging song is relatively common in popular music, there are clear antecedents within the blues canon – Muddy Waters's 'Mannish Boy' and '(I'm Your) Hoochie Coochie Man' being obvious examples. As described, it is Prince's vocal and guitar work which firmly places this song in the blues camp; he is the central protagonist, and the interplay between his voice and guitar is reminiscent of performances of B. B. King – particularly his use of exclamatory single notes in the higher registers of the instrument during a solo which owes as much to physical and gestural pantomime as to musical and stylistic content.

While on the one hand 'If I Had a Harem' may seem to be a song about the preponderance of Prince's sexual prowess in line with a stereotyping of Black male (Davis and Cross; Rogers), the punchline of the song reveals that ultimately, it would be the harem that would be delivering the satisfaction rather than Prince himself. This playful abnegation of sexual responsibility is present in another blues staple – Muddy Waters's '(I'm Your) Hoochie Coochie Man'. Often delivered as a strutting, boastful hymn to masculinity, Waters himself explained that 'that's supposed to be a funny song' (Wald 177). In other words, while on the surface the song may seem to be about the artist's physical power and potency, closer contextual examination of the lyrical content reveals that it is the prospective lover who has the power; after all, it is they who are being begged for congress, and in the bragging of Waters and the miming of the lack of control of Prince, it is the singer who is at a disadvantage and unlikely (or unable) to provide ultimate satisfaction.

The blues aesthetic

The concepts of postmodernity and aesthetics have provided many writers and cultural commentators with ontological challenges in terms of definition. Nonetheless, scholars and artists such as Langston Hughes, Toni Morrison, Amiri Baraka, Houston J. Baker, James Baldwin and Ralph Ellison have described the blues aesthetic by bounding it firmly within the African American experience. Writer Kalamu Ya Salaam offers a succinct description, drawing attention to six key points: (i) stylization of process; (ii) the deliberate use of exaggeration to call attention to key qualities; (iii) brutal honesty clothed in metaphorical grace; (iv) acceptance of the contradictory nature of life; (v) an optimistic faith in the ultimate triumph of justice in the form of karma; and (vi) celebration of the sensual and erotic elements of life.

Each of these elements is present in the work of Prince in general, but also in pieces which draw on the stylistic and genre-based traditions of the blues in particular. For example, adoption of the blues as a stylistic context represents *stylization of process*, since this is a deliberate choice concerning the form of the music in terms of timbre, instrumentation, harmony and melody. In the example quoted, the *deliberate exaggeration of the power* of Prince's guitar – throwing him bodily across the stage, having the power to strike Cat Glover to the ground – embodies the key notion of the guitar as both a potent phallic symbol and powerful weapon. This particular trope is one which binds Prince not just as a musician in an evocation of the bluesman but also as the libidinous man-with-the-guitar presence in popular culture. Similar exaggerations are to be found in the ostensibly comedic lyric to 'Beggin' Woman Blues' which on the one hand invites laughter at the brazenness of a cash-strapped lover but on the other highlights the vicissitudes of modern poverty. Of note is that this song is essentially a re-working of the 1973 recording, 'Beggin' Woman' by blues artist Cousin Joe. It is possible to read *brutal honesty and acceptance of the contradictory nature of life* in many Prince compositions, but most baldly and clearly in 1987's *Sign o' the Times*, where the artist describes various contemporary urban scenes of depravity, loss, predestined failure and abuse. These themes themselves are staples in many blues, and Prince delivers his observations of Black and lower-class social reality in a style akin to a talking blues over a backing which features a blues-inflected pentatonic ostinato from the bass in the key of C, while the growling outro solo calls to mind blues guitarists Buddy Guy and Stevie Ray Vaughan in equal measure (Jack Hamilton, *Just around Midnight: Rock and Roll and the Racial Imagination*). *An optimistic faith in the triumph of justice in the form of karma* underpins the opening track on the scrapped 1997 album *The Truth*, in which Prince offers one of his most obviously blues-inspired recorded performances. The song is a twelve-bar sequence played in the key of E, and Prince performs the piece with only an acoustic guitar accompanying his voice. This sparse yet powerful texture is immediately evocative of the early- to mid-twentieth century practitioners of African American acoustic blues music such as Charlie Patton, Son House, Robert Johnson and Muddy Waters, a comparison compounded by the production on the song which emphasizes the solo nature of the performance by foregrounding Prince's plaintive and blues-inflected vocal, and surrounding the whole in a generous solitude-inferring reverberation effect reminiscent of Muddy Waters's 'Feel Like Goin' Home'. Finally, Prince's recorded and performed repertoire is replete with music which *celebrates the sensual and erotic elements of life*. For this chapter, we turn to the 1996 song 'Zannalee'. A twelve-bar sequence played in the key of E, the song is a straightforward narrative about group sex and voyeurism in which Prince describes being 'double-teamed' by the eponymous girl and her (twin) sister after drinking strong liquor, watching pornography and playing pool (itself a metaphor for sexual congress) – all the while being observed by the police. A further stylistic indication of the blues influence beyond the harmonic and melodic structure comes in the third verse of the song following the electric guitar solo. The drums and bass fall away, with the rhythmic pulse of the song coming from a low thumping sound evocative of a foot stomping on a wooden floor. The distorted and effected electric guitar is replaced by a clean guitar sound played with a slide, and these are the only accompaniments to Prince's voice. As with the song *The Truth*, the sonic representation is that of a solo acoustic blues player in the mould of Robert Johnson or Bukka White. The representation of Prince as a hypersexual buck is reinforced by the accompanying video, in which Prince is presented as living in a mansion, drinking heavily with the female protagonists of the song, being served up as a meal on a banquet table, before finally following the two women up a twisting, purple-carpeted stairway into a bedroom – where the video narrative of the song ends.

Postmodernity

'Postmodern' is a contested term in cultural studies. Broadly, it refers to a period in history which follows the modern era, itself a post-medieval period of the evolution of sociocultural norms of European origin which followed the Renaissance and included the Enlightenment and industrialization, and which took in the existential and subjective experience engendered by these epochs (Berman; Giddens). Postmodernity then might be regarded as the prevailing contemporary sociocultural orthodoxy in the Western world, with a starting point anywhere between the end of the Second World War and the widespread ascendancy of the information age in the mid-1980s (Bauman; Castells). Theorists variously characterize postmodernity as 'an incredulity towards metanarratives', (Lyotard; Lyotard et al.); 'the cultural logic of late-capitalism', (Jameson, *Postmodernism, or, the Cultural Logic of Late Capitalism*); pastiche privileged over parody (Jameson, 'Postmodernism and Consumer Society'); a predilection for nostalgia and the tendency to use the past as a context-free 'dressing-up box' (Jameson 'Postmodernism and Consumer Society'; Reynolds); a fixation for the never-ending 'now' and a perpetual present (Jameson 'Postmodernism and Consumer Society'; Reynolds); an emphasis on intertextuality (Barthes et al.; Kristeva); eclecticism

(Goodwin); and a lack of distinction between reality and representation (Auslander; Baudrillard).

How then should we view Prince through a postmodern lens? As Holland suggests, Prince represents 'the deconstruction of ... hierarchical oppositions such as God/Mortal, male/female, mind/body. ... His music provides the basis for deconstructing the obvious hierarchies of race, gender, and sexuality, but also those of the sacred and the profane, the writer/composer/producer and the performer, and even Self and the Other.' How does this marry to notions of the blues? Bluesmen occupy a privileged space in secular society, not unlike that of priests within a sacred context – a reality borne out by blues performers such as Son House and Rubin Lacey, both preachers in their time as well as renowned bluesmen. In other words, blues performers can be seen as secular celebrants, calling together the audience as a congregation and directing an antiphonal ceremony which celebrates and interrogates the realities of the participant's lives. Additionally, the blues player occupies the fluid nexus of performer-persona-protagonist (Moore, *Song Means : Analysing and Interpreting Recorded Popular Song* 181–2); specifically, the real-world *performer* takes on the *persona* of the bluesman, who in turn becomes the *protagonist* within the song being delivered. While this is true for many performing artists, blues players seem to carry an added burden of authenticity as part of their cultural capital as musicians, with audiences collapsing persona and protagonist into the real-world existence of the performer – in other words, audiences seem to expect the performer to be singing about the reality of their own lives (Pearson, 122–4). Prince embodies this particular element of postmodernity on several fronts. The artist's portrayal of 'The Kid' in *Purple Rain* is an act of signification (Brackett 311) which, for many, blurs the line between the performer and the character portrayed on screen as a persona and protagonist. This ownership and creation of image and character is characteristic of the blues artist's approach to satire, signifying, and intertextuality, and can be regarded as part of the bluesperson's *stylization of process*, that is, whatever blues people did, 'it was done with a style that emphasised the collective tastes and at the same time demonstrated the individual variation on the collective statement' (Ya Salaam 67). Specifically, bluespeople – particularly the blues*men* of the middle twentieth century appeared to walk the line between character and caricature in pursuit of their performance. Several cases are instructive in this instance. Huddie Ledbetter (1888–1949) – also known as Leadbelly – was initially discovered by John Lomax while serving time in Angola prison during the mid-1930s. Despite his prodigious musical talent, Leadbelly was often portrayed as a rural wild man with his criminal past being placed to the fore as a marketing stripe. Additionally, Leadbelly was famously photographed barefoot, in rural worker's dungarees and among barrels and burlap sacks for early publicity photographs – these at odds with the political activism and urban sophistication which characterized not only his early musical development but also his later career. Similarly, Lee Conley Bradley (1903–48) worked as a musician under the name Big Bill Broonzy. In contrast with Leadbelly, Broonzy developed his career as an urban sophisticate songwriter, authoring blues standards such as *Key to the Highway* and standing in for the deceased Robert Johnson in the From Spirituals to Swing concert of 1938. However, by the time of his European tours, Broonzy was presenting as a sharecropper in performance, while delivering acerbic and unequivocal protest songs such as 'Get Back', which spoke openly of the racial discrimination of the time. Finally, McKinley Morganfield (1918–83) performed under the name Muddy Waters and during early career presented as a slick urban performer as his sound came to define the beat-driven electric blues of the 1950s. However, by the 1960s and in search of a consistent national and international audience, Waters was re-recording acoustic music as a response to the folk boom, as well as flirting briefly with psychedelia in the wake of Jimi Hendrix on the *Electric Mud* album (Gordon).

These examples illustrate briefly that three of the seminal blues performers of the twentieth century worked within the stereotypes of Black masculinity that were most common at their time of prominence. The chapter now turns to a figure who was influenced by these individuals as musicians and in turn visibly influenced Prince – Jimi Hendrix.

'5 Women'/'The Thrill Is Gone'

As previously mentioned, the blues does not exist solely in a single musical and/or lyrical form. Also, while the blues had its origins in the African American communities of the United States, as Jeff Todd Titon notes, by the end of the twentieth century, the blues had moved from 'a music by and chiefly for black Americans' to 'a music by black and white Americans primarily for white Americans and Europeans' (Titon 207–8), assisted by the blues boom of the 1960s which brought an influx of youthful energy and performers to the style who labelled their amplified and largely guitar-led output as 'blues'. Within this context, Riley 'B. B.' King is regarded as one of the seminal crossover figures of blues music during the second half of the twentieth century. His 1969 recording of 'The Thrill Is Gone' marks a moment of commercial and critical success within American popular music, often considered as the point at which the blues finally departed from a majority Black audience towards a more mixed and White-consumer-oriented 'mainstream' (Adelt, 'Black, White, and Blue: Racial Politics in B.B. King's Music from the 1960s').

'The Thrill Is Gone' is a mid-tempo blues ballad in B minor, arranged for guitar, bass, drums, keys and strings. Originally written and recorded by Roy Hawkins in 1951, King's recording is arguably his best-known, becoming his first million-selling song when released as a single in December 1969. The song marked a departure in style and arrangement from King's previous material, featuring a standard blues-pop ensemble of guitar, bass, drums, keys and voice, but with the addition of strings at the suggestion of producer Bill Szymczyk (King and Ritz 249–50).

Originally conceived as a slower vamp in the Cab Calloway/Cotton Club big band style, King's version is altogether smoother and foregrounds the blues singer's signature barrel-chested roar, contrasted with his smooth, clean lead guitar lines – a texture used by Prince in the performance of 'Blues in C (If I Had a Harem)'. Essentially, King's take on the song is sophisticated and urbane; in the bitter reprimand to his lost love there is subtlety as well as strength, and there is dignity in despair.

The structure of 'The Thrill Is Gone' is a twelve-bar minor blues in B. Prince's '5 Women' is built on a similar minor blues harmonic structure but extends the form to a sixteen-bar blues.

Aside from the thematic similarity of the song – a tale of lost love being a staple in popular music, not just blues – the choice of minor blues and melodic phrasing in the vocal calls to mind King's performance. This is significant since King was a well-known blues player and, as indicated before, played a role in the cultural shift between audiences for blues music at the end of the 1960s. In '5 Women', Prince echoes the texture, tonality and timbre of King's multi-award-winning breakthrough arrangement and performance of a sophisticated, urban blues – while extending the form and harmonic structure of the material. Additionally, with specific regard to the harmony of the piece, the choice of 7#9 chords is a harmonic nod to Jimi Hendrix (Tippett 15). Also, the extension of the band to include a brass section which features the use of mutes refers to the sonic textures of 1970s urban Blaxploitation films such as *Across 110th Street* (Shear) and *Shaft*(Parks), thus 'using horns to negotiate the intertwined tension between the musical past and present and between competing versions of black masculinity' (Woodworth 120).

Finally, for blues-influenced songs, Prince also paid homage to Muddy Waters by working the lyrics to 'Electric Man' into his own minor blues vamp 'The Question of U'. A recording of the May 2015 Baltimore 'Rally 4 Peace' indicates a performance sensibility directly related to that of B. B. King, with specific reference to King's landmark concert recording *Live at the Regal*. Specifically, Prince directly addresses the audience, particularly the female contingent through the lyrical structure of the song, emphasizing the single entendres of 'plugging in to [your] socket', and conducting a group-singing session in addition to the call and response between his own voice and his guitar during the piece, a staple of blues performance.

Jimi Hendrix

It's just because we're both black.

Prince to Neal Karlen, 1985

Despite Prince's auto-ethnographic negation of the stylistic influence of Jimi Hendrix on his work, comparisons between the two musicians persist beyond noting their shared ethnic origin. It is possible to suggest that Prince's denial of Hendrix's influence is a long-running satire, whose punchline is found both in the younger artist's music and stage presentation, a stylistic double-voiced utterance which both refutes and confirms Hendrix's significance to Prince's work (Brackett). Clearly, flamboyance and advanced creativity underpinned the work of both musicians, and the lack of a significant African American guitar hero – with the possible exception of Nile Rodgers during the 1970s – also highlighted the dearth of credible heirs to Jimi Hendrix within the cultural landscape of popular music in the years since 1970 (Jack Hamilton, 'Why Prince May Have Been the Greatest Guitarist since Hendrix (and Why That Shouldn't Seem Like a Surprise)'). In terms of similarities, yes, they came from geographic locations which were not previously nationally noted for their popular music output – Prince from Minneapolis and Jimi from Seattle. In both areas, the Black population was in a minority. Yes, they were both African American males. Yes, they both came from broken homes, and artistically, they transgressed arbitrary musical genre lines. Additionally, Hendrix and Prince represent a challenging musical presence in that there is no obvious consistent pigeonhole in music marketing for either artist beyond filing under the umbrella term of 'popular' (Cutler); they are both, in their own ways, groundbreaking. Hendrix's clear blues influence mixed with psychedelia, jazz and folk and performed using what was for the time cutting-edge technology in an innovative style defies easy categorization; Prince's development of the Minneapolis Sound and in full possession of a grand vision for musical orchestration similarly challenges the musical popular music landscape by being genre fluid across several years of creativity (Murray 125).

However, the differences are also significant. The popular music recording and touring industry, certainly in terms of rock music and large-scale theatre and festival performances and their attendant technologies is in formation while Jimi is working in the late 1960s. By Prince's debut in 1978 it is well-established and certainly the tours undertaken by Prince are testament to the strides made in lighting, amplification and PA technology since the 1960s; Jimi is primarily a guitarist whereas Prince's large-scale visions are supported by his multi-instrumentality – this underlined perhaps by the Piano and a Microphone tour; Jimi is well-defined as a hypersexual heterosexual male – a notion given weight by the original UK cover of the *Electric Ladyland* album which featured a harem of naked young women, an image and design detested by Hendrix at the time of its release (Cross 238). On this point, however, Prince appears to revel in a sexual ambiguity brought to the fore by the postmodern lyrics of *Controversy*: Is the artist male or female, Black or White, straight or gay? Prince is further characterized by a certain knowingness; Jimi may have coquettishly asked, 'Are you experienced?', but the rejoinder from Prince, based on his recorded output and stage presence, would be, 'Hell, yes'. Further, this sense of sexuality is indelibly stamped through both artists' work, often underpinned by an overt Dionysian imperative inherent in the phallic symbolism of the electric guitar. Hendrix repeatedly made capital of this in live performance, a famous image from a show in Newport in 1969 showing Jimi playing the guitar behind his back with its neck protruding between his legs like a substitute penis, emphasizing his technical instrumental and sexual prowess and creating a 'technophallus' (Waksman 188). This idea is further extended by Prince, as demonstrated in the following two examples. In the first instance, during the 1984–5 Purple Rain concert tour, Prince's guitar was wired to ejaculate water onto the crowd during the climax of the opening song 'Let's Go Crazy' leaving little ambiguity regarding the nature of the imagery in play (Associated Press). In the second instance, during the acclaimed 2007 Super Bowl half-time performance, Prince's shadow was projected onto a large, flowing beige sheet, casting a shadow which carried phallic connotations for some (Coyle), and led others to complain that their sons had been turned to homosexuality by the power of the image (Lee). It is also worth noting that this performance contained a brief snatch of the Bob Dylan song 'All Along the Watchtower', a piece famously re-imagined by and associated with Jimi Hendrix since 1968.

The man with the guitar

The libidinous, molten guitar work of Jimi Hendrix is a clear touchstone of Prince's work as a performing musician. The significance of this influence lies in Jimi's role as a blues-influenced musician who used the style as a launch-pad for his own musical creativity. As Charles Shaar Murray notes,

> [Early Hendrix contains] performances which display a fully-formed and individual 'voice', both utterly steeped in the richest juices of the post-T-Bone [Walker] tradition and restlessly eager to create within it. From B.B. King Hendrix had learned to form long, smooth, elegantly flowing lines; from Buddy Guy he derived jagged, angry, spitting clusters of notes; from Albert Collins and Albert King he inherited a ferocious, snapping attack at the leading edge of a note; and from Bo Diddley an eagerness to incorporate both electronic effects and the 'bad' noises that most guitarists strive to eliminate ... finally, he was more than capable of travelling back to the earliest ... Delta blues, incorporating the rolling bass riffing of [Muddy] Waters and John Lee Hooker into the more modern styles. (Murray 171)

While Prince denied any ostensible link to Hendrix when questioned directly, he also made clear his stylistic debt in other interviews as well as musically. In the first instance, with reference to Hendrix's landmark performance of *The Star Spangled Banner*, Prince explained that to learn this specific piece of music was a rite of passage, and that no one who could not play this tune had a right to call themselves a guitarist (Murray 265, 270).

That Prince refuted what was an obvious link to the older musician is a trait of African American signifying, specifically, that the outright denial of something that appears obvious is a part of meaning-making (Gates). The African tradition aims at circumlocution rather than at an exact definition. The direct statement is considered crude and unimaginative; the veiling of all contents in ever-changing paraphrases is considered the criterion of intelligence and personality (Borneman). This in itself is evidence of a bluesperson's approach to reality: to be part of a situation, and to define it from the inside out, in opposition to externally imposed meaning (Jones; Levine).

It is in Prince's music that the presence of Jimi Hendrix's blues is most clearly felt. The first example is the Jimi Hendrix set-piece 'Hear My Train A-Comin'.' This piece was often featured in Hendrix's live shows and introduced variously as 'Getting My Heart Back Together Again' or 'Get My Heart Back Together' (Shapiro and Glebbeek). The song served as an open-ended blues jam on stage and in the recording studio as a showcase for Jimi's improvisational talents (Cross).

The image of the train in the song is also subject to a double meaning common in African American music. The train has presence in Negro spirituals and early blues as a means of escape and as a symbol of transport and transition from a situation of subjugation, invoking a sense of autonomy and self-determination in the ability to travel (McGeachy 46). This sense of salvation and redemption is further underlined by Jimi's lyrical description of leaving a town where his life is confused and unsatisfactory. The guitar makes the first statement of an E minor pentatonic ostinato phrase, before this is doubled by Noel Redding's electric bass, the whole emphasizing the rhythm of a slow train in motion. Additional to the imagery of transition and redemption inherent in the song and lyric is the psychosexual image of the train as a latent-Freudian, Hitchcockian phallic symbol (Pomerance 57; Sterritt 63).

Prince develops this psychosexual imagery as he performs the Hendrix-indebted blues jam *The Ride*. Both songs rely on their pulsing ostinato for structure while the guitar moves in essentially pentatonic shapes above the band. In fact, Prince directly confirms the blues influence in several performances, for example, in the *3 Nites in Miami Glam Slam 94* performance:

> PRINCE: 'Is this a blues crowd? [cheers] turn all these lights in here to blue.'
> ... and from *the VH1 Love 4 One Another TV Special*;
> PRINCE: 'How many of you like the blues in here tonight?'
> ... and from a 2015 show in Manchester
> PRINCE: 'It's Saturday night, can I play the blues?'

He echoes Jimi's line from 1967 – 'We're gonna throw a little bit of blues on you tonight' – and inhabits the position of performer-as-preacher, another element inherent in blues performances where the central performer encourages call and response (antiphony) and personification of the crowd as a single entity in their response to cues (heterophony).

Also in the key of E, the ostinato riff underpinning *The Ride* recalls the Jimi Hendrix line. Similarly, the slow grind of both tunes eventually reaches a climax as the train reaches its station – a metaphor for the conclusion of a sexual encounter or the realization of the freedom symbolized by the train.

Clearly, the song refers to the rocking motion of a train in motion; the crotchet/quaver pattern suggesting the rhythm of a train moving down the line. In common vernacular; the 'ride' is also a way of describing having sex – something underpinned by Prince's innuendo-laden lyrics.

'Purple House'/'Red House'

Prince's decision to record a re-working of the Jimi Hendrix song 'Red House' – re-titled as 'Purple House' for the 2004 *Power of Soul: A Tribute to Jimi Hendrix* album – is perhaps the clearest indication of the artist's regard for Hendrix's work. Recorded in 1966 as part of the *Are You Experienced* album, Hendrix derived 'Red House' from a well-established slow blues template. The Hendrix rendition of the song makes explicit his foundation in the blues in terms of twelve-bar structure, dependence on the I-IV-V chord structure, A-A-B lyric form, interplay between lead vocal and guitar, and featured guitar solo. Hendrix's original version of the song is in the key of Bb. Prince shifts the song to the key of E – a more obviously guitar-friendly key – and embellishes the performance with both backing vocals and a synthetic horn section. Of interest is that the backing vocals and all instruments with the – exception of the bass – all appear to be overdubs by Prince himself. This has two effects: First, that there appears to be a choir on the track, bringing into play a sense of a congregation and alluding to the sacred through an inference to the gospel vocal in the arrangement of the music. Second, the use of multiple overdubs highlights a postmodernist notion of multiplicity, intertextuality and construction. Specifically, the multiple voices sound like a single performance of a choir when in reality they are built from multiple takes of a single artist. This is further emphasized by the guitar lines in the Prince recording, which are layered harmonically during the solo and in the antiphonal responses to the vocals in the latter half of the song. In other words – the recording of 'Red House' by Hendrix is essentially a live capture of a blues trio on the 1966 production. Prince's 'Purple House' is a postmodernist blues in that the recording emphasizes multiple roles for the individual within the construction of what is presented as an ensemble piece.

Conclusion

Prince's explicit use of the blues as a framework for creativity does not limit his output to a single style or genre of music. His use of the blues emphasizes his status as a master musician in the popular style. Like Jimi Hendrix, Prince extends the blues form beyond the twelve-bar, three chords I-IV-V harmonic structure and lyrics in A-A-B format. Critically, with each of the examples given here, Prince takes artistic possession of crossover moments in the music's sociocultural and sociopolitical history and bends them to his own artistic purpose. In so doing, the artist brings questions of identity, ontology and ownership to the fore. While it is possible to recognize the blues quite distinctly in Prince's work, it is a foundational element of the music rather than its total content. In quoting, developing and extending the musical and cultural work of Muddy Waters, B. B. King and Jimi Hendrix, Prince positions himself as the embodiment of the postmodern blues aesthetic.

Notes

1 Creative production, especially of a work of art; an instance of this.
2 Mandingo – a sexual stereotype of Black masculinity common in the representation of African Americans from the nineteenth century.
3 A musical ensemble technique in which the rhythm section stops playing for one or more beats each measure while and instrumental soloist continues to play, or a vocalist continues to sing. See 'Hoochie Coochie Man', 'I Want to Be Loved' and so on https://www.collinsdictionary.com/dictionary/english/stop-time

Works cited

Adelt, Ulrich. 'Black, White, and Blue: Racial Politics in B.B. King's Music from the 1960s'. *Journal of Popular Culture*, 44.2 (2011): 195–216, aph, doi:10.1111/j.1540-5931.2011.00828.x.

Adelt, Ulrich. *Blues Music in the Sixties: A Story in Black and White*. Rutgers University Press, 2010.
The Associated Press. 'Some See Phallic Imagery in Prince's Show'. 2007. https://www.today.com/popculture/some-see-phallic-imagery-prince-s-show-wbna17013425.
Auslander, Philip. *Liveness: Performance in a Mediatized Culture*. 2nd ed. Routledge, 2008.
Baker, Houston A., Jr. *Blues, Ideology, and Afro-American Literature: A Vernacular Theory*. University of Chicago Press, 1984.
Baldwin, James. *No Name in the Street*. Joseph, 1972.
Baraka, Amiri. 'The "Blues Aesthetic" and the "Black Aesthetic": Aesthetics as the Continuing Political History of a Culture'. *Black Music Research Journal*, 11.2 (1991): 9, doi:10.2307/779261.
Barthes, Roland et al. *S-Z*. Cape, 1975.
Baudrillard, Jean. *Simulacra and Simulation*. University of Michigan Press, 1994.
Bauman, Zygmunt. *Liquid Modernity*. Polity Press, 2000.
Berman, Marshall. *All That Is Solid Melts into Air: The Experience of Modernity*. Verso, 1983.
Borneman, Ernest Jules. 'The Roots of Jazz'. *Jazz: New Perspectives on the History of Jazz by Twelve of the World's Foremost Jazz Critics and Scholars*. Ed. Nat Hentoff and Albert J. McCarthy, Da Capo Press, 1974.
Brackett, David. 'James Brown's "Superbad" and the Double-Voiced Utterance'. *Popular Music*, 11.3 (1992): 309–24, http://www.jstor.org/stable/931312.
Castells, Manuel. *The Rise of the Network Society*. 2nd ed., with a new pref. edition, Wiley-Blackwell, 2010.
Charters, Samuel Barclay. *The Country Blues. [with Plates.]*. Michael Joseph, 1959.
Coyle, Jake. 'Prince's Halftime Imagery Questioned'. *Washington Post*, 2007. http://www.washingtonpost.com/wp-dyn/content/article/2007/02/06/AR2007020601182.html.
Cross, Charles R. *Room Full of Mirrors: A Biography of Jimi Hendrix*. Sceptre, 2006.
Cutler, Chris. *File under Popular: Theoretical and Critical Writings on Music*. 2nd ed., November 1989.
Davis, Angela Y. *Blues Legacies and Black Feminism: Gertrude 'Ma' Rainey, Bessie Smith, and Billie Holiday*. Pantheon Books, 1998.
Davis, G. L, and H. J. Cross. 'Sexual Stereotyping of Black Males in Interracial Sex'. *Archives of Sexual Behavior*, 8.3 (1979): 269–79, doi:doi.org/10.1007/BF01541243.
Dylan, Bob. 'All Along the Watchtower'. *Composer – Bob Dylan*, CBS, 3872, 1968. https://www.discogs.com/Bob-Dylan-All-Along-The-Watchtower/release/2608196.
Ellison, Ralph. *Invisible Man*. Random House, 1952.
Garon, Paul. 'White Blues'. *Race Traitor*, 4.1 (1995), http://racetraitor.org/blues.html.
Gates, Henry Louis, Jr. *The Signifying Monkey: A Theory of Afro-American Literary Criticism*. Oxford University Press, 1988.
Gellert, Lawrence, and Elie Siegmeister. *Negro Songs of Protest*. American Music League, 1936.
Giddens, Anthony. *Modernity and Self-Identity: Self and Society in the Late Modern Age*. Polity Press, 1991.
Goodwin, Andrew. 'Popular Music and Postmodern Theory'. *Cultural Studies*, 5.2 (1991): 174–90, doi:10.1080/09502389100490151.
Gordon, Robert. *Can't Be Satisfied: The Life and Times of Muddy Waters*. Pimlico, 2003.

Grazian, David. *Blue Chicago: The Search for Authenticity in Urban Blues Clubs*. University of Chicago Press, 2003.

Hamilton, Jack. *Just around Midnight: Rock and Roll and the Racial Imagination*. Harvard University Press, 2016.

Hamilton, Jack. 'Why Prince May Have Been the Greatest Guitarist since Hendrix (and Why That Shouldn't Seem Like a Surprise)'. Web. 16 May 2017. slate.com http://www.slate.com/blogs/browbeat/2016/04/28/why_prince_was_the_greatest_guitarist_since_jimi_hendrix.html.

Hamilton, Marybeth. *In Search of the Blues: Black Voices, White Visions*. Jonathan Cape, 2007.

Harris, Corey. 'Can White People Play the Blues?' *Blues Is Black Music!*, 2015, Blogspot, http://bluesisblackmusic.blogspot.co.uk/2015/05/can-white-people-play-blues.html. Accessed 26 March 2015.

Harrison, Daphne Duval. *Black Pearls: Blues Queens of the 1920s*. Rutgers University Press, 1988.

Hendrix, Jimi. 'Are You Experienced'. composer – Jimi Hendrix, Reprise Records, RS 6261, 1967. https://www.discogs.com/The-Jimi-Hendrix-Experience-Are-You-Experienced/release/1435384.

Hendrix, Jimi. 'Electric Ladyland'. *Electric Ladyland*, composer – Jimi Hendrix, Reprise Records, 2RS 6307, 1968. https://www.discogs.com/The-Jimi-Hendrix-Experience-Electric-Ladyland/release/399579.

Hendrix, Jimi. 'Hear My Train a' Comin''. *BBC Sessions*, Experience Hendrix, MCA3-11742, 1998. https://www.discogs.com/The-Jimi-Hendrix-Experience-BBC-Sessions/release/518461.

Hendrix, Jimi. 'Red House'. *The Best of Jimi Hendrix*, composer – Jimi Hendrix, Experience Hendrix, 111 671–2, 1997. https://www.discogs.com/Jimi-Hendrix-Experience-Hendrix-The-Best-Of-Jimi-Hendrix/release/4813706.

Hendrix, Jimi. 'The Star Spangled Banner'. *Woodstock*, composer – John Stafford Smith, Polydor, 523 384–2, 1994. https://www.discogs.com/Jimi-Hendrix-Woodstock/release/433023.

Hodges, Johnny, and Rex Stewart. 'Things Ain't What They Used to Be'. *Things Ain't What They Used To Be*, composer – Mercer Ellington, RCA Victor, RD-7829, 1967. https://www.discogs.com/Johnny-Hodges-Rex-Stewart-Things-Aint-What-They-Used-To-Be/release/2577145.

Hoffman, Lawrence. 'At the Crossroads'. *Guitar Player*, 1990.

Holland, Nancy J. 'Prince: Postmodern Icon'. *Journal of African American Studies*, 21.3 (2017): 320–36, doi:10.1007/s12111-017-9363-7.

Hughes, Langston. 'The Negro Artist and the Racial Mountain'. *The Nation*, 1926.

Jameson, Fredric. 'Postmodernism and Consumer Society'. *Postmodern Culture*. Ed. Hal Ed Foster, Pluto Press, 1985. 111–25.

Jameson, Fredric. *Postmodernism, or, the Cultural Logic of Late Capitalism*. Verso, 1991.

Joe, Cousin. 'Beggin' Woman'. *Cousin Joe of New Orleans*, composer – Joseph Pleasant, Bluesway, BLS-6078, 1973. https://www.discogs.com/Cousin-Joe-Cousin-Joe-Of-New-Orleans/release/4787443.

Jones, Le Roi. *Blues People: Negro Music in White America*. Morrow, 1963.

Keil, Charles. *Urban Blues*. University of Chicago Press, 1966.

King, B. B. 'Live at the Regal'. composer – B. B. King, ABC-Paramount, ABC-509, 1964. https://www.discogs.com/BB-King-Live-At-The-Regal/release/5984765.

King, B. B. 'The Thrill Is Gone'. composer – A Benson and D Pettie, Bluesway, 45–61032, 1969. https://www.discogs.com/BB-King-The-Thrill-Is-Gone/release/1770713.
King, B. B., and David Ritz. *Blues All around Me: The Autobiography of B.B. King*. Sceptre, 1997.
King, Stephen A. *I'm Feeling the Blues Right Now: Blues Tourism and the Mississippi Delta*. University Press of Mississippi, 2011. American Made Music Series.
Kristeva, Julia. 'Word, Dialogue, and Novel'. *The Kristeva Reader*. Ed. Toril Moi, Basil Blackwell, 1986.
Lacava, Jacques D. 'The Theatricality of the Blues'. *Black Music Research Journal*, 12.1 (1992): 127–39, doi:10.2307/779286.
Lee, Adrian. 'Why the 2007 Super Bowl Was an Act of Peak Prince'. 21 Apr. 2016. http://www.macleans.ca/culture/arts/why-the-2007-super-bowl-was-an-act-of-peak-prince/.
Levine, Lawrence W. *Black Culture and Black Consciousness: Afro-American Folk Thought from Slavery to Freedom*. 30th anniversary ed., Oxford University Press, 2007.
Lieb, Sandra R. *Mother of the Blues: A Study of Ma Rainey*. University of Massachusetts Press, 1981.
Lomax, Alan. *The Land Where the Blues Began*. Methuen, 1993.
Lyotard, Jean-François. *The Postmodern Condition: A Report on Knowledge*. Manchester University Press, 1984.
Lyotard, Jean-François et al. *Toward the Postmodern*. Humanities Press International, 1993.
Mack, Kimberly. '"There's No Home for You Here": Jack White and the Unsolvable Problem of Blues Authenticity'. *Popular Music and Society*, 38.2 (2015): 176–93, doi:10.1080/03007766.2014.994323.
Magnoli, Albert. 'Purple Rain'. Producer, by Robert Cavallo, 1984. https://www.imdb.com/title/tt0087957/fullcredits/?ref_=tt_ov_st_sm.
McGeachy, M. G. *Lonesome Words: The Vocal Poetics of the Old English Lament and the African-American Blues Song*. 1st ed., Palgrave Macmillan, 2006.
Moore, Allan F. 'Authenticity as Authentication'. *Popular Music*, 21.2 (2002): 209–23, http://www.jstor.org/stable/853683.
Moore, Allan F. *Song Means: Analysing and Interpreting Recorded Popular Song*. Ashgate, 2012.
Morrison, Toni. *Playing in the Dark: Whiteness and the Literary Imagination*. Harvard University Press, 1992.
Murray, Charles Shaar. *Crosstown Traffic: Jimi Hendrix and Post-War Pop*. New ed., Canongate, 2012.
Oakley, Giles. *The Devil's Music: A History of the Blues*. Rev. ed., British Broadcasting Corporation, 1983.
Oliver, Paul. *Blues Fell This Morning: The Meaning of the Blues*. Jazz Book Club by arrangement with Cassell, 1960.
Palmer, R. *Deep Blues: A Musical and Cultural History from the Mississippi Delta to Chicago's South Side to the World*. New York: Penguin Books, 1981.
Parker, Charlie. 'Billie's Bounce'. *The Charlie Parker Story*, composer – Charlie Parker, Savoy Records, MG-12079, 1956. https://www.discogs.com/Charlie-Parker-The-Charlie-Parker-Story/release/3584405.
Parks, Gordon. 'Shaft'. 1974. Producer, Joel Freeman. https://www.imdb.com/title/tt0067741/fullcredits/?ref_=tt_ov_st_smhttps://www.imdb.com/title/tt0067741/fullcredits/?ref_=tt_ov_st_sm.

Pearson, Barry Lee. *'Sounds So Good to Me': The Bluesman's Story*. University of Pennsylvania Press, 1984.

Petrusich, Amanda. *Do Not Sell at Any Price: The Wild, Obsessive Hunt for the World's Rarest 78rpm Records*. First Scribner hardcover edition, 2015.

Pomerance, Murray. *An Eye for Hitchcock*. Rutgers University Press, 2004.

Prince. '5 Women'. Controversy Music, PRO1588, 1999. https://www.discogs.com/Prince-5-Women/release/4439326.

Prince. 'Beggin' Woman Blues'. *Indigo Nights / Live Sessions*, composer – Prince, NPG Records, 2008. https://www.discogs.com/Prince-Indigo-Nights-Live-Sessions/release/5509778.

Prince. 'Blues in C (If I Had a Harem)'. PolyGram Music Video, 081 202–3, 1988. https://www.discogs.com/Prince-Lovesexy-Live/release/9051454.

Prince. 'Controversy'. *Controversy*, composer – Prince, Warner Bros. Records, BSK 3601, 1981. https://www.discogs.com/Prince-Controversy/release/7682833.

Prince. 'Purple House'. *Power of Soul – A Tribute To Jimi Hendrix*, composer – Jimi Hendrix, Experience Hendrix, 01704-2012-1, 2004. https://www.discogs.com/Various-Power-Of-Soul-A-Tribute-To-Jimi-Hendrix/release/2708985.

Prince. 'The Question of U'. *Grafiti Bridge*, composer – Prince, Paisley Park, 9 27493–1, 1990. https://www.discogs.com/Prince-Graffiti-Bridge/release/1335397.

Prince. 'The Ride'. *3 Nites In Miami Glam Slam '94*, composer – Prince, Rox Vox, 1994. https://www.discogs.com/Prince-3-Nites-In-Miami-Glam-Slam-94/release/8835821.

Prince. 'The Ride'. *Love Symbol's Interactive Night*, composer – Prince, Frontline, FLCD-12, 1994. https://www.discogs.com/Prince-And-The-New-Power-Generation-Love-Symbols-Interactive-Night/release/7351828.

Prince. 'Sign o' the Times'. *Sign o' the Times*, composer – Prince, Paisley Park, 9 25577–1, 1987. https://www.discogs.com/Prince-Sign-O-The-Times/release/123915.

Prince. 'The Truth'. *The Truth*, NPG Records, 1997. https://www.discogs.com/Prince-The-Truth/release/8638971.

Prince. 'Zannalee'. *The Undertaker*, Warner Music Vision, 7599 38398–3, 1994. https://www.discogs.com/Prince-The-Undertaker/release/2186861.

Prince and the Revolution. 'Let's Go Crazy'. *Purple Rain OST*, composer – Prince, Warner Bros. Records, 9 29216–7, 1984. https://www.discogs.com/Prince-And-The-Revolution-Lets-Go-Crazy-Erotic-City/release/6013423.

Reynolds, Simon. *Retromania: Pop Culture's Addiction to Its Own Past*. 1st American ed., Faber, 2011.

Ripani, Richard J. *The New Blue Music: Changes in Rhythm & Blues, 1950–1999*. 1st ed., University Press of Mississippi, 2006. *American Made Music Series*.

Rogers, J. A. *Sex and Race: Vol 3: Why White and Black Mix in Spite of Opposition*. 5th ed., S.l.: H M Rogers, [1944] 1972.

Rudinow, Joel. 'Race, Ethnicity, Expressive Authenticity: Can White People Sing the Blues?' *The Journal of Aesthetics and Art Criticism*, 52.1 (1994): 127–37, http://www.jstor.org/stable/431591.

Ryan, Jennifer. 'Beale Street Blues? Tourism, Musical Labor, and the Fetishization of Poverty in Blues'. *Ethnomusicology*, 55.3 (2011): 473–503.

Shapiro, Harry, and Caesar Glebbeek. *Jimi Hendrix: Electric Gypsy*. Rev. and updated ed., Mandarin, 1995.

Shear, Barry. 'Across 110th Street', 1973. Producer, Anthony Quinn. https://www.imdb.com/title/tt0068168/?ref_=nv_sr_1?ref_=nv_sr_1https://www.imdb.com/title/tt0068168/?ref_=nv_sr_1?ref_=nv_sr_1.

Sterritt, David. *The Films of Alfred Hitchcock*. Cambridge University Press, 1993.
Tippett, Graham. *50 Guitar Hacks: For the Advancing Guitarist*. Tippett, 2016.
Titon, Jeff Todd. 'Reconstructing the Blues: Reflections on the 1960s Blues Revival'. *Transforming Tradition: Folk Music Revivals Examined*. Ed. Neil V. Rosenberg, University of Illinois Press, 1993.
Waksman, Steve. *Instruments of Desire: The Electric Guitar and the Shaping of Musical Experience*. Harvard University Press, 2000.
Wald, Elijah. *Escaping the Delta: Robert Johnson and the Invention of the Blues*. 1st ed., Amistad, 2004.
Waters, Muddy. 'Electric Man'. *'Unk' in Funk*, composer – Muddy Waters, Chess, CH 60031, 1974. https://www.discogs.com/Muddy-Waters-Unk-In-Funk/release/2310610.
Waters, Muddy. *Electric Mud*, Chess, CRLS 4542, 1968. https://www.discogs.com/Muddy-Waters-Electric-Mud/release/3075275.
Waters, Muddy. 'Feel Like Going Home'. *Folk Singer*, composer – Muddy Waters, Chess, LP-1483, 1964. https://www.discogs.com/Muddy-Waters-Folk-Singer/release/4487456.
Waters, Muddy. '(I'm Your) Hoochie Coochie Man'. composer – Muddy Waters, Chess, 1560, 1954. https://www.discogs.com/Muddy-Waters-And-His-Guitar-Im-Your-Hoochie-Cooche-Man-Shes-So-Pretty/release/4201802.
Waters, Muddy. 'Mannish Boy'. composer – Muddy Waters et al., Chess, 1602, 1955. https://www.discogs.com/Muddy-Waters-And-His-Guitar-Manish-Boy/release/7774033.
Woodworth, Griffin. 'Prince, Miles, and Maceo: Horns, Masculinity, and the Anxiety of Influence'. *Black Music Research Journal*, 33.2 (2013): 34, doi:10.5406/blacmusiresej.33.2.0117.
Ya Salaam, Kalamu. 'The Blues Aesthetic'. *Bluesspeak: The Best of the Original Chicago Blues Annual*. Ed. Lincoln T. Beauchamp, University of Illinois Press, 2010, https://www.amazon.co.uk/BluesSpeak-Original-Chicago-Blues-Annual/dp/0252076923.

9

'Tears go here'[1]

Commemorating the Minneapolis Prince and the international Prince

Suzanne Wint

On 21 April 2016, images of Minnesotans placing purple flowers and balloons on the fence at Paisley Park spread around the world. Soon, Upper Midwesterners[2] in driving distance joined them; later, those from farther afield flew in. Fans danced away their grief and celebrated the life of Prince Rogers Nelson for three nights outside First Avenue club in downtown Minneapolis.[3] Since Prince's untimely death, the Twin Cities have continued to host visitors paying their respects in contemplative and joyful ways, at large-scale ticketed events such as the Official Prince Tribute Concert on 13 October 2016 at Xcel Energy Center in St. Paul and Celebration 2017, held from 20 through to 23 April at Paisley Park. At the same time there have been numerous smaller-scale, unticketed remembrances with a decidedly local focus, often with a DIY or charitable component.

Impressed by the volume and the character of commemoration, I set out in May 2016 to understand the significance of public mourning in the wake of Prince's untimely passing. Remembrances did not seem to wane through the summer of 2016. The number of memorial events in Minnesota was particularly striking, given that its regional culture is typically perceived within the United States as quiet, humble, modest and even-tempered – diametrically opposed to Prince's stage persona and to public displays of grief. It became clear through ethnographic fieldwork that mourning Prince among Minnesotans and among visitors, though in many respects a shared experience, also differs in significant ways. In this chapter, I examine the importance of the local in mourning Prince in the year following his death, as well as the significance of the local in shaping his future legacy.

Mourning, methodologically

Few objects of fandom have been linked to place as strongly as Prince. Though he had other residences, and lived in Los Angeles from 2007 to 2009, he was based in

Minneapolis or its suburbs for most of his life and career. He made his love for his home state public through his costuming, lyrics and frequent shout-outs to Minneapolis in live concerts, and through his own fandom for local sports teams. But he also showed his commitment to his home through his professional and philanthropic support of local arts scenes and local community.

To understand the mechanics of mourning Prince, I use ethnography to bring together studies of fan cultures, popular music, posthumous fame, public mourning and celebrity culture. Though I draw on online journalism, blogs and fan forums, podcasts and social media, it is through participant observation at dozens of events – large and small, ticketed and free to the public – that I have been able to tease out the significance of place and belonging in mourning Prince. I have conducted semi-structured interviews by telephone or in person with fans, artists, arts organizers and other cultural workers. These individuals have several subject positions – for instance, a long-time fan and native Minnesotan who teaches in an art department at a branch of a state university, and was commissioned to paint a portrait of Prince that is displayed prominently in a Minneapolis stadium. Investment in fandom varies widely among participants, from superfans who travel to Minnesota to find closure after Prince's unexpected death to those who do not consider themselves fans at all, but wanted to pay respect to Prince for his impact on the music industry and music technology, his philanthropy, his work ethic or his message of being unabashedly oneself.

Anthropological research regularly focuses on relationships between local and global cultures, while fan studies has more frequently dealt with a defined work transmitted transnationally or globally, and the participatory fan activities responding to that work (e.g. fan fiction, mashups and cosplay). New considerations of popular music in heritage studies such as Cohen et al.'s *Sites of Popular Music Heritage* or Fry's 'Becoming a "True Blues Fan"' address issues of the local such as how genre and style are linked to place through heritage tourism. Though such work is likely to take place in the Twin Cities in the future, it was not a cultural focus in the acute period of mourning through mid-2017.[4]

Certainly, local and visiting constituencies exist and intermingle at many events, and some tributes have been aimed at national audiences, such as those during televised awards shows and sporting events. When I speak of events emphasizing the local, I mean events unlikely to be destination events due to the scheduling or scope – for instance, an opening reception mid-week in late winter – or events that specifically speak to local customs (the Minnesota State Fair Unite in Purple Day serving purple local foods) or local exhibitors (Lost Literary Center's Minnesota Poets on Prince), while still welcoming the public to participate in viewing or listening.

The small-scale and the local

Though larger, official events drew visitors to the Twin Cities, smaller-scale events have been popular among visitors and locals alike. Small-scale events in galleries and clubs popped up around 7 June 2016, which was the 58th anniversary of Prince's birth.

Having adopted the Jehovah's Witness faith in his forties, Prince stopped celebrating birthdays; however, at almost seven weeks after the musician's death, many fans were hungry for a form of ritual send-off, as there had been no official public memorial or funeral. Venues chose to celebrate Prince's life with his music, in most cases in the form of dance parties. The events I attended – all advertised by The Current blog[5] (Johnson) – were free to attend, or asked for a small entry fee that supported local non-profit organizations focusing on youth music programmes in honour of Prince's own support of such programmes in the region.

Small-scale events also emerged in October 2016 in conjunction with the opening of Paisley Park for public tours and the Official Prince Tribute Concert. When the status of each event became uncertain, fans who had booked non-refundable travel and hotel rooms began planning meet-ups to take the place of the events they feared would not happen. Venues followed suit with small club concerts by Prince associates, or dance parties with special guests from Prince's orbit.

As the anniversary of Prince's death approached in April 2017, similar programming again emerged around Celebration 2017, the four-day event at Paisley Park. At around $500 for general admission and $1000 for VIP, the cost of tickets was too exorbitant for many, and the smaller-scale events became reason for fans to travel to Minneapolis during that week.

Local residents and visitors cited many reasons for attending only the satellite events at these times. Many were not able to obtain tickets because events sold out so quickly. Especially for local residents who had not taken time off to travel to Minneapolis, the concerts ran too late during the work week. Others felt the events were too commercial. Still others could not imagine attending a Prince concert from which Prince would be conspicuously absent. For these mourners, the smaller, more intimate events better served their needs.

Many of these smaller-scale events, as well as those that took place throughout the year between official commemorations, served to emphasize the local, and to allow Minnesotans to mourn Prince as a community member. I examine three such events that, though coinciding with the lifecycle dates, very much focused on what Prince meant to Minnesotans, and how Minnesotans might mourn and celebrate him.

BlueNose Coffee (from Friday, 21 April to Sunday, 23 April 2017)

BlueNose Coffee held a three-day showing of nine pieces of designer Kristin D. Hensen's Prince-themed artwork and offered four Prince-themed specialty espresso drinks: the Little Red Corvette, Pancake, and Raspberry Beret lattés, and the Purple Vanilla frappé. Purple and lavender paper raindrops were suspended from the café's décor, and a chalkboard on the patio advertised the tribute. The café is located about 30 miles (48 kilometres) south of the Twin Cities in Farmington, Minnesota, home to approximately 22,000.

Though The Current advertised this event widely, the distance from Minneapolis/ St. Paul made it an unlikely destination for visitors, especially since Farmington is not located on an interstate highway. Owner Sarah said, in fact, that she wanted to host an event that was local, for those who could not make it into Minneapolis for late-night events, and affordable, for those whose budgets could not accommodate expensive official commemorations and concerts.

Prince's pursuit of his dreams had been an inspiration to Sarah and her friend designer Hensen as they grew up south of the Cities. They respected his sustained support of local arts scenes and education in the Metro area, so they decided to hold a small tribute in the café. Sarah told me that the weekend after his death, she had gathered with neighbours in Farmington to listen to Prince's music and celebrate his life. She hoped similarly to create a community remembrance at the café on the anniversary of his passing.

Remembering Prince Coloring Party (Sunday, 23 April 2017)

Though her shop was usually closed on Sundays, Tammy Ortegón opened her ColorWheel Gallery from 2:00 to 6:00 p.m. to host a colouring party with snacks, purple hibiscus lemonade and an all-Prince playlist. ColorWheel regularly hosts DIY art-making events at a common table in the back of the shop under the motto 'create community' (ColorWheel Gallery). On this particular day, participants could select art pages from Ortegón's 'Rated P 4 Funky' colouring book, a collection of drawings of the performer that Ortegón had made in her youth. Inspired by the ways Prince encouraged people to exercise their creativity, she wanted to offer an opportunity for people to gather for free to remember Prince while also creating.

ColorWheel also committed to carrying on Prince's support of and solidarity with the arts community in many ways. In contrast with imported Prince colouring books available online, Ortegón worked with a Minneapolis printer who used high-quality art paper for the book. She wanted this to be a quality remembrance that emphasized his local roots. Part of the proceeds from the book go to Sabathani Community Center, formerly Bryant Junior High School, which Prince attended. In fact, during the whole month of April 2017, the shop donated a percentage of sales and contents of a donation jar to Sabathani's Horizons Youth Program, which Prince himself supported. The sign over the jar read, 'For the month of April – In Honor of Prince – the #ColorWheelGallery will be donating a percentage of sales to #HorizonsYouth at Sabathani Community Center … Sabathani has been offering programs for neighborhood youth in art, music, social/emotional development, academic enrichment & more for 50 years. Prince was a Big Supporter of these programs & so are We!' (ColorWheel Gallery).

Where Purple Reigns: Minnesota Artists on Prince (from Tuesday, 7 June to Sunday, 17 July 2016)

Located in the North Minneapolis community that was Prince's home for part of his youth, the University of Minnesota Robert J. Jones Urban Research and Outreach-Engagement Center (UROC) partners with the community to address issues of economic and social inequality through a variety of projects, including those in performing and visual arts. UROC hosted a six-week exhibit of visual art by Minnesota artists with a presentation of literary arts at the 7 June opening by Minnesota poets. The exhibit included a variety of media, such as photographs of April 2016 commemorations in Minneapolis, illuminated glass sculpture, a 'zine, an eight-foot-tall Prince puppet created for Minneapolis' 2016 May Day parade, a portrait that hung in Prince's Minneapolis night club Glam Slam and an embellished jeans jacket. Artists could sell their work commission-free, and twelve pieces were sold over the run of the exhibition (Janzen). Entry to the exhibit was free and it was open to the public, with the opening event, 'Where Purple Reigns: Minnesota Poets on Prince', curated by Program Director Bao Phi of Loft Literary Center.

UROC gallery curator and special projects coordinator Hawona Sullivan Janzen explained that there was a strong desire to host an event commemorating Prince because the centre is located in the North Side neighbourhood where Prince spent much of his youth. As someone from the neighbourhood who 'made it', he is respected by and inspires community members. Employees of the centre also have ties to Prince's siblings and the Anderson family with whom he lived as a teenager. So, when a cancellation in the gallery's schedule coincided with the anniversary of Prince's birth, UROC sent out a call for Prince-inspired artwork by Minnesotans and put together the show in two-and-a-half weeks. Though the jury originally hoped for 25 to 30 pieces, Janzen said the response was so great, the jury accepted far more in order to represent as many Minnesotans as possible.

The literary arts event sponsored by Loft Literary Center had been scheduled later in June, as space allowed, but with the cancellation came the opportunity to incorporate the spoken word performances into a memorial as the exhibit opening[6] on a date significant to Prince's life. Janzen wanted to create small moments of ritual for attendees, but focused these moments on Prince's and the contributors' art so as not to conflict with Prince's Jehovah's Witness beliefs, or the belief or non-belief of attendees.

Janzen estimated attendance at the opening at around 200, which is three- to fourfold the usual attendance at UROC event openings. This was due in part to out-of-town visitors who heard about the event through The Current, but ties between Prince and the community, and the fact that community members' art was displayed also contributed to the larger-than-usual crowd.

☙ ☙ ☙

The three events I describe here were focused on community commemoration of Prince's support of the arts. Though each celebrated the local community of artists so dear to Prince, all of the events were inclusive of visitors. Each event was organized around local mourning, not merely because of pride in a local resident achieving success and fame, but because of very concrete ties to Prince as a neighbour. Sarah had attended events at Paisley Park; Tammy Ortegón had Prince's mother as a home economics teacher in Minneapolis public schools; UROC has numerous ties to Prince's extended family. A much larger circle of Minnesotans feels a neighbourly bond to Prince because his philanthropy extended to so many arts and youth programmes, and he turned to Minneapolitans to DJ parties or do design work for one-off events.

So even though Prince was not a physical presence in the community in the way an average resident might be, his presence was very much felt. For instance, when Chanhassen Elementary School publicly requested donations from the community for enrichment programs, Prince sent a sizeable donation despite not having children in his local school. As principal Greg Lange said, 'He was the neighbor down the road' (Smith).

Prince from Minnesota

Throughout his career, Prince openly displayed his hometown pride and identified himself with Minnesota. He introduced listeners to the geography of Minneapolis through songs like 'Uptown', 'Calhoun Square' and 'Northside', and he proclaimed his allegiance to the city and the state through the bold graphics of his Minneapolis Sound costumes on the *Lovesexy* tour and shout-outs to the city in concerts abroad. Spanning his career, his lyrics refer to many typical – and stereotypical – characteristics of Minnesotan culture, from the (White) Minnesotan accent he uses in 'Zannalee' to a land covered in snow in 'White Mansion' and 'Rock 'n' Roll Is Alive (and It Lives in Minneapolis)'. In 'Laydown', Prince sings, 'From the heart of Minnesota here come the Purple Yoda.' 'Yoda' and 'Minnesota' rhyme properly in a strong Minnesota accent, rather than being a slant rhyme. By choosing the word, 'heart', Prince locates himself (the Purple Yoda) both geographically and metaphorically within the state and its culture. By representing himself as akin to *Star Wars* character Yoda, he employs a typically Minnesotan rhetorical device of following a boastful statement with self-deprecating humour in order to forestall the charge of immodesty.[7] Yoda is both a revered Jedi master and an elderly, homely figure of short stature. He expresses himself cryptically, which many journalists wrote of Prince. With this metaphor, Prince intimates that it is the wise who speak cryptically, thus admonishing the journalists with a sly smile, a characteristic of 'Minnesota nice'.

The impact Prince has had on Minnesotans by remaining in Minneapolis simply cannot be overstated. The Midwest region of the United States is referred to as 'flyover country' – a part of the country that one flies over on the way from the highly populated commercial and cultural centres on the East and West Coasts. The Midwest is often seen as far less cosmopolitan than New York City or Los Angeles. Because most famous Minnesotans have left the state in the pursuit of fame or after attaining it, the message Prince sent to at least two generations of Minnesotans is very strong. His staying bolstered a sense of civic pride, but also endeared Prince to many Minnesotans. In a remembrance entitled 'What Prince Meant to Minnesota and the World', Aaron Rupar explains, 'Though he became an international pop music and cultural icon, … Prince, unlike *certain other legendary Minnesota musicians*, always reserved a special place in his heart for his home state.' The italicized text indicates a hyperlink to a Minnesota-penned article on Bob Dylan's decision to house his archive in Oklahoma. Inevitably, any conversation about the Hibbing-born Nobel laureate includes the remark, 'But Prince stayed.'

Prince as Minnesotan

Prince is often described as transcending categories. Since his death, many stories have emerged that point to his life as an international rock star, and as a typical Minnesotan. Speaking to *The New York Times*, Paisley Park director of archives Angie Marchese made note of how many of Prince's accessories were dramatic statement pieces without being made of precious stones, or by expensive designers. She described them as 'everyday' and 'simple' (Matos). Just as he traversed societal categories of gender, sexuality, race and genre in his career, Prince also straddled the worlds of rock star extravagance and Midwestern practicality.

On a visit to the Minnesota History Center in St. Paul on 14 February 2017, I spoke to various staff members about the Center's involvement in commemoration. Acquisitions and Outreach Coordinator Lori Williamson told me about the Center's work to help remove items from the Paisley Park fence and catalogue them.[8] Paisley Park has since put together a museum exhibit that recreates the outdoor fence, rotating through the archived items. When we finished talking about the project, I asked Williamson how Prince's death affected her as a native Minnesotan. She told me she always expected she would run into him walking around one of the many lakes in town. 'I'd say, "Hey." He'd say, "Hey", and we'd both keep going. And now that will never happen.' Running into an international music star on a walk around the lake sounds highly improbable to most fans, but this sort of encounter with Prince happened regularly enough in Minneapolis and in the western suburbs for there to be a saying that every Minnesotan has a Prince story (see, for example, Rushin; Brooker).

Though I embarked on this research considering fandom as a performance of belonging – being part of the Purple Army – exchanges like the one with Williamson revealed a more interesting performance of belonging: that is, claiming Prince's belonging as a Minnesotan, a Minneapolitan and a neighbour first and foremost. Rather than saying, 'I am part of him as a fan,' through such stories and through iconography Minnesotans are saying, 'Prince is part of us.'

While at the History Center, I also spoke to the library's front desk staff, Nancy and John, about attendance patterns at the free exhibit of the Purple Rain suit and other holdings through August 2016. Discussion soon shifted to the fence and Paisley Park, and Nancy pulled out her phone to show me pictures of handcrafted items people had left that day. 'I'm not a fan', she said. 'But you had to go.' John joked about their age, saying they had been too busy listening to Elvis to have discovered Prince, but it was clear they knew about and had great respect for him. For Minnesotans, Prince very much embodied Minnesota values. He was a hardworking, community-minded neighbour, who went to church and kept his lawn trimmed. 'You had to go,' Nancy had said: paying respects to a good neighbour was the right thing to do.

The events around First Avenue are another measure of Prince's belonging as a neighbour and a Minneapolitan. General Manager of First Avenue Nate Krantz spoke with me about organizing the three-night block party in April 2016, among other events. As soon as it was announced that the body found at Paisley Park was Prince's, Krantz and Dave Safar of The Current (Minnesota Public Radio's local-music station and blog) were on the telephone, and within fifteen minutes, they decided to co-host a block party in the unseasonably pleasant weather in order to accommodate as many guests as possible. The Current would enlist performers and set up gear, while First Avenue would apply for the city permits. Krantz told me that the city of Minneapolis has absolutely no permitting provisions for dance parties to take place beyond 2:00 a.m. As Krantz spoke with the permits office, they recognized Prince's significance to the local community, and uncharacteristically created city permits out of thin air that would allow three nights of dancing until 7:00 a.m. inside First Avenue and on the streets surrounding the building.

Displaying the local to the world

Prince's own fandom for Minnesota's professional sports teams was reciprocated in the 2016–17 season during which they all honoured him publicly. The US Bank Stadium had been in talks with Prince for him to perform on 12 August 2016, as the very first event in the new facility. This then became the initial date and location for the Official Prince Tribute Concert. So it was no surprise when the Minnesota Vikings, the American football team for which the stadium serves as home field, dedicated the first home game's half-time show to Prince.[9]

The half-time show begins with the Minnesota Orchestra playing an abbreviated version of the first movement from Beethoven's Fifth Symphony from a stage on the field. Animations of Minnesota history are projected on a screen in front of the stage, and also on the scoreboard. As the crowd applauds at the end of the piece, the Vikings' logo is projected on the screen. Thunder echoes through the stadium speakers and rain begins to fall in the purple background of the logo. More musicians enter the stage to the announcement, 'Please welcome members of Prince's New Power Generation and Prince collaborators The Steeles, as we pay tribute to our native son and the state he loved' (Minnesota Orchestra et al. 4:09–4:20). The orchestra and the NPG intone the familiar first chords of 'Purple Rain' and an iconic purple silhouette of Prince appears on a screen in front of the stage (4:23). This turns into a purple nebula (4:27), which then bursts into white doves flying away (4:33). The camera focuses on soloist Jevetta Steele as the first verse begins and remains on the musicians through the beginning of the first chorus. Images then shift between the performers, images of recognizable sites in Minnesota and of Minnesotans working and playing. As a truncated guitar solo begins, we see the guitarist on screen (6:56), but the image changes to Prince's silhouette from his iconic Superbowl half-time performance (6:59), and then turns back to the NPG (7:13). In the coda (the 'woo-hoo-hoo-hoo' section), the video screen shows a famous silhouette of Prince's head, with the First Avenue star superimposed (7:25), and we see various images of Prince within the state of Minnesota (7:30–7:46). The final image shows many Minnesotans in the state outline, with Prince among them (7:47–7:59).

In contrast with many visual tributes that focus only on his Purple Rain era, this tribute includes photos from his entire career. The sixth photo in the sequence of Prince images inside the shape of Minnesota (7:42) appears to be from 2015, or possibly even early 2016. This is significant because work on posthumous fame would predict the use of images from the height of commercial success, youth and beauty – think 1950s movie-star Elvis as opposed to jumpsuit-era Elvis. In this tribute, we see Prince among his fellow Minnesotans, who claim him for his entire lifespan, much as one might with neighbours, friends and family.

Visiting Minneapolis

Once visitors started making extended trips to Minneapolis for the purpose of remembering Prince, the Minneapolis Convention and Visitors Association published a free map for self-guided tours of twenty-one Prince-related sites, from the buildings that formerly housed the hospital where he was born, to the Hard Rock Café that displays one of Prince's concert suits with 'Minneapolis' on the arm of the jacket. Fan pilgrimages to these sites are driven by what Les Roberts has called 'contagious magic' (12), or the properties or qualities of a celebrity that 'rub off' onto an object or a place, thus transforming it (Bickerdike 50). By visiting these sites – or indeed by visiting Minneapolis – fans might be imbued with some of the magic Prince left behind.

The façade of First Avenue has been an important site for visitors and locals alike to access this contagious magic, as the venue is intimately linked with Prince's rise to superstardom in the movie *Purple Rain*. The stars painted on the side of First Avenue honour acts that have sold out the venue, but as Dan Corrigan explained during a tour of the facilities, an act must also be a 'friend of the house' in order to merit a star. In other words, the star honours the relationship with fans and with club, showing that the act has established some sense of belonging, and has not merely touched down, sung and left without interacting with the stage crew. Shortly after Prince's death was announced, Corrigan saw a woman on her lunch hour approach the club, and place just three or four white tulips under Prince's star, the first in a stream of notes, pictures, artwork and even functioning guitars, that confirmed the bond between performer and place that the First Avenue stars represent. Prince's star became a place of veneration, where fans could feel a kind of proximity to him – and indeed, photographs of mourners touching the star appear across news sources.[10]

Reclaiming the local from the world

The morning of Wednesday, 4 May 2016, commuters passing First Avenue found that Prince's star was now gold. First Avenue denied involvement, and noted that security cameras had recorded the culprits, though none of the small group could be identified. The club also announced that Prince's star would remain gold. International press recounted the intrigue, but no one took credit. The act itself is indicative of the special relationship between Prince and Minneapolis, but it is also noteworthy that the artist responsible revealed himself in the local press. In the December 2016 issue of *Mpls St Paul* dedicated to Prince, artist Peyton Russell came forward to tell that he had not merely painted the star gold, but that he and his former teacher had applied gold leaf to the painted brick wall (Wood 92).

With the death of any celebrity begins the clamber for legacy formation, and it is no different with Prince. Who gets to claim Prince, and how will he be represented? Jensen notes that in reading a celebrity's legacy, different groups bring various ideological agendas, in terms of identities (among them, race, class, gender, ethnicity), but also in terms of who plays what role in constructing or constraining celebrity image (fans, critics, journalists, family, industry, other interest groups) (xviii). This is amplified by the fluidity Prince purposely embodied in both courting and confounding identities throughout his career: indeed, he asks the listener, 'Was I what you wanted me to be?' ('Controversy'). Considering Prince through a particular identity – in this case, as a Minnesotan – need not negate the many other identities with which followers and fans identify. Examining Prince's relationship to his home state does, however, bring more nuance to our understanding of an artist often described as mysterious, enigmatic or reclusive. When asked in an interview what the greatest misconception is that the public has about Prince, Revolution drummer and native Minnesotan Bobby Z stated, 'That he's not a normal person. He is a normal person. He's an extraordinary person, but he's still a human' (Singer). Some of Prince's behaviours that seemed unusual for an international rock star, such as keeping his personal life and philanthropy out of the public eye and basing his business empire in the Upper Midwest, very much align with Minnesotan culture.

Examining the relationship between Prince and Minnesota is also important to understanding the construction of his legacy. I assert that if Minneapolis possesses the contagious magic tourists and pilgrims seek, then so too do Minneapolitans embody some of this contagious magic. Steve Rushin writes, 'Prince sang about Uptown. We had been to Uptown. Prince was cool, so we were too.' Each retelling of a Prince story, each local commemoration, each investment in the local arts scene, regenerates that contagious magic and solidifies Prince's legacy. His commitment to Minnesota built Minnesotans' commitment to his legacy. As a local mourner posted under Prince's First Avenue star, 'You never left us and we'll never leave you'[11] (Wood).

Notes

1   'Tears go here' is the final line of Prince's song 'Comeback', widely believed to have been written in response to the death of his infant son.
2   The Upper Midwest is a term used to refer to Minnesota, Wisconsin and Michigan. Adjoining northern regions of Illinois, Indiana, Iowa and Ohio, as well as all of North and South Dakota are also frequently included.
3   See, for instance, the lower photograph from Scott Olsen on the MPR News website: <https://www.mprnews.org/story/2016/04/22/prince-fans-party-all-night-first-avenue>.
4   In the time since Prince's death, local-music journalists and photographers have published over half a dozen books on the Minneapolis music scene from the 1960s

onward. Together with the tourism arising from Prince's life and death, this may well mark the beginning of Minnesota Popular Music Heritage.
5 The Current is a non-commercial radio station based in St Paul that puts an emphasis on local music. See the list in question here: <https://blog.thecurrent.org/2016/06/where-to-celebrate-princes-birthday-in-the-twin-cities/>.
6 Video of some of the spoken word performances can be viewed online in the Vimeo album 'Where Purple Reigns: Minnesota Artists on Prince', https://vimeo.com/album/3987655.
7 I thank Susan Campion, fellow conference delegate and native Minnesotan, for pointing out this rhetorical strategy as typically Minnesotan during Dez Dickerson's keynote on 24 May 2017 at the University of Salford's Purple Reign conference.
8 Several local history societies cooperated on this initiative.
9 In the discussion that follows, I refer to the 8'01" video uploaded to the official YouTube channel of the Minnesota Orchestra: <https://www.youtube.com/watch?v=7Jti7jqAVh0>.
10 See *StarTribune* coverage throughout April 2016: for instance, the first photo (by Jim Gehrz) in the gallery of the 23 April 2016 article: http://www.startribune.com/photos-fans-continue-to-mourn-prince/376726201/#grid.
11 See Jim Mone's photograph in the 5 December 2016 issue of *Mpls St Paul Magazine* dedicated to Prince (subtitled 'Funkiest. Minnesotan. Ever'): http://mspmag.com/arts-and-culture/prince-everlasting/.

Works cited

Bickerdike, Jennifer Otter. *The Secular Religion of Fandom: Pop Culture Pilgrim*. Sage, 2016.

Brooker, Ira. 'Why Does Minnesota Still Go Crazy for Prince?' *MN Artists*, 30 October 2013. http://www.mnartists.org/article/why-does-minnesota-still-go-crazy-prince.

Cohen, Sara, Robert Knifton, Marion Leonard, and Les Roberts, eds. *Sites of Popular Music Heritage: Memories, Histories, Places*. Routledge, 2013.

ColorWheel Gallery. [Remembering Prince]. *Facebook*, 9 April 2017, 12: 56 a.m. https://www.facebook.com/ColorWheelGalleryMpls/.

Corrigan, Dan. Personal interview. 19 January 2017.

Fry, R. W. 'Becoming a "True Blues Fan": Blues Tourism and Performances of the King Biscuit Blues Festival'. *Tourist Studies*, 14.1 (2014): 66–85.

Gehrz, Jim. 'Photos: Fans Continue to Mourn Prince'. *StarTribune*, 23 April 2016. http://www.startribune.com/photos-fans-continue-to-mourn-prince/376726201/#grid.

Janzen, Hawona Sullivan. Personal interview. 14 July 2016.

Jensen, Joli. 'Introduction: On Fandom, Celebrity, and Mediation: Posthumous Possibilities'. *Afterlife as Afterimage: Understanding Posthumous Fame*. Ed. Steve Jones, Joli Jensen, and Peter Lang, 2005. xv–xxiii.

Johnson, Celia. 'Where to Celebrate Prince's Birthday in the Twin Cities'. *The Current Blog*, 3 June 2016. https://blog.thecurrent.org/2016/06/where-to-celebrate-princes-birthday-in-the-twin-cities/.

Jones, Steve. 'Better Off Dead: Or, Making It the Hard Way'. *Afterlife as Afterimage: Understanding Posthumous Fame*. Ed. Steve Jones and Joli Jensen, Peter Lang, 2005. 3–16.

Jones, Steve, and Joli Jensen, eds. *Afterlife as Afterimage: Understanding Posthumous Fame*. Peter Lang, 2005.
Krantz, Nate. Personal interview. 20 February 2017.
Llewellyn, Farrington. 'Where Purple Reigns: Minnesota Artists on Prince'. *Vimeo*. n.d. https://vimeo.com/album/3987655.
Matos, Michaelangelo. 'Inside Prince's Paisley Park Archives: 7,000 Artifacts Catalogued, Many More to Go'. *The New York Times*, 20 April 2017. https://www.nytimes.com/2017/04/20/arts/music/prince-paisley-park-archives.html.
Minneapolis Convention & Visitors Association. *Prince's Minneapolis*. Minneapolis Convention & Visitors Association, 2016.
Minnesota Orchestra, New Power Generation and The Steeles. 'The Minnesota Orchestra Performs at the Minnesota Vikings Halftime Show'. *YouTube*, uploaded by Minnesota Orchestra, 23 September 2016. https://www.youtube.com/watch?v=7Jti7jqAVh0.
Nancy and John of Minnesota History Center. Personal interview. 14 February 2017.
Olsen, Scott. [Photograph]. *MPR News*, 22 April 2016. https://www.mprnews.org/story/2016/04/22/prince-fans-party-all-night-first-avenue.
Ortegón, Tammy. Personal interview. 23 April 2017.
Prince [as Love Symbol]. 'Calhoun Square'. *Crystal Ball*, NPG Records, 1998.
Prince [as Love Symbol]. 'Comeback'. *The Truth*, NPG Records, 1998.
Prince. 'Controversy'. *Controversy*, Warner Bros. Records, 1981.
Prince. 'Laydown'. *20TEN*, NPG Records, 2010.
Prince. 'Northside'. *The Slaughterhouse*, NPG Records, 2004.
Prince [as Love Symbol]. 'Rock 'n' Roll Is Alive (and It Lives in Minneapolis)'. *Gold single*, Warner Bros. / NPG Records, 1995.
Prince. 'Uptown'. *Dirty Mind*, Warner Bros. Records, 1980.
Prince [as Love Symbol]. 'White Mansion'. *Emancipation*, NPG Records, 1996.
Prince [as Love Symbol]. 'Zannalee'. Chaos and Disorder, Warner Bros., 1996.
Roberts, Les. 'Marketing Music Scales, or the Political Economy of Contagious Magic'. *Tourist Studies*, 14.1 (2014): 10–29.
Rupar, Aaron. 'What Prince Meant to Minnesota and the World'. *ThinkProgress*, 21 April 2016. https://thinkprogress.org/what-prince-meant-to-minnesota-and-the-world-e1b4be4700f7.
Rushin, Steve. 'Why Minneapolis Loved Prince, and He Loved His Hometown'. *Time*, 4 May 2016. http://time.com/4314125/prince-minneapolis-hometown/.
Sarah of BlueNose Coffee. Personal interview. 21 April 2017.
Singer, Matthew. 'Prince Had Many Backing Bands in His Career, but He Only Led One Revolution'. *Willamette Weekly*, 12 July 2017. http://www.wweek.com/music/2017/07/12/prince-had-many-backing-bands-in-his-career-but-he-only-led-one-revolution/.
Smith, Kelly. 'Creative Ways to Mourn Prince Blossom Saturday in Twin Cities'. *StarTribune*, 25 April 2016. http://www.startribune.com/a-significant-impact/376863811/.
Williamson, Lori. Personal interview. 14 February 2017.
Wood, Drew. 'The Man Who Made It Gold'. *Mpls St Paul*, December 2016. 92–7.

Part Three

Gender

10

Re-imagining masculinity

Prince's impact on millennial attitudes regarding gender expression

Natalie Clifford

Although I was not alive when Prince first graced the world with his purple presence, my adoration for him dates back to my childhood, when my father would turn up the stereo in our basement in suburban Minnesota for family dance parties. I came of age in a religious, dogmatic environment in a conservative suburb of Minneapolis. I grappled with coming to terms with my own queer sexuality, as I had internalized homophobia and did not believe that queer people existed as living, breathing beings whom I could encounter in everyday life. Rather, in my day-to-day experience, LGBTQ+ folks were mainly described through the prism of religiously based judgement and dehumanization. As such, I am motivated to support young people through realizing the necessity of self-love and self-determination in a society which often shuns nonconformity. I have Prince in large part to thank for this realization.

At the University of Minnesota, I studied gender, women and sexuality studies, as well as comparative race and ethnicity. I was privileged to do so, yet I also know that these fields of study truly impact matters of life and death around the world. Language transforms our ability to understand ourselves, the world around us and the significance of our relationships with each other. Having an honest grasp of these realities cultivates our ability to empathize with rather than resort to violence when confronted with what we perceive as difference. Naming Prince's role in carving space for queer and gender non-conforming youth provides an opportunity to push back against oppressive norms and embrace fluid self-expression.

At the time of the Purple Reign conference in Manchester, UK – the origin of papers comprising this anthology – I was working as a sexual violence prevention educator at the Rape Crisis Center of Central New Mexico in Albuquerque, New Mexico. Through this role, I facilitated programmes with middle- and high-school-aged students to discuss healthy and unhealthy norms around masculinity, sexuality and gender identity and expression overall. According to the American Psychological Association, the term 'gender expression' describes 'the presentation of an individual, including physical appearance, clothing choice and accessories, and behaviors that express aspects of gender identity or role. Gender expression may or may not conform to a person's gender identity' or how they feel inside (American Psychological Association).

Using the aforementioned ways of knowing, I argue that over the course of his career, Prince's risk-taking in his own gender expression created space for youth to find freedom in exploring expressions of gender nonconformity and in inventing new possibilities within masculinity. When I use the term 'masculinity', I refer to gender as a constructed binary with presumed dominance and social power granted to normative masculinity. I am committed to developing practices that function in the lives of youth every day. As bell hooks writes in her book *Teaching to Transgress: Education as the Practice of Freedom*:

> Children make the best theorists, since they have not yet been educated into accepting our routine social practices as 'natural', and so insist on posing to those practices the most embarrassingly general and fundamental questions, regarding them with a wondering estrangement which we adults have long forgotten. Since they do not yet grasp our social practices as inevitable, they do not see why we might not do things differently. (hooks, 59)

Theory that is not grounded within reality is empty of meaning and exists only for its own self-congratulation. As James Baldwin wrote, 'I think all theories are suspect ... and that one must find, therefore, one's own moral center and move through the world hoping that this center will guide one aright' (Baldwin). Similarly, as many scholar-activists such as Angela Davis, Gloria Anzaldúa and Grace Lee Boggs have articulated throughout history, it is essential to centre those most impacted by various systems of violence in discussions regarding solutions to undo said violence. Accordingly, these matters bear material consequences of life and death, given the violent backlash which occurs against those who challenge the status quo. Thus, in this chapter, I carry an enormous responsibility to centre the lives of the youth and communities with whom I have worked and will continue to work.

First, I will examine particular examples of Prince's non-conforming gender expression throughout his career. I will assess the ways in which Prince refused to be confined to normative understandings and expressions of masculinity and sexuality. In this exploration, I define masculinity in terms of its formation through and relationship with White supremacy, capitalism, ableism and heteronormativity.

Second, I will review recent research regarding millennial attitudes on gender and gender expression. Specifically, I will explore the ways in which millennials and Generation Z demonstrate high acceptance of the idea of gender existing along a spectrum, as well as overall acceptance of gender expression beyond traditionally binary expectations or limitations. Furthermore, I will analyse several millennial musical artists, their non-conforming gender expression, and how they reflect Prince's legacy in that regard. I argue that these trends both generationally and musically reflect Prince's continued influence in carving space for younger generations to explore gender nonconformity and expand possibilities for non-conforming gender expression.

Third, I will consider the context of the work I have done critically discussing masculinity with self-identified young men in Albuquerque, New Mexico. Given Prince's own practices in terms of gender expression, in addition to current generations' greater acceptance of non-conforming gender expression, I will address the gaps and challenges in youth work confronting normative masculinity. I will speak to the violent consequences that still exist as punishment for transgressing socially accepted gender norms.

First, when I refer to masculinity, I am addressing normative expectations of men which have developed through the interlocking oppressions of colonialism, White supremacy, heteronormativity and capitalism. The history of masculinity and its evolution have shaped individual and communal ideas regarding what is acceptable in terms of men's gender expression and display of emotions. Throughout his career as an artist, Prince explicitly stated his adamant disregard for societal expectations not only in terms of gender but also in terms of his other overlapping and layered, multiple identities such as artist and Black. I capitalize the word Black in recognition that 'Black with a capital B refers to people of the African diaspora. Lowercase black is simply a color' (Tharps). Black feminists such as Audre Lorde and Kimberlé Crenshaw have asserted for centuries the importance of recognizing intersectional approaches to undoing oppressive systems:

> We must face with clarity and insight the lessons to be learned from the oversimplification of any struggle for self-awareness and liberation, or we will not rally the force we need to face the multidimensional threats to our survival. There is no such thing as a single-issue struggle because we do not lead single-issue lives. (Lorde 138)

In other words, a person cannot separate aspects of their identity from each other through a single-lens analysis. Rather, one's race, class, gender and sexuality all mutually shape each other as we navigate the world. It is impossible to separate Prince's gender expression from his Blackness, class identity, geographic location and so on because these factors all simultaneously influenced how he experienced the world.

Particularly early on in his career, Prince was outspoken lyrically in his refusal to be boxed into normative assumptions about who he should be and how he should express himself. The 1980 song 'Uptown' reflects Prince's desire to take charge of his own self-expression and his advocacy for others to have that same right to transgress what is expected without fear of violence. Additionally, his referral to gender expression and clothing as 'drag' in the song indicates his understanding of gender as public performance. Similarly, in the 1981 song 'Controversy', Prince uses his lyrics to challenge society's instinct to define others based on narrow, binary, normative ideas of gender identity and expression.

Catapulting himself into worldwide fame with the classic 1984 film *Purple Rain*, Prince boldly equated himself with something beyond the human invention of binary gender in songs such as 'I Would Die 4 U'. The 1986 song 'Kiss' reflects Prince's unique ability to pair his effeminate gender expression and androgyny with his sexual attraction to women. In the music video, Prince is baring his midriff while flaunting a crop top, wearing high heels and singing in a tender falsetto to a half-clothed woman. For Prince, these reflections of himself were only contradictory to those limiting their understanding of gender expression through the constructed, binary system.

'If I Was Your Girlfriend' showed a side of Prince which interwove the sensual with bent boundaries of desire and gender. He croons about his wish to perform emotionally intimate activities with his female lover such as helping her choose the clothes she wears. Here, Prince reveals his appreciation for emotional intimacy within romantic relationships – pushing back on normative narratives which associate this emphasis on emotionality as reserved for women. He blends his masculine sexuality with his desire to centre feminine energy. In 1988, Prince released the album *Lovesexy*, whose cover features Prince nude and seated atop life-size flowers, his hair almost shoulder-length and blowing in the breeze. Looking back on Prince's dozens of album covers after his death, the internet opined that 'the cover for *Lovesexy* was amongst Prince's more outrageous' due to his 'emulation of [Sandro] Botticelli's *The Birth of Venus*, butt-naked' (Wiener and Hay). Alluding to the Greek and Roman goddess of love portrayed in Botticelli's classic work of art, Prince confidently exudes an ethereal aura. Gazing towards the sky in contemplation, Prince blends his masculine sexuality with feminine energy. Ultimately, the cover of this album demonstrates some of the ways in which Prince rejected the binary conceptions of gender, seeing masculinity and femininity as interconnected and fluid, rather than rigid opposites.

There were certainly Black men who challenged heteronormative White masculinity and accompanying expectations before Prince, such as Little Richard and Rick James. Yet Prince found ways to re-claim and own his gender expression in a unique way. He sexualized himself in a way that was both autonomous and continuously self-reflexive, in contrast to the historical hyper-sexualization of Black men. Furthermore, queer, trans and gender non-conforming people of colour have existed throughout history and were resisting oppressive, compulsory gender assignment prior to Prince's arrival (Ellison). Nevertheless, Prince created his own platform to bring his nonconformity to a new level, and therefore played an enormous role in shifting norms around masculinity and femininity within gender expression.

Prince used his influence as an artist to rebuke the notion that men – particularly Black men – must conform to socially constructed expectations of masculinity, or that non-conforming gender expression illegitimates a man's sexual attraction to women. Rather, Prince uplifted, centred and revered femininity. He expanded the notion that expression of and access to femininity was not limited to those coercively assigned female at birth. Prince pushed the boundaries of conflating sex and gender as binaries to be rigidly followed. Not only that, but Prince also shifted understandings of emotional intimacy in recognition that masculine-of-centre folks could and should also perform this emotional labour typically assumed to be reserved for women. Throughout his career, Prince celebrated, explored and lived within these contradictions. His choices have had significant impact upon generations coming of age ever since his arrival onto the music scene.

Second, the legacy of Prince's boundary-breaking self-expression is reflected in attitudes held by young people regarding gender expression, as well as expectations surrounding gender overall. Research conducted in the last five years indicates that millennials (born between 1980 and 1996) and those classified as Generation Z (born 1996 – present) hold highly open, accepting views regarding gender and sexuality. Moreover, 50 per cent of millennials believe that gender exists on a spectrum and cannot be conflated with the constructed notion of biological sex, defined as male and female (Rivas, *Fusion*). Across a variety of platforms within the United States, gender inclusivity – specifically, recognition that there are more than two genders – is on the rise. In 2015, Facebook expanded beyond the fifty-eight gender options they had added in 2014 to allow users to fill in their own gender. The year 2013 was proclaimed the 'Year of Unisex Names', with a rise in popularity for gender-neutral names given by millennial parents to their children (Jayson).

According to a 2016 study conducted by the Innovation Group, 28 per cent of millennials aged between twenty-eight and thirty-four at the time reported knowing someone who uses gender-neutral pronouns such as 'they'. According to research conducted through the Harris Poll on behalf of the Gay and Lesbian Alliance against Defamation (GLAAD), 20 per cent of millennials aged between eighteen and thirty-five identify as LGBTQ; 8 per cent identify as cisgender but not strictly heterosexual, 4 per cent as non-cisgender but strictly heterosexual, and 8 per cent identify as both non-cisgender and non-heterosexual. Folks born since 1985 overwhelmingly demonstrate an acceptance of and openness to non-conforming gender expression, and to sexuality as fluid: 54 per cent of millennials surveyed stated that they buy clothing associated with the sex they were assigned at birth, as conflated societally with a binary gender system (Tsjeng).

In terms of Generation Z, 56 per cent of Generation Z aged between thirteen and twenty reported knowing someone who uses gender-neutral pronouns, 52 per cent identified as non-heterosexual, and only 44 per cent bought clothing associated with the sex they were assigned at birth. According to GLAAD's survey, 'young people ... increasingly reject traditional labels like gay / straight and man / woman, and instead talk about themselves in words that are beyond the binary' ('Accelerating Acceptance 2017: A Harris Poll Survey of Americans' Acceptance of LGBTQ People'). In March, *Time* magazine's cover story was entitled 'Beyond He or She' and highlighted modern youth's rejection of traditionally understood norms around gender identity, gender expression and sexuality ('Accelerating Acceptance' 2017).

These results reflect a generational shift in openness to non-conforming gender expression as well as an expansion of possibilities beyond society's narratives of heteronormative expectations. Prince's refusal to ascribe meaning to these binaries and instead to implode them through his own unique gender expression and performance have continued to play an important role in shifting what seemed acceptable, possible and even attractive for those coming of age since the 1980s until the present. As has been the case for decades since the riots at Compton's Cafeteria and Stonewall Inn, queer, trans and gender expansive people of colour are leading social movements in the modern age. Nevertheless, we must *all* recognize the ways in which gender and sexuality are irrevocably intertwined with race, class, ethnicity, ability and other aspects of identity. The Black Lives Matter movement was founded by three queer Black women, and subsequent chapters around the world have made the centring of queer and trans folks of colour a key priority in ending racist violence ('A Herstory of the Black Lives Matter Movement'). Movements for immigrants' rights centre the voices of queer, trans and gender non-conforming youth of colour ('Undocuqueer Movement').

Musical artists of the millennial generation as well as Generation Z have also embraced a shift towards increased openness to reflect their gender in ways considered non-conforming, both in terms of physical gender expression as well as emotional or verbal expression. Most notably, Janelle Monáe – a close friend and mentee of Prince, who is moreover a trailblazing artist in her own right – has challenged norms around gender, sexuality and race in the music industry from the beginning of her career. Consistently, wearing a tuxedo for the first few years of her time in the public eye, and only wearing the colours black and white, Monáe chose to concurrently honour her elders – who worked for the post office, collected trash and as a janitor respectively – while defying the notion that women must be sexualized through the male gaze in order to be successful as musical artists (Rivas, *Colorlines*). Through her intentional clothing decisions, Monáe has embraced, claimed and subverted normative, restrictive, White masculinity as a Black woman – reinventing it on her own terms. Additionally, in response to inquiries regarding her sexuality, she stated for years that she 'only date[s] androids' (Hoard) – in defiance of attempts to make assumptions about her sexuality in association with her gender expression. As she has grown throughout her career, however, Monáe has shifted and experimented with her gender expression, as well as become more open in discussing her sexuality. With the release of her groundbreaking album *Dirty Computer*, Monáe came out as pansexual – powerfully defining herself on her own terms as 'a free-ass motherfucker' (Spano). Monáe has been outspoken in critiquing the limits and expectations placed upon her as a Black queer woman and artist; following in the footsteps of Prince, she has boldly carved out space for queer and Black artists alike to pursue success through living their truth.

Frank Ocean, who came to fame through his critically acclaimed sophomore album *Channel Orange*, crooned of his first love – a man – on the aforementioned album in the song 'Thinkin bout You'. Similar to Prince and Monáe's aversion to questions aimed to pin down and define on terms other than their own, Ocean has staunchly avoided attempts to pigeonhole and label his sexuality in interviews. Ocean nonchalantly infuses queerness throughout the album by referencing same gender relationships seamlessly within the lyrics. The title of Ocean's most recent album, 'Blond(e)', implies a reference to the dual gender system through Ocean's refusal to identify with either, yet his desire to align himself with both simultaneously. Although his physical gender expression is not noticeably non-conforming, Ocean's open and vulnerable expression of his love for a man challenges the idea that men cannot be emotionally sensitive, particularly in connection with other men.

Angel Haze, the rapper and singer known for such singles as 'Werkin Girls' and 'New York', identifies as agender, meaning they do not feel aligned with any specific gender. Haze has been outspoken of their rejection of the gender binary system as oppressive and limiting. Haze has stated that they should not need to justify their existence as a non-binary person in the world, and should simply be able to live freely as such (Keating).

There are countless other musical artists – both millennials and those from Generation Z – who have benefited from Prince's influence on non-conforming gender expression. As one of the most famous and uncompromisingly unconventional musicians and artists of the last forty years, Prince's visibility and success contributed to an expansion of what was possible and acceptable to be, and to centre the voices of those who are marginalized and therefore have most insight into the ways in which our society must change. Although he certainly was not solely responsible for these significant attitudinal shifts, Prince was a possibility model – to use Laverne Cox's term – and major contributor to recent generations' recognition of who and what they could be in terms of self-expression (Rude).

Third, despite Prince's consistent rejection of heteronormativity and binary gender expression, as well as his clear impact on millennial acceptance of and explorations towards expanding possibilities within gender, there nevertheless remains much work to undo toxic masculinity as well as the accompanying violence inflicted upon our young people. As a sexual violence prevention educator, I spent every week working with a different group of self-identified young men to critically discuss masculinity, gender and sexuality. While I occupied this professional role, I resided in Albuquerque, New Mexico, where the majority of students are Latinx, multiracial or Native American. Prior to that role, I worked in the fields of college access, youth theatre and mentoring with elementary, middle and high school students.

While working in New Mexico, I had countless conversations with youth regarding the inflexibility that exists for young men in terms of gender expression and sexuality. More specifically, gender nonconformity often brings dangerous and violent social consequences, especially for self-identified young men and those assigned male at birth who do not identify with the gender into which they were coerced. At one middle school, a student who held significant social clout with his peers confidently informed me with a smirk that 'there aren't any boys who are gay here at our school, miss. They'd get bullied.' The other boys eagerly chimed in, 'Yea, there's definitely girls who are lesbian or bisexual, but no guys.' I challenged them to explain why they thought a male-identified person who might be LGBTQ+ – or perceived to be LGBTQ+ – would be bullied. We referred back to assumptions that boys and men cannot cry, ask for help or display weakness – all characteristics which are conflated negatively with femininity and therefore are devalued and seen as inferior. Sadly, the degree to which young men internalize homophobia and transphobia begins at quite a young age, which requires that we who are committed to the work further dedicate ourselves to undo these harmful ideologies with due vigilance.

I would always 'come out' as queer to students during my presentations, as I found it humanized the conversation around sexuality – making it more three-dimensional by granting youth witness to a queer adult existing in the world. Although I am fairly gender conforming in my daily presentation, I would express myself in a more androgynous fashion via my clothing style at times, in an effort to bridge the gap across the various identities which distinguish myself from the young men, such as race and class. I utilize the term 'tomboy femme' to define my identity, while also recognizing the privilege of fluidity and visibility. As a result, students occasionally asked me with genuine curiosity about my gender identity, particularly in connection with my gender expression. At the same school mentioned previously, one student who had been acting somewhat aloof for the first few days grew to become so comfortable that he casually suggested aloud amid discussion on LGBTQ+ folks, 'I could be gay.' The other students held the space for that youth to be vulnerable and share his potential truth. Another student inquired cautiously: 'Do you think there are trans students at our school?' and I assured them that there were. The space in naming these multiple identities is profoundly important towards eliminating violence.

I collaborated with young men in these conversations to analyse why we assume that men cannot have feelings or cannot express emotions. We considered false stereotypes that men cannot be abused or violated within romantic relationships or otherwise. I asked the youth if every man they have met is strong, buff, unfeeling and straight. They always assured me vehemently that no, not all men fit into this rigid box, which assurance built their investment into the discussion. From there we began to break down the constructed walls of hyper-masculinity and heteronormativity. Debunking the myth that men and boys cannot experience sexual violence gets to the root of our assumptions as a society that gendered violence only directly impacts women, when in fact men are also uniquely impacted by the violence of a rigid, binary gender system. The constrictive regulations of normative masculinity – as manufactured through White supremacist heteropatriarchy and capitalism – often limit young men's ability to express their need for help and to recognize when they are being victimized or harmed. When there is not language in place to name and express the pain that rigid masculinity causes young men to internalize, there can be fatal consequences. Although Prince did not explicitly acknowledge this pain, his challenges to the constructed boundaries of masculinity via his gender-fluid self-representation undeniably opened space for younger generations to continue rejecting these same boundaries and live as their authentic selves.

Overall, despite the reflection that a majority of young people who are either millennials or part of Generation Z express openness and tolerance of gender non-conformity, to equate this with true equity and justice for queer and gender expansive people is false. The trauma inflicted upon those socialized and often coerced to identify as young men reflects the need for more role models like Prince to openly reveal the power, strength and vital significance of emotional expression and femininity for people of all genders. Trans women of colour face the highest murder rates in the United States. After twenty-seven trans people were killed in 2016, considered the deadliest year on record (Schmider), 2017 tragically exceeded that record, as twenty-nine trans people were killed. The Human Rights Campaign reported twenty-two known deaths of trans people in 2018, and as of this chapter's submission for final editing in January 2020, twenty-four trans people were known to have been found dead in 2019 (Human Rights Campaign). Nearly all trans people killed were women of colour, and a majority of the women of colour were Black – highlighting the lethal combination of racism and heterosexism which exposes trans women of colour to deadly violence. These statistics do not include those who were mis-gendered at the time of their death, or whom the police did not correctly identify as trans.

Furthermore, LGB youth are four times as likely as their straight peers to have attempted suicide (Centers for Disease Control and Prevention) while 40 per cent of all trans adults reported attempting suicide (The Trevor Project). Queer and gender non-conforming youth are more likely to be homeless, bullied, harassed, experience sexual violence, feel unsafe at school, and fall into substance abuse as a coping mechanism in response to various traumatic experiences (The Williams Institute). Trans and gender-fluid or gender non-conforming youth are much more likely to encounter 'multiple, overlapping forms of violence' in various spheres of their lives (Sterling et al., cited by Anwar). As adults, trans folks 'are three times more likely than the general population to be unemployed' while '38% of Black transgender Americans are living in poverty' (James et al., cited by Sosin). The levels of violence experienced by trans women of colour especially are compounded given the interlocking layers of systems of oppression. Troublingly, our society severely normalizes violence against trans and gender expansive folks to the point that their deaths do not make headlines or cause the level of outrage that other deaths do. Thus, despite Prince's positive influence on younger generations' wider acceptance of queer and gender expansive people, there remains much work to be done for our society to ensure safety, autonomy and dignity for all members of the LGBTQ+ community.

In conclusion, throughout his lifetime, Prince's insistence on self-determination within self-expression as well as his sheer confidence in challenging norms carved space for upcoming generations to pursue their own means of self-expression outside of what is expected. A film like *Moonlight*, for example, would not have been possible without Prince's legacy as an artist and activist advocating by his own example for the dismantling of constrictive masculinity, particularly for Black men. First, Prince defied normative expectations regarding masculinity and its accompanying performance. He embraced contradiction and opened the door for future generations to make bold explorations of self and to begin to de-construct rigid norms around gender expression. Second, Prince's choices left an enormous impact on the attitudes of millennials and Generation Z regarding what is socially acceptable in terms of gender expression – particularly within the music industry – as intersecting with race, class and other identities. Third, despite Prince's significant influence on current generations through his innovative and inimitable androgynous style, there nevertheless remains much work to be done in the field of preventing violence against queer, trans and gender non-conforming people, especially those of colour. In my role as a sexual violence prevention educator in New Mexico, I witnessed the social regulation which young men exert upon each other to discourage nonconformity and to perpetuate myths regarding the necessity of hyper-masculinity.

Conversations around unlearning toxic masculinity are key to support young men in becoming their whole selves. Our society sends messages that forbid displays of vulnerability at the risk of social punishment and violence. In this chapter I was not able to explore research on millennial attitudes broken down by race, gender, class, ability, geographic location and so on. Additionally, I did not theorize extensively about the origins of rigid masculinity and explore the deep-rooted connections between hyper-masculinity, patriarchy, racism and capitalism. My main goal has been to provide insights into the consequences of work in sexual violence prevention as juxtaposed with Prince's impact. Lastly, I did not address Prince's comments later in his life regarding LGBTQ+ people in general – comments which many believe may have stemmed from his conversion to a devout follower of the Jehovah's Witness faith, and have sometimes been interpreted as homophobic or biphobic. On the Arsenio Hall Show in March 2014, Prince expressed disdain regarding male-on-male physical contact (Juzwiak), and 'dodged questions about marriage equality' when interviewed by the *Minneapolis Star Tribune* (Bream). In 2013, Prince released a song entitled 'Da Bourgeoisie' which was widely interpreted as homophobic (Smith). Yet regardless of Prince's own private beliefs later in his life, his impact upon the lives of the generations that followed him – whether LGBTQ+ identified, or simply exploring themselves via newfound possibilities for self-expression – is undeniably significant. Prince's enormous legacy therefore reflects the importance of researching the effect of cultural figures on youth attitudes.

We have a long way to go as a society to not only accept but also celebrate expanded understandings of gender. We must create language beyond tolerance towards fully recognizing the humanity of queer, trans and gender non-conforming people. We need to support youth in innovating towards a world free from violence against trans women, LGBTQ+ youth, Black youth, immigrant youth and indigenous youth. Prince was an outspoken advocate for youth later in life, and saw the value of developing young leaders through his support of the Black Lives Matter movement and other social justice movements ('Beyond Music, Prince's Legacy Includes Black Activism'). As Tarell Alvin McCraney, the playwright behind *Moonlight*, expressed in an awards acceptance speech: 'We can see our way towards limitless' when we show up for each other and encourage our youth to live fully as themselves ('"Moonlight" Receives the HRC [Human Rights Campaign] Visionary Arts Award'). Prince challenged norms and rejected them as oppressive and limiting. We owe it to our youth to continue his legacy by doing the same and uplifting each other towards freedom (Human Rights Campaign 2017).

Works cited

American Psychological Association. 'Definitions Related to Sexual Orientation and Gender Diversity in APA Documents'. Web. 26 May 2019. https://www.apa.org/pi/lgbt/resources/sexuality-definitions.pdf.

American Psychological Association. 'Guidelines for Psychological Practice with Transgender and Gender Nonconforming People'. *American Psychologist*, Dec. 2015. Web. 26 May 2019. https://www.apa.org/practice/guidelines/transgender.pdf.

Anzaldúa, Gloria, and Cherríe Moraga. *This Bridge Called My Back: Writings by Radical Women of Color*. New York: Kitchen Table: Women of Color Press, 1981.

Associated Press. 'Beyond Music, Prince's Legacy Includes Black Activism'. *Billboard*, 24 Apr. 2016. Web. 1 Aug. 2017. http://www.billboard.com/articles/news/7341802/beyond-music-prince-legacy-includes-black-lives-matter-activism.

Baldwin, James. *Autobiographical Notes* (1952) republished in *Notes of a Native Son*. Bantam Books: New York, 1964.

Black Lives Matter. 'A Herstory of the Black Lives Matter Movement'. Web. 16 Apr. 2017. http://blacklivesmatter.com/herstory/.

Boggs, Grace Lee. *The Next American Revolution: Sustainable Activism for the Twenty-First Century*. Los Angeles: University of California Press, 2011.

Bream, Jon. 'A Rejuvenated Prince Looks Forward Again'. *Star Tribune*, 16 May 2013. Web. 1 Aug. 2017. http://www.startribune.com/rejuvenated-prince-looks-forward-i-want-to-work-with-young-people/207478531/.

Centers for Disease Control and Prevention. 'LGBT Youth – Experiences with Violence'. Web. 7 Apr. 2017. https://www.cdc.gov/lgbthealth/youth.htm.

Crenshaw, Kimberlé Williams. 'Demarginalizing the Intersection of Race and Sex: A Black Feminist Critique of Antidiscrimination Doctrine, Feminist Theory and Antiracist Politics'. *University of Chicago Legal Forum*. University of Chicago Law School, 1989. 139–68.

Davis, Angela Y. *Women, Race and Class*. New York: Vintage Press, 1981.

Ellison, J. M. 'When Were You Mine? Prince's Legacy in the Context of Transgender History'. Web. 1 Aug. 2017. https://jmellison.net/if-we-knew-trans-history/when-were-you-mine-princes-legacy-in-the-context-of-transgender-history/.

Equality Archive. 'Undocuqueer Movement'. Web. 16 Apr. 2017. https://equalityarchive.com/issues/undocuqueer-movement/.

Gay and Lesbian Alliance against Defamation (GLAAD). 'Accelerating Acceptance 2017: A Harris Poll Survey of Americans' Acceptance of LGBTQ People'. Web. 17 May 2017. http://www.glaad.org/files/aa/2017_GLAAD_Accelerating_Acceptance.pdf.

Hoard, Christian. 'Artist of the Week: Janelle Monáe'. *Rolling Stone*, 30 June 2010. Web. 1 Aug. 2017. http://www.rollingstone.com/music/news/artist-of-the-week-janelle-monae-20100630.

hooks, bell. *Teaching to Transgress: Education as the Practice of Freedom*. New York: Routledge, 1994.

Human Rights Campaign. '"Moonlight" Receives the HRC [Human Rights Campaign] Visionary Arts Award'. 11 Feb. 2017. Web. 16 Apr. 2017. https://youtu.be/bGa65oBM8LI.

Human Rights Campaign. 'Violence against the Transgender Community in 2018'. 1 Nov. 2018. Web. 8 June 2019. https://www.hrc.org/resources/violence-against-the-transgender-community-in-2018.

Human Rights Campaign. 'Violence against the Transgender Community in 2019'. 31 December 2019. Web. 1 January 2020. https://www.hrc.org/resources/violence-against-the-transgender-community-in-2019.

James, S. E. et al. *The Report of the 2015 U.S. Transgender Survey*. Washington, DC: National Center for Transgender Equality, 2016.

Jayson, Sharon. 'Gender Loses Its Impact with the Young'. *USA Today*, 21 June 2014. Web. 17 Jan. 2017. https://www.usatoday.com/story/news/nation/2014/06/21/gender-millennials-dormitories-sex/10573099/.

Juzwiak, Rich. 'Prince and His Gay Panic Took over Last Night's *Arsenio*'. *Gawker*, 6 Mar. 2014. Web. 1 Aug. 2017. http://gawker.com/prince-and-his-gay-panic-took-over-last-nights-arsenio-1537896202.

Keating, Shannon. 'The Evolution of Angel Haze'. *Buzzfeed*, 27 March 2015. Web. 1 Aug. 2017, http://www.buzzfeed.com/shannonkeating/the-evolution-of-angel-haze.

Lorde, Audre. *Sister Outsider: Essays and Speeches by Audre Lorde*. Berkeley, CA: Crossing Press, 2007.

Rivas, Jorge. 'Half of Young People Believe Gender Isn't Limited to Male and Female'. *Fusion*, 3 Feb. 2015. Web. 17 Jan. 2017. http://fusion.net/story/42216/half-of-young-people-believe-gender-isnt-limited-to-male-and-female/.

Rivas, Jorge. 'Janelle Monáe on Being a Former Maid and Why She Still Wears a Uniform'. *Colorlines*, 5 Nov. 2012. Web. 10 June 2019. https://www.colorlines.com/articles/janelle-mon%C3%A1e-being-former-maid-and-why-she-still-wears-uniform.

Rude, Mey. 'Flawless Trans Women Carmen Carrera and Laverne Cox Respond to Katie Couric's Invasive Questions'. *Autostraddle*, 7 Jan. 2014. Web. 13 May 2017. https://www.autostraddle.com/flawless-trans-women-carmen-carrera-and-laverne-cox-respond-flawlessly-to-katie-courics-invasive-questions-215855/.

Schmider, Alex. '2016 Was the Deadliest Year on Record for Transgender People,' *GLAAD*, 9 Nov. 2016. Web. 9 Apr. 2017. http://www.glaad.org/blog/2016-was-deadliest-year-record-transgender-people.

Smith, Rob. 'Prince's New Song Is Funky, Sexy, and Kind of Homophobic'. *Queerty*, 19 Nov. 2013. Web. 1 Aug. 2017. https://www.queerty.com/princes-new-song-is-funky-sexy-and-kind-of-homophobic-2031119.

Sosin, Kate. 'Murders of Black Transgender Women in Dallas Raise Fears in LGBTQ Community'. *NBC News*, 10 June 2019. Web. 10 June 2019. https://www.nbcnews.com/feature/nbc-out/murders-black-transgender-women-dallas-raise-fears-lgbtq-community.

Spanos, Brittany. 'Janelle Monáe Frees Herself'. *Rolling Stone*, 26 April 2018. Web. 8 June 2019. https://www.rollingstone.com/music/music-features/janelle-monae-frees-herself-629204/.

Sterling, Paul et al. 'Social Ecological Correlates of Polyvictimization among a National Sample of Transgender, Genderqueer, and Cisgender Sexual Minority Adolescents', *Child Abuse & Neglect* Volume 67, pages 1–12, 1 May 2017, UC Berkeley, Web. 14 May 2017. Cited by Yasmin Anwar, 'Trans and Gender-Fluid Teens Left with Few 'Safe Harbors'. *Berkeley News*, 27 Feb. 2017. Web. 14 May 2017. http://news.berkeley.edu/2017/02/27/gender-fluid/.

Tharps, Lori L. 'The Case for Black with a Capital B'. *The New York Times*, 18 Nov. 2014. Web. 1 Jan. 2020. https://www.nytimes.com/2014/11/19/opinion/the-case-for-black-with-a-capital-b.html.

The Trevor Project. 'Facts about Suicide'. Web. 9 Apr. 2017. http://www.thetrevorproject.org/pages/facts-about-suicide.

Tsjeng, Zing. 'Teens These Days Are Queer AF, New Study Says'. *Broadly*, 10 March 2016. Web. 17 Jan. 2017. https://broadly.vice.com/en_us/article/teens-these-days-are-queer-af-new-study-says.

Wiener, Moses, and Kameron Hay. 'A Visual History of Prince's Album Covers'. *Complex*, 7 June 2018. Web. 26 May 2019. https://www.complex.com/style/2018/06/visual-history-of-princes-album-covers/.

The Williams Institute. 'Serving Our Youth: Findings from a National Survey of Services Providers Working with Lesbian, Gay, Bisexual and Transgender Youth Who Are Homeless or at Risk of Becoming Homeless'. July 2012. Web. 19 May 2017. http://williamsinstitute.law.ucla.edu/wp-content/uploads/Durso-Gates-LGBT-Homeless-Youth-Survey-July-2012.pdf.

11

'We can't hate you, because we love you'
A look at Prince, queerness, misogyny and feminism

Leah Stone McDaniel and Shannan Wilson

Preface

This chapter seeks to explore the complex relationship between Prince's love for women physically and musically and his actual treatment of them in his daily life, as well as to offer a newer theory regarding Prince's gender-bending persona and its overall effect on the Black American community and his influence on current Black artists. This examination of his background, significant relationships and lyrics is an attempt to answer the question, was Prince a misogynist or a feminist?

Queerness, misogyny and acceptance in the Black American community

Prince Rogers Nelson is a unique entity in music, particularly in Black American music. For many music lovers, Prince is considered unique because of his gender-bending, queer persona. Prince's outward expressions present a harrowing complexity because, as a Black American male, it conflicts with the often hypermasculine persona that is both stereotypical and defines the Black American community. The emergence of Prince on the music scene challenged Black America because it brought forth an ultimatum with the choice of either accepting the undeniable talent of Prince with all of his queerness or utilizing the default mechanism of disowning a Black man because of his confidence with his queerness. The Black American community, however, chose to embrace Prince and accepted his queerness under the conditional basis that his queerness is steeped in misogyny, thus making Prince's queerness tolerable for the Black American community.

In order to understand the complexity of the acceptance of Prince's queerness in the Black community, it is imperative to understand what the terminology of queer is. According to Parents, Families and Friends of Lesbians and Gays (PFLAG), queer is defined as 'anyone that does not identify under the rigid binaries of straight/gay or male/female. An umbrella term for sexual and gender minorities. Queer as an identity represents freedom and acceptance which allows space for individuality and acknowledges that each person's sexuality and identity is different from every other' (www.pflag.org). In his book, *Your Average Nigga: Performing Race, Literacy and Masculinity*, American scholar Dr Vershawn Young exerts that Black boys and young men in America perform what they believe is to be the ideal persona of Black masculinity, as a way to be accepted in the Black American community. The performance of this hyper-masculinity is often a rebellion against education, sociolinguistics, sexuality and queerness. Young asserts that this performance can be considered a 'coping mechanism' or 'survival tactic', because, if there is any inkling of queerness, homosexuality or the rejection of Blackness, such as using standard English as opposed to African American vernacular, young men may be attacked emotionally, physically or both by members of his own community.

Prince's rising star was a crucial moment in music. R&B music was moving away from the traditional Motown Sound and disco was beginning to die out in the late 1970s. Hip hop music was conceived in the Bronx, New York, and was beginning on its quest to reign. The 1970s proved to be very influential as it portrayed Black people on television and in films, as evident from the Blaxploitation films of the 1970s that often depicted Black urban life and had central characters that exude Black male hyper-masculinity. Prince's affiliation with Morris Day and The Time was a highly significant component to his acceptance in the Black American community. Morris Day and The Time represented all things depicted and glorified in the urban Black community. Morris Day, clad in his flashy suits and spewing out his playful, charismatic banter, is certainly synonymous to the hypermasculine characters in the 1970s Blaxplotation films, always surrounded by money, material things and lots of beautiful women. Although Prince is credited for essentially 'discovering' Morris Day and The Time, his affiliation with Day can actually be considered a vetting process, because the Black American community can accept Prince because he was 'with' Morris Day. Moreover, Prince and Day's partnership is the evidence that the Black American community needed in order to accept the fact Prince wore feminine clothing and make-up because, although he is androgynous, he still has relationships with women only. Prince's complex love life was on display in the hugely popular, autobiographical film *Purple Rain* (Magnoli, Purple Rain 1984), which propelled Prince to superstar status. The film showcased that behind Prince's queerness, he was still an 'alpha male', thus solidifying himself as a mainstay in the Black American community.

Prince's legacy can be seen all over the music industry. As hip hop progressed through the 1980s and 1990s, it began to take on a misogynistic tone, often objectifying women as mere sex objects. In 2017, there were new hip hop artists who are pushing the boundaries and embracing their queerness in regard to outward appearance in addition to sexuality. One example is Frank Ocean, a Black American singer and songwriter who released his first solo album in 2012. Ocean wrote an open letter disclosing his relationship with a man when he was nineteen years old. Another is Young Thug, a Black American hip hop artist who claims to have been wearing women's clothing since the age of twelve, including dresses, and that he does not believe in gender. Lil Uzi Vert is also a new millennium Black American hip hop artist who recently caused a social media buzz because he wore a women's blouse and carried a handbag to the Billboard Awards. Finally, Young M.A is a Black American rapper who identifies as female, is openly gay and presents a masculine image. Although Prince's influence can be seen throughout all of the aforementioned artists, it can be argued that Ocean and Young M.A are embraced more by the Black American community because their queerness, much like that of Prince, is associated with masculinity, as Ocean is not as fashionably flamboyant as Thug and Uzi Vert. Vert and Young Thug come under fire because their queerness is not exclusively linked to masculinity; therefore, they are often highly criticized and attacked within the Black American community, as evident from and concurrent with Dr. Vershawn Young's research.

Prince has had a profound effect on the way the Black American community views male artists: as long as the queerness incorporates masculinity it is tolerable. As a community, Black people should be inclusive of all Black identities. Activist Audre Lorde said it best: 'It is not our differences that divide us. It is our ability to recognize, accept and celebrate those differences.'

Misogyny and feminism

The lyrics to 1987's 'Strange Relationship' from the *Sign o' the Times* album delves into Prince's take on what appears to be an interaction he just cannot shake. Despite knowing that he is toxic for his romantic partner, he continues to long to be with them. This tug of war between the head and the heart, decency and discourtesy and morality and immorality were themes that wove themselves through Prince's lyrics and life throughout his illustrious career.

The only thing more cryptic than Prince's lyrics was the lifestyle that fuelled them. From his early fame, Prince was linked to a variety of women, each more famous and intriguing than the last. However fleeting these relationships were, they seemed the only place Prince could be honest with himself, and often his harem was through song and performance. Were his talent and his celebrity status able to help overshadow the expectations of morals and values in his personal relationship?

To understand a person's viewpoint on relationships, it is necessary to delve into their past. Prince's early context of relationships could be rooted in his parents' widely documented tumultuous union. The pair met in 1956 through their joint love of music, at a show in Minneapolis. Mattie Shaw was a jazz singer in John Nelson's band, The Prince Rogers Trio with a voice that was comparable to Billie Holiday. Despite being 16 years Nelson's junior, Shaw would marry Nelson and bear two children, Prince in 1958 and Tyka in 1960. Nelson would continue to pursue his musical dreams, while Shaw would shelve hers to care for her family. While it is not documented whether Shaw harboured any ill will at doing so, Nelson's conflict over pursuing his passion and caring for his family has been recorded. Prince himself may have felt that it would be impossible to fully give oneself to music if one had the responsibility of a family. In

1981, Prince told *New York Newsday*, '[that his father] felt hurt that he never got his break, because of having the wife and kids and stuff'. This anger and hurt led his father to abuse his mother, both physically and mentally, ultimately leading to their divorce in 1968. During this time, Prince watched his mother take on the full responsibility of the household until she married Heyward Baker. However, the abandonment he felt that began with the departure of his father continued despite having a somewhat 'normal' household.

While Prince did not often speak about his mother, in a 1985 *Rolling Stone* interview, he remarked, 'My mom's the wild side of me; she's like that all the time. My dad's real serene; it takes music to get him going. My father and me, we're one and the same. He's a little sick, just like I am.' As Prince would advance through his career, that 'wild side' would slowly begin to dim as he embraced religion and the teachings of Jehovah, leaving some of his scandalous history behind. In identifying the wildness in himself with his mother, a natural divide would have been created between peace and serenity that could be associated with music and his father. From an early point in his life, without even consciously realizing it, Prince would begin to identify women with wildness and chaos. To balance that, he would seek women who were creatively his contemporaries when entering into working relationships that often turned romantic. An internal struggle built from loving his mother, but watching her be wild and social, would lead to an evolved 'Madonna-whore complex' (20). Freud's theory that men's anxiety towards women's sexuality causes them to cast women into one of two categories, the 'Madonna' – women to be admired and respected – and the 'whore' – women to be attracted to and ultimately disrespect – seemingly crept into Prince's world in childhood. However, the complex is not traditional as Prince found a way to disassociate characteristics within the same woman by casting her creatively as a 'Madonna' and relishing in her through lyrics and musical genius, but treating her as a 'whore' in personal dealings.

The divide with his mother increased as she was not supportive of his musical aspirations and wanted him to focus on his education. From Prince's perspective, he felt music had ultimately destroyed his parents' marriage, and she did not want that life for him. With the love of music being a call that he could not escape, Prince would continue to feel a strain with his mother that would later emerge in personal relationships.

Finally, the abandonment that Prince felt from his mother would shape how he would later become involved with members of the opposite sex. After her remarriage, Prince and his stepfather did not get along well and he left his mother's house beginning a somewhat nomadic existence as he bounced from relatives to friends before finding a permanent home with long-time friend André Anderson, who later became his bandmate André Cymone (Ro 2011). During this time, it is not documented whether his mother ever made the effort to bring Prince back into her household, even after learning that his father had forced him to move out after finding him in bed with a girl. This period would make Prince cling to his music even more as it became the fuel that would propel him to stability in his mind. His mother's inability to put him first would create a hollow that would not allow him to fully embrace women in the future.

From early in his musical career, Prince's lyrics constructed an almost awe of women that ranged from physical adoration to conflicted glorification. One could hypothesize that this stemmed from the feelings of abandonment that Prince felt from his mother and the sense that he could never truly receive the love that he needed from her long term. In Prince's own words, his early relationships ended abruptly: 'I was very bitter when I was young. I was insecure and I'd attack anybody. I couldn't keep a girlfriend for two weeks. We'd argue about anything.' He channelled most of that bitterness into music and began writing songs about women as early as his high school days, penning lyrics about 'two-timing women who would leave him for his best friend', inspired by a then ongoing rivalry with his half-brother, Duane Nelson. Other songs from the early days were pure fantasy as Prince wrote prophetically about a life that he would one day actually experience.

As Prince's fame grew, his voracious appetite for women seemed to follow suit. While known as a rock lothario, he was actually very much a serial relationship pursuer. Unfortunately, these relationships often overlapped with women being discarded in the process. Still, the way in which previous lovers discuss Prince is interesting as many are adamant about the level of respect he had for each of them and the love that they felt he harboured for them long after the relationship, like Mayte Garcia, Prince's first wife. Some of these women almost seem to view themselves as a sorority of sorts maintaining that once you have dated Prince you are initiated into a fold that you never quite escape. After his passing, Garcia wrote in her autobiography *The Most Beautiful: My Life with Prince*: 'There was a post-apocalyptic moment right after Prince's death when we were all kind to one another, but it didn't take long for the side-eyes and not-so-subtle digs to pop up on Facebook and Twitter … .When I hear one of his old flames say, "I feel like his widow", I'm sad for her because in so many ways that matter, I feel like he's still with me.' This further shows the power that a relationship, no matter how brief, with this man had over women.

For women whom Prince creatively thrived with, he created a pedestal that became almost worship-like but would soon crumble when they were no longer the object of his affection. Former fiancée Susannah Melvoin spoke of how 'tender' Prince could be when sharing time with her and their bandmates Lisa and Wendy, Melvoin's twin sister. She found herself the inspiration for several popular Prince ballads, including 'Nothing Compares 2 U' and 'The Beautiful Ones' which included heartfelt haunting lyrics regarding finding true and fleeting love only to be scarred in the process (Swensson 2016).

These lyrics could again display Prince's defiance when faced with potential abandonment. Melvoin has never shared the reason for their break-up, but timing indicates an overlap with other women, including backup singer Jill Jones and drummer Sheila E. Another popular song, 'I Hate U' features scathing lyrics that model/actress Carmen Electra believes are about her, the song describing falling in love a foolish thing that can only lead to hate in the end.

Prompted by Electra going on a date with another man while touring, Prince immediately recoiled and ended the relationship when any semblance of imperfection arose. Despite the fact that, at the time of its recording, he was already involved in a serious relationship with his first wife Mayte Garcia. Mayte reflected on this saying, 'The girl [herself] in Minneapolis is the girl on her way in. The girl who leaves Minneapolis [Carmen Electra] is the girl on her way out.' This revolving door was a characteristic of Prince's relationships over many years, when one woman's time expired, another waited in the wings to take her place.

This rotation of women begs the question whether these women were merely props in his life used to fuel his insatiable desires? Working through all of these overlapping relationships, was there an undercurrent of misogyny present, likely sparked by unresolved issues with his relationship with his mother? Further, we sometimes see in his lyrics that he could be outright brutal. From 1979's 'Bambi' which touched on sexual violence to 1982's 'Extraloveable' which threatened rape with lyrics that spoke of being on the verge of the act with detail on how to carry it out, there are times that Prince has crossed the line and there are rumours that similar songs exist in 'The Vault' with Prince feeling the content was too dark to be released to mainstream audience. This line-crossing was also existent in his personal life with multiple exes, from Sheila E. to Mayte – while he respected and cared for them, he could also be cruel at times, even if unintentional. During the time that led to their divorce, when Prince had already begun courting his second wife Manuela Testolini, Garcia expressed feeling 'banished … as if he expected me to simply disappear'.

However, for every time Prince displayed these misogynistic tendencies, we also see him exalt and liberate women. If we go back to his lyrics, we will find that Prince sought to elevate women and liberate them from normal societal constructs. In her essay 'Purple Passion: Images of Female Desire in "When Doves Cry"', Nancy J. Holland touches on the three codes of sexuality found within the song's lyrics. Here she cites that Prince has touched upon something she deems the 'uncanny code', which is defined as a counter-code to the usual male-oriented sexuality of rock music and represents an attempt to elicit a non-stereotypical female sexuality, which is not related to male sexual economy. We see this uncanny code resurface in many songs, notably in 1991's 'Gett Off', which glorifies the female orgasm.

Here Prince comes across as almost feminist with the liberated viewpoint that a woman should be able to 'gett off' just as much as a man. There seems to be a no-strings-attached approach that suggests Prince was open to his partner experiencing pleasure in whatever way she saw fit. Susanna Hoffs, of The Bangles for which Prince wrote the '80s hit 'Manic Monday', was often a collaborator and rumoured love interest, and maintains in Cochrane and Davies Hannah's article 'The women behind Prince: "The respect he showed us speaks volumes"' that Prince was 'in awe of women'. She believed that his support of women artists creatively and expressing female sexuality in his own music make him a feminist. 'Everyone has different interpretations, but, yes, [for] his support of the Bangles, his genuine interest in our music. We were not manufactured;

we had thrift-store clothes, formed in a garage. I think he really respected that and understood it and liked it.'

After examining his background, significant relationships and lyrics the question remains, was Prince a misogynist or feminist? The evidence in his lyrics and all accounts of those who knew him best suggest that, like most, he was multidimensional. His personality was made of all of these characteristics, which led to his creative genius. He was a lover of women both physically and mentally which led to him seeking out those that could further him creatively. Whether it was collaborating with Sheila E.'s powerful percussion, Lisa Coleman's instrumentation, Mayte's belly dancing or even Manuela's charitable efforts, his female counterparts were left with some of their best professional work while finding a way to inspire Prince. His artistry, however, reigned supreme throughout his too short life and relationships would always play second fiddle to his music. Perhaps rumoured girlfriend and *Purple Rain* co-star Apollonia Kotero said it best: 'He loves his women but music comes first. He is married to his music and no woman can compete with that.'

Works cited

Aswad, Jem. 'Sheila E. Looks Back on Prince: Their Collaborations, Engagement and Lifelong Love'. 26 Apr. 2016. https://www.billboard.com/articles/news/7341899/sheila-e-prince-memorial.

Cleary, Tom. 'John L. Nelson & Mattie Shaw. Prince's Parents: Five Fast Facts You Need to Know'. 21 Apr. 2016. https://heavy.com/news/2016/04/john-nelson-mattie-shaw-who-are-were-prince-parents-deaths-bios-divorce-children-marriage-musicians-jazz-band/.

Cochrane, Lauren, and J. Davies Hannah. 'The Women behind Prince: The Respect He Showed Us Speaks Volumes'. 24 Apr. 2017. https://www.theguardian.com/lifeandstyle/2017/apr/24/the-women-behind-prince-the-respect-he-showed-us-speaks-volumes.

Definition of 'Queer'. Dec. 2016. www.pflag.org.

Garcia, Mayte. *The Most Beautiful: My Life with Prince*. New York: Hachette Book Group Inc., 2017.

Holland, Nancy J. 'Purple Passion: Images of Female Desire in "When Doves Cry"'. 1988. https://www.jstor.org/stable/1354108?seq=1#page_scan_tab_contents.

Karlen, Neal. 'Prince Talks: The Silence Is Broken'. 12 Sept. 1985. https://www.rollingstone.com/music/news/prince-talks-the-silence-is-broken-19850912.

Perkins, Nichole. 'How Prince Taught Me about Female Sexuality'. 8 Feb. 2015. https://www.buzzfeed.com/tnwhiskeywoman/do-me-baby?utm_term=.naGpZaPo8#.rra25E3G1.

Prince. 'Sign o' the Times; Strange Relationship'. *NPG Music*, 1987. Vinyl Album.

Prince. 'Purple Rain; The Beautiful Ones'. Warner Bros., 1983. Vinyl Album.

Prince. 'The Gold Experience; I Hate U'. NPG/Warner Bros., 1995. Compact Disc.

Prince. 'Extraloveable'. Warner Bros., 1982. Vinyl Album.

Prince. 'Diamonds and Pearls; Gett Off'. Prince, Paisley Park/Warner Bros., 1991. Compact Disc.

Purple Rain. Dir. Albert Magnoli. Warner Bros., 1984. Film.

Ro, Ronin. *Prince: Inside the Music and the Masks*. New York: St Martin's Press, 2011.

Swensson, Andrea. 'Susannah Melvoin on the Hidden Tenderness of Prince and the Story behind "Starfish and Coffee"'. 7 Nov. 2016. https://blog.thecurrent.org/2016/11/susannah-melvoin-on-the-hidden-tenderness-of-prince-and-the-story-behind-starfish-and-coffee/.

Unknown Author. 'Madonna-Whore Complex'. Psych 424 blog. https://sites.psu.edu/aspsy/2015/10/03/madonna-whore-complex/.

Young, Vershawn Ashanti. *Your Average Nigga: Performing Race, Literacy, and Masculinity*. Detroit: Wayne State Press, 2007.

12

'Flying the Seduction 747'

Prince, humour and horizontal erotics

Annie Potts

In his 1991 performance of 'Gett Off' at MTV's Video Music Awards, Prince Rogers Nelson wore a bright yellow suit with elaborate holes in the fabric through which his very hairy chest could be seen. The onstage act resembled an orgy of heaving sweaty bodies involved in different erotic dances and positions. 'Gett Off' (from 1991's *Diamonds and Pearls*) is one of Prince's raunchier offerings but even the indelicate lyrics of this gangsta glam song, which (to the beat of a woman's moans) extol the virtue of twenty-three positions in a one night stand, didn't prepare the audience for the ultimate moment of humour/shock – when at three minutes into the performance, as he commands his would-be lover to move her 'big ass' around so he can undo her zipper, Prince turns his back to the stage revealing 'ventilated' pants with holes in the seat to expose his own bare (and hairless) buttocks. Such parody of 'peacock strutting' masculinity is typical of Prince's modus operandi.

In fact, Prince played with many forms of humour as well as parody – irony, camp, slap-dash, idiosyncratic – in a variety of ways and across contexts throughout his career. He also used his wide vocal range (particularly his falsetto) – as well as disco and funk sounds – to appeal to listeners' and viewers' sense of (transgressive) humour, quirkiness and playfulness. Humour appears in superficial asides in otherwise serious ballads ('Adore', *1999*, 1982), rap within songs ('Incense and Candles', *3121*, 2006), acting and dance routines ('Kiss', *Parade*, 1986), and sometimes via self-deprecating or self-aggrandizing lyrics in songs ('Satisfied', *3121*, 2006).

In the first section of this chapter I will explore some of the ways that Prince has employed humour in his lyrics and performances to facilitate the transgression of sexual, gender, class, race and religious norms, assumptions and prejudices. The second section involves a closer analysis of one of Prince's most amusing songs 'International Lover' (*1999*, 1982). My reading of this song's subversive appeal will be influenced by Deleuzian theory on desire as experimental and inventive. In Deleuzian terms, the word 'bodies' refers not so much to individual corporeal forms as to the connections made among materialities of various kinds: in this instance, then, connections between the musician, his music (including lyrics and vocal range and use of instruments), sartorial sense, performance, the band, the instruments, technology and the audience. 'Bodies' are understood more in terms of what they do, rather than 'who they are'. I will explore how what I call the 'Body with Humour' produced through Prince's wit – including his use of self-parody – has the potential to disrupt both the affective dimension of his music and our assumptions about heteronormative masculinity.

Humour is, of course, a matter of taste. Some of the ways I find Prince's music comedic and uplifting will not necessarily appeal to others. Humour is also a personal experience, and, in my case, appreciation of Prince's music is very much related to its playful and comedic energy. Early on, I was riveted by his gender-blurring sartorial style, electrifying performances and subversive lyrics; however, my favourite Prince songs have always been those that use humour playfully to disrupt orthodox notions of 'manliness' and 'womanliness', as well as normative (hetero)sexuality, mind and body, the sacred and the profane. Prince created songs that spoke of physical pleasures beyond simplistic binaries. His music generates a sense of confidence to wear otherness and eccentricity proudly and strongly. Much of his repertoire disrupts tired imperatives about active masculinity versus passive femininity: the women in his tales about lust and love are, if anything, more knowing and assertive about their sexual pleasures than their male counterpart (that is, Prince himself – or at least the Prince persona he adopts for his performances). They are independent women who determine their own desires and encounters. This kind of woman is best represented by the protagonist in 'Pussy Control' (*The Gold Experience*, 1995), a song which tells the story of an impoverished bullied girl who grows up and educates herself to take charge of her life in a way that excludes men who would exploit her, or leech off her self-made wealth and status (perhaps not surprisingly we later learn only Prince makes the grade as a man worthy of Pussy's romantic attentions – a finale that always brings a smile to my face).

When Prince emerged as a musical tour de force, the genres of glam rock and new wave were popular, mainly exemplified by White male musicians such as Freddy Mercury, David Bowie, and groups such as Queen, ABC and the Human League, all of whom (albeit in different ways) played with versions of the 'dandified' male image (Hawkins and Niblock 2011); even some punk-rockers, such as Adam Ant, did the same. Like these others, Prince toyed with and performatively decoded dominant images of masculinity, but with his diminutive slender figure and unique sartorial style, he produced an inimitable on- and off-stage identity that was attractive to Black or White, straight or queer men or women, as well as to those between and outside binary identities. He appeared liminal – on the edge of something that could be recognized as gendered but difficult to decipher and therefore to capture or contain: Prince was a gender and a sexuality unto himself. As early as 1994 Robert Walser points out in an article entitled 'Prince as Queer Poststructuralist' the radical affective impact of this artist:

> Prince invites men to imagine different modes of eroticism and relations [and] women to imagine men who could imagine such things. Most important, though, he invites everyone to be interpellated into structures of desire that are not territorialized by rigid patriarchal distinctions. Like Deleuze and Guattari, he is

after a sort of body without organs that can escape Oedipal structures. He is much more intelligible than they because he is able to enact recodings of desire through music and image rather than having to critique them through language. (Walser 1994: 85)

Prince employed signs, images, lyrics, fashion and movement conventionally read as feminine in his re-imagining and enactment of alternative masculinities and male sexual pleasures. Whether wearing a sleeveless tee, thigh-highs and black underwear (1981), a high-collared ruffled shirt and pearl-studded pastel jacket (1985), a pyjama striped suit with gold medallions (1993) or a flowing white tunic with beaded trim (2008) (Billboard 2013), Prince embodied revolution. He was not in drag but rather experimenting with and reconstructing (a predominantly heterosexual) masculine sexuality beyond the confines of gender ideals.

Moreover, and importantly, he worked with, while radically disrupting, formulaic ideas about Black masculine sexuality, in particular. When Prince's eroticized performances mimic the stereotypical hypersexualized notion of African American masculinity (and there are many of them) they ultimately undercut this fantasy by simultaneously embracing the opposite of such machismo – powerful, sexually assertive women being pursued by an androgynous sex symbol in high heels, frills, make-up and (as in his 1991 performance of 'Gett Off') 'ventilated' yellow pants with holes in the seat to expose his buttocks.

This effect/affect can best be summed up by those it had the most impact on. African American journalist Terryn Hall writes in his online tribute to Prince in *The Guardian*, April 2016:

> Prince's music exposed me to a masculine sensuality that allowed a space for vulnerability, ambiguity and fluidity. All this acted as a counter-narrative to what I saw at home and in rap music. … Prince's voice, his music, his entire artistic being existed in a liminal space between the sexual and spiritual, something that I had, and have, heard all too rarely.

Similarly, the *US Guardian*'s Steven W. Thrasher describes the emancipatory impact for him of Prince's performative subversion of Black masculinity:

> He really frightened me as a young man, and yet I couldn't look away. … Prince really spoke to me, both in the way that he dealt with race in a very explicit way and [also] as a queer person who didn't know that I was gay when I was quite young, I found Prince just titillating and really frightening. … He was trying to expand the notion of what it meant to be a man, and yet, at the same time, he was really deconstructing gender. … I realize seeing Prince was one of the first times I saw someone who refused to live in a binary. (Thrasher, *US Guardian* 21 April 2016)

While Prince had a transformative influence on Black masculinity, his music also impacted profoundly on women listeners and viewers. During the Reagan era when conventional gender norms were being (re)entrenched, early Prince songs such as 'The Ballad of Dorothy Parker', 'If I Was Your Girlfriend' (both from *Sign o' the Times,* 1987), and 'Darling Nikki' (*Purple Rain,* 1984) spoke brazenly of the power of women. In these highly sexualized and provocative songs, women (like the protagonist in 'Pussy Control') are not represented as passive objects of masculine sexual conquest (as is the case in much conventional rap and rock made by men) but instead as independent self-determining individuals who express their active desires confidently and shamelessly; and, if in his songs, women fall in love with Prince, they have fallen for a genderfucking[1] lover who respects and feels enriched by their desires and wants to learn from them.[2] Emma Gardner, assistant editor of *Noisey* e-zine, writes,

> One of the most important [things that Prince taught me] was that there is no right way to be a man, no right way to be a woman. And, to a queer white girl with a different set of problems and privileges, Prince was and continues to be a beacon of fluidity and rebellion, standing defiant in a studded jacket and a G-string, amid a world hell bent on trying to categorise women's experiences and silence their voices. No matter how grim or gross the world might be, I can escape into one of Prince's many, many worlds, and feel equal. (Gardner, *Noisey* 25 April 2016)

While the critics quoted here are taking very seriously Prince's radical disruptions of gender and sexuality, the emotional dispositions they register in response to his music include vulnerability, fear, titillation and defiance. These responses all seem appropriate and accurate to me, but I would also want to add recognition of another pervasive response generated by Prince's performances, one seldom discussed by critics: *laughter*. My argument is that Prince's ability to, as Gardner states, 'transport us to other worlds' is often by means of another of his characteristic boundary-mixing and paradoxical effects: Prince was able to enact these very serious and potentially dangerous disruptions alongside and by means of humour and irreverence.

Indeed, with graphically sexualized songs such as 'Head' (*Dirty Mind,* 1980), 'My Private Joy', 'Jack U Off' (both on *Controversy,* 1981) and 'Darling Nikki' (*Purple Rain,* 1984), Prince sealed a reputation early on for his contravention of received moral standards in music. These four songs subverted conventional ideas about gender, race and propriety while employing various forms of humour and playfulness to facilitate the sense of transgression. 'Private Joy', 'Jack U Off' and 'Darling Nikki' all reference masturbation, while 'Head' is, as the name suggests, about oral sex; in this latter song, Prince (as protagonist) seduces a would-be bride away from her wedding when she fellates him (and he comes on her wedding gown). And, while some have read 'Private Joy' as a song about a secret lover of Prince's (speculation continues about who this might be), I prefer an interpretation favouring masturbation. The lyrics are deliberately ambiguous, but however you read it, the song subverts notions of sexual propriety (especially in the early 1980s). When read through the lens of Prince's masturbatory talent, however, the song refers to a secret toy that brings private joy – something that belongs to him and he won't let others play with – suggesting the joke is on Prince's amorous relationship with his own penis.

Humour is also influenced by context and tone, of course. For example, 'Private Joy' has an upbeat disco pop sound, and when performed at The Summit venue, Houston, in 1981, Prince wore a faux-leopard skin jacket and a black choker collar (no shirt) and was accompanied by guitarist Dez Dickerson who at one stage played his guitar with his mouth; during the performance the audience is asked to clap and sing along when Prince demands (of his private joy) to 'get up'!

In 'Jack U Off' the joke comes at the end (pun intended) when, after several verses of Prince enthusiastically offering to jack *u* off (in a restaurant, a movie show, the back seat of a car), the song's conclusion implies this generosity may all have been in the ultimate service of getting exactly what *he* wants: someone to jack *him* off! This song's blatantly crude and funny lyrics, accompanied by Prince's suggestive performance, undermine cultural understandings of masturbation as a taboo and 'undignified' activity that were still prevalent in late-1970s and early-1980s America.

Humour also emerges in Prince's music with respect to racial difference, as exemplified in 'Black Sweat' (*3121*, 2006*)*. A reading of both the content and video performance of this song is vital to an understanding of its light-hearted appeal. In the video, which is filmed in black-and-white in a minimalist setting, Prince, dressed in a stylish suit, first looks at and beckons the viewer. An African American woman (played by Celestina Aledakoba) wearing a love symbol pendant dances flirtatiously around him. With a mischievous look Prince begins by singing in his falsetto that he *doesn't want to* take his clothes off, but he *does*; and he *doesn't want* to feel 'turned on' but he *does*. At various times in the video he is more or less interested in the dancer, at one point feigning indifference while holding a cup and saucer and politely sipping tea. The performances are playful and teasing. Prince acts sexily confident if not a little flummoxed at times by the equally energetic advances of his stage-mate. While 'working' up a 'black sweat', Prince announces he's hot, the groove is sweet (no point in 'acting hard') and that the dancer on screen will be screaming like a 'white lady' when he counts to three. After three beats Aledakoba's character opens her mouth and lets loose a long high-pitched scream (actually made by the keyboard riff). At this point Prince's face screws up in disgust as he looks at the camera/viewer and moves away from her.

Aside from the mischievous connotation about White women and Black masculinity this moment is also funny because throughout the song Prince has been self-assuredly suggestive – if not cocky. In fact, much of his humour (in 'Black Sweat', 'Private Joy', 'Jack U Off' and 'Head') relies on performative self-aggrandizement. As Fuchs points out above, such masculine sexual arrogance takes on a different meaning when referring to a dandified or glammed up diminutive man and/or a queer performance. In this case, then, there are two layers of self-irony involved: the first is the self-ironization of Prince himself, claiming to be every woman's dream while being both tiny and very non-macho; the second, involves the ironization of the codes of Black hetero machismo, being voiced by a beautiful tiny figure in high heels and make-up.

Many times sexual and spiritual themes intersect in Prince's songs – for example, in 'Controversy' (*Controversy*, 1981), 'Let's Pretend We're Married' (*1999*, 1982), 'The Human Body' (*Emancipation*, 1996) and 'Satisfied' (*3121*, 2006) where the struggle between divine transcendence and base sexual energy is depicted, and even celebrated. 'Temptation' (*Emancipation*, 1996) is one of Prince's songs that more clearly demonstrates a complicated relationship between sex/body/animal/the profane and god/spirit/the sacred (Potts 2016). The protagonist (Prince) growls his enjoyment of 'animal lust' throughout the track; however, his carnal pleasure is curtailed by a God-like presence at the end of this song that admonishes sex without love and tells him he must die (in other words, his pleasure-seeking body will be taken from him). 'Temptation' finishes with Prince's childlike and regretful apology and acknowledgement that love is more important than sex, and his promise that he will be good next time.

This kind of song stages the Christian division and hierarchical privileging of the spiritual or transcendent over the bodily or animal, thereby requiring the mastery and repudiation of both non-human animals and those parts of the human thought to be too close to the animal. But while that makes sense in Christian terms, it exists in a contradictory tension with for a musical tradition like funk that empowers the spontaneous movement of the body and the freer expression of its desires and pleasures (see Reed 2003). Moreover, those places in songs like 'Temptation' which connect human sexuality with 'animality' appear lyrically, vocally and instrumentally much more expansive, fun and definitely more desirable than those moments when 'a higher power' admonishes or curbs pleasurable physical experiences. Here I would argue that Prince employs humour to defuse the potentially alarming or certainly pleasure-killing effect of having Christian sexual morality intrude into celebrations of bodily pleasure.

The prominence of religious/spiritual and sexual/physical ideas, narratives and imagery in Prince's music resonates with the presence of similar themes – and struggles – in the lives and works of other prominent African American male musicians such as Marvin Gaye, Al Green and Michael Jackson (see Friskics-Warren 2005). While other African American artists have persistently wrestled with – and sometimes agonized over – the dissonance between the sacred and the profane in their lives, Stan Hawkins and Sarah Noblick (2011) have convincingly identified how the apparently deep theological message conveyed in Prince's songs like 'Anna Stesia' (*Lovesexy*, 1988) and 'The Holy River' (*Emancipation*, 1996) is actually undercut by his blatant erotic delivery. They suggest that this propensity, in conjunction with extra-musical quasi-religious imagery appearing on album covers, ultimately renders Prince's affiliation to faith 'ambiguous and [verging] on self-parody' (Hawkins and Noblick 2011: 56).

Having discussed some of the ways in which humour in Prince's music has the effect of rendering taboo, unpopular or uncomfortable subjects more accessible and palatable, I want to focus next on a reading of one particular song with reference to the (sometimes also humorous) theory of anti-psychoanalytic of French philosopher Gilles Deleuze and his sometimes co-author Felix Guattari.

Deleuze and Guattari (1983, 1987) reconceptualize desire as positive and productive, an approach that challenges and disrupts the normative phallocentric model of lack or loss associated with psychoanalysis, in which desire is understood as the response to a need. Instead of viewing desire in terms of lack or loss (and thereby the need to complete oneself; or if male, to find completion with female, and vice versa), Deleuze and Guattari prefer to think of desire as active and potentially liberating – desire has no goal apart from its own expansion or proliferation (Potts 2001, 2004).

Likewise, instead of focusing on Masters and Johnson's (1966) influential model of the 'human sexual response cycle' which follows a teleological approach to 'normal' sexual experiences, where both the end point of sexual relations and the measure of 'sexual health' and 'function' is the 'achievement' of orgasm, Deleuze and Guattari favour rhizomatic relations. Such horizontal erotics disturb conventional modes of sexuality and sexual pleasure through the shattering of hierarchical binaries such as masculine/feminine, subject/object, inside/outside, active/passive, heterosexual/homosexual and even sex/non-sex.

Deleuze and Guattari's affirmative theory of desire is developed in the neo-concepts of 'desiring-production' and 'desiring machines'. The term desiring-production refers to the fundamental properties of desire as positive, active and inventive, in the sense that it proliferates difference and novelty: desire is 'neither good or bad, sexual or non-sexual, but creative' (Jordan 1995: 127). It is non-teleological and unpredictable. Desiring-machines are the assemblages or aggregations where desire 'exists'. Like 'bodies' in Deleuzian theory, desiring-machines are not to be interpreted according to *who they are* (identity) but rather with respect to *what they do*, what their function is (Buchanan 1996).

Schizoanalysis, Deleuze and Guattari's alternative to psychoanalysis, seeks to provide routes of escape from domination and repression. As a theoretical strategy it is characterized by the aforementioned rhizomatics – these are non-hierarchical flows which, rather than re-territorializing an experience within familiar binary configurations, operate by deterritorializating, by non-directional invention. The nomadic wandering endorsed by Deleuze and Guattari involves fleeing in multiple directions out from central power sources. As Goodchild (1996: 81) explains, 'Any move or thought or social relation is desirable, so long as it does not lead back into an old or new convention, obligation or institution.' Such trajectories constitute 'lines of flight', the most liberated modes of 'thought' or 'becoming' in Deleuze and Guattari's theoretical trilogy of lines which stratify society. Lines of flight are nomadic: they 'deterritorialize' by disturbing boundaries and demarcations.

The other two trajectories relevant to an understanding of the relationship between the individual and society are the molar and the molecular. Molar lines represent those macroforces in society which divide, define, control and regulate. They follow particular pathways or patterns associated with categorization and stratification. It is the molar lines that produce power differentials between men and women, for example. Molecular lines are associated with micro-processes. Like molar lines, they subscribe to a determinate arrangement of connections, but they are not as rigid or structured. Lines of flight may escape the molar, but they do so, in Deleuzian theory, not 'by running away from the world [but by] causing runoffs' (Deleuze and Guattari 1987: 204). This phenomenon is likened to the process of drilling holes in a pipe: 'there is no social system that does not leak from all directions, even if it makes its segments increasingly rigid in order to seal its lines of flight' (ibid). Lines of flight surge through the space between the molar and molecular lines; they occur where these lines have been ruptured and broken down, and they signal something different and new.

I would argue that some escapes from the molar and molecular occur through humour, especially where humour transgresses, disrupts or 'deterritorializes' a 'given' or 'taken for granted' fact, meaning or experience. Prince's use of humour, as I have suggested, manifests in a range of musical contexts and across diverse subject domains – from sexuality, gender and race to propriety, religion and politics; it is not always able to be read as radically disruptive,[3] but there are occasions where the molar and molecular stratifications in society are challenged by a novel feeling or meaning. Instead of the expected trajectories of gender or sexuality, a 'line of flight' is enabled – in Prince's performances such moments are often marked by laughter, emerging through wit, irony, parody or irreverence.

In the following reading of 'International Lover', the final track on the 1982 album *1999*, I propose that humour plays a key part in dismantling heteronormative masculine sexual prowess and creating an experience for the listener based on uplifting transgression. In particular, I argue that 'International Lover' subverts through humour several assumptions about active masculine sexpertise. This song of nearly seven minutes duration was written, composed, produced, sung and all instruments played by Prince, and it gave the artist his first Grammy nomination (in the R&B section) at the 26th Grammy Awards ('International Lover' lost to Michael Jackson's 'Billie Jean').

The first part of the song, narrated in his characteristic falsetto, follows the seduction of an unnamed 'passenger' tempted into taking a flight on Prince's 'plane' – here he uses a conventional vehicular or machinic metaphor that is prevalent in some of his other songs about sex such as 'Little Red Corvette' (*1999*, 1982), and, most humorously, in 'Lovesexy' (off the album of the same name), where Prince likens smelling his lover to race cars burning rubber in his pants.

In 'International Lover' double entendres prevail; prior to boarding, Prince's lover is reassured that he won't fly too fast, he's got too much class for that (this inference confirms that *he* doesn't suffer from the stereotyped masculinist need to race to climax or 'come first'; nor does he suffer from premature descents; instead he will provide the perfect slow ride). However, this self-aggrandizement is undercut somewhat by his having asked earlier in the song if she thinks he's 'qualified' (as a body, as a lover) – Is *Prince*, of all people, now doubting his expertise? And meanwhile, at the level of the 'vehicle' of the metaphor, how might the passenger feel, hearing the pilot wonder out loud about his competence?

The song changes tone around three and a half minutes in. Here the narrative turns to imitate the aviation safety instructions performed by flight attendants before take-off, and the incongruity of the situation emerges through theatricized masculinity and self-parody. 'Pilot Prince' introduces himself and officially welcomes his lover aboard the 'Seduction 747', a plane he boasts is equipped to satisfy any carnal desire. He assures his paramour that if cabin pressure is lost, he will willingly drop down to apply more. With increasing vocal avidity he commands they 'turn on' the flow of excitement by 'extinguishing' their clothes and bringing their bodies together. Wresting back control of this flight (his arousal), while continuing to mimic the protocol of flight safety talks,

Prince then instructs that in the event of an emergency (too much excitement) his partner's 'seat cushion' may be used as a 'floatation device'. She must now hold on fast as he anticipates turbulence along the way! Prince's demeanour becomes more and more exhilarated – he breathlessly declares they are about to arrive at satisfaction! She must bring her hips, arms and lips to the upright and locked position! And at this point the pseudo-professional simulation of the flight safety narrative collapses entirely into the loud and prolonged 'announcement' of Prince's own 'landing', which, once completed successfully and very noisily, is followed by his slower non-falsetto welcome to 'satisfaction'. Dutifully continuing the safety talk despite this return to earth, Pilot Prince requests his passenger to stay awake until the aircraft comes to a complete stop … before thanking her (in breathy bursts as he slows down and stops) … for flying… Prince … International.[4]

During this performance, our Pilot Prince positions himself as the ultimate sexpert – the previous doubts about his qualifications seem to be forgotten. Once his passenger is 'on board', he subjects her to his sexual know-how through a series of polite – but through innuendo, deeply rude – guidelines and moves. As he tells her what he will do to arouse and excite, Prince, as the narrator, plays with and mocks his own sexual response, and also the male sexual expertise discourse prevalent in vocabularies of heterosex (Potts 2003). The song ends after Prince's orgasm (unequivocally pronounced in a long line of 'yeah', 'yeah', 'YEAH's), and this may seem like a capitulation to the conventional linear version of the authoritative sexological model of human sexual response (where male orgasm signals both the end point of male response and the end point of sexuality activity per se); however, in songs like 'International Lover', 'Automatic' and 'Delirious', all from the *1999* album, and 'The Beautiful Ones' (*Purple Rain*, 1984), Prince shakes off orthodox constructions of masculine sexual control and dominance by loudly and passionately and over-theatrically enacting his *own* loss of control in the face of desire. The conventional, if somewhat silly, trajectory of heterosex – where male orgasm signals the end of activity – is subverted in another way too – when Pilot Prince asks his sexual partner to stay awake until the plane has stopped moving. This line of the song suggests that *she* is in danger of falling asleep straight after *he* 'lands'. This reverses the more usual assumption that it is the man who falls asleep straight after he climaxes. It also hints at the radically undermining possibility that she may not have been fully engaged or delighted or pleased by his 'ride'; indeed, it is Prince as the pilot who 'gets off' in this song; we are not sure whether his lover is actually welcoming 'satisfaction' at all.

The whole tone of this song is making fun of the intensity of the situation (a passionate sexual exchange), and the authority of masculine confidence that may accompany heterosexual 'conquests'. In its musical genre, that of the R&B ballad, the song also parodies soul maestros such as Barry White whose erotic speaking in songs occurs as a means to invest the songs with more meaning, more substance and more gravity.

But what does 'International Lover' produce in or for the listener? This is what Deleuze and Guattari would be interested in. Does this work re-establish the mundane territories of heterosex, or does it produce something different?

Certainly, if the listener hears or reads the song straight, then its representation of sex is masculinist, teleological and heteronormative. But that can only happen if no humorous tone is ascribed to the song, its lyrics, or its treatment of the genre whatsoever. It is only the humour of the song that allows the listener to *veer off the flightpath*, and thereby to recognize what is produced is a light-hearted but thoroughgoing mockery of clichéd ideas of heterosex; the authoritative model of sex is parodied and ridiculed. The combination of lyrics, music and queer masculine vocal performance renders this song, rather than a heteronormative love ride, an alternative line of flight. Or, to use another Deleuzo-Guattarian idiom, the molecular 'leakages' generated by the humorous tone create rhizomatic discharges of energy, simultaneously erotic and funny, along the molar hydraulic pipeline of a Masters-and-Johnson-style sexual response mechanism.

In romantic discourse, sex is constructed as a meaningful connection of bodies and souls, an intimate and serious experience. In normative sexological discourse, sex follows a more or less linear trajectory based on the masculine human sexual response cycle (arousal, orgasm, resolution); and in evolutionary discourse, sex is primarily about masculine dominance and feminine submission in the service of reproduction. But our Pilot Prince subverts these imperatives through parody – parody of normative sexual discourses and self-parody of macho masculinity. 'International Lover' is precisely not part of that hydraulic model of sex, even at the same time as it refers to it and enacts it, because it produces laughter.

So, yes, Prince queered sex, but he also made it funny, light, superficial and rather than a hierarchical or vertical relationship between active men and passive women seeking to complete each other through penile-vaginal sex, he created horizontal erotics where the expected masculine sexpertise is mocked and the power and difference of women's sexual pleasure is often paramount. Prince's music is all about experimental lines of flight: purple runways are there if we want to take them, and laughter is one way to travel.

Notes

1. 'Genderfuck' is a concept in June Reich's work, which Cynthia J. Fuchs picks up in her reading of sex and death in Prince's performances. Reich (pp. 113, 125) says of genderfuck: 'To "get over yourself" is counter-identity politics … we are defined not by who we are but by what we do. … Genderfuck could be said to be the effect of unstable signifying practices in a libidinal economy of multiple sexualities.' Fuchs (1996: 146) refers to genderfuck as performance that questions the notion of identity aggressively, 'poking at its limits, reimagining its possibilities'.
2. David Bowie having represented a similar transgressive image earlier, Prince became the gender-fluid figure of Generation X (1965–81) (Touré 2012).
3. Nor should it be thought that humour is necessarily transgressive. Humour may of course also be used in the reinforcement of dominant power relations.
4. The reader is advised to listen to the full version of 'International Lover' to appreciate the nuances of this song.

Works cited

Billboard Staff. 'Prince's Fashion Evolution'. *Billboard*, 13 Jan. 2013. Web. 15 July 2018. http://www.billboard.com/photos/1500115/prince-fashion-evolution-photos.
Buchanan, Ian. 'The Problem of the Body in Deleuze and Guattari, Or, What Can a Body Do?' *Body & Society* 3 (1996): 73–91.
Deleuze, Gilles, and Felix Guattari. *A Thousand Plateaus: Capitalism and Schizophrenia*. Tran. Brian Massumi, Minneapolis, University of Minnesota Press, 1987 [1980].
Deleuze, Gilles, and Felix Guattari. *Anti-Oedipus: Capitalism and Schizophrenia*. Trans. Robert Hurley, Mark Seem and Helen R. Lane, Minneapolis, University of Minnesota Press, 1983 [1972].
Friskics-Warren, B. *I'll Take You There: Music and the Urge for Transcendence*. New York, Bloomsbury, 2005.
Fuchs, C. J. (1996), 'I Wanna Be Your Fantasy: Sex, Death, and the Artist Formerly Known as Prince'. *Women & Performance: A Journal of Feminist Theory* 8.2 (1996): 137–51.
Gardner, E. 'Prince Wrote about Women in a Way That Most Contemporary Male Artists Still Can't'. *Noisey*, 25 April 2016. 15 July 2018. http://noisey.vice.com/blog/prince-and-the-power-of-women.
Goodchild, P. *Gilles Deleuze and the Question of Philosophy*. Cranbury, NJ, Associated University Presses, 1996.
Hall, T. 'When I Saw Prince I Saw a Vital New Masculinity'. *The Guardian*, 26 Apr. 2016. Web. 15 July 2018. http://www.theguardian.com/commentisfree/2016/apr/24/prince-vital-new-black-masculinity.
Hawkins, Stan, and Sarah Niblock. *Prince: The Making of a Pop Music Phenomenon*. London, Ashgate, 2011.
Jordan, Tim. 'Collective Bodies: Raving and the Politics of Gilles Deleuze and Félix Guattari'. *Body & Society* 1.1 (1995): 125–44.
Masters, William H., and Virginia E. Johnson. *Human Sexual Response*. Boston, Little, Brown, 1966.
Potts, Annie. 'The Body without Orgasm: Becoming Erotic with Deleuze and Guattari'. *International Journal of Critical Psychology* 1.3 (2001): 140–64.
Potts, Annie. 'Deleuze on Viagra (Or, What Can a "Viagra-Body" Do?)'. *Body & Society* 10.1 (2004): 17–36.
Potts, Annie. 'The Intersectional Influences of Prince: A Human-Animal Tribute'. *Animal Studies Journal* 5.1 (2016): 152–86.
Potts, Annie. *The Science/Fiction of Sex: Feminist Deconstruction and the Vocabularies of Heterosex*. London, Routledge, 2003.
Prince. *1999*, Warner Bros, 1982.
Prince. *3121*, NPG, 2006.
Prince. *Around the World in a Day*, Paisley Park, 1985.
Prince. *Controversy*, Warner Bros, 1981.
Prince. *Diamonds and Pearls*, Paisley Park, 1991.
Prince. *Dirty Mind*, Warner Bros, 1980.
Prince. *Emancipation*, Paisley Park, 1996.
Prince. *The Gold Experience*, NPG, 1995.
Prince. *Lovesexy*, Paisley Park, 1988.
Prince. *Parade*, Paisley Park, 1986.

Prince. *Purple Rain*, Warner Bros, 1984.
Prince. *Sign o' the Times*, Paisley Park, 1987.
Reed, T. L. *The Holy Profane: Religion in Black Popular Music*. Lexington, The University Press of Kentucky, 2003.
Reich, J. L. 'Genderfuck: The Law of the Dildo'. *Discourse* 15.1 (1992): 112–27.
Thrasher, S. W. 'Prince Broke all the Rules about What Black American Men Should Be'. *The Guardian*, 21 Apr. 2016. 15 July 2018. https://www.theguardian.com/music/2016/apr/21/prince-broke-expectations-black-american-men-musical-genius-performances.
Touré. *I Would Die For You: Why Prince Became an Icon*. New York, Atria, 2012.
Walser, R. 'Prince as Queer Poststructuralist'. *Popular Music & Society* 18.2 (1994): 79–89.

13

When were you mine?

Prince's legacy in the context of transgender history

Joy Ellison

When Prince passed, transgender people, like many others, mourned his loss by sharing the images and lyrics by which we wanted to remember him. I watched as my transgender friends posted pictures of Prince in feminine clothing, gifs of his best eye-rolls, links to the songs in which he seemed to express gender identifications similar to our own. Andrea Jenkins, the first Black transgender woman elected to the city council of Minneapolis, Minnesota, cited Prince's song 'I Would Die 4 U' in an interview following his death, saying, 'He opened up a whole lot of space for people' (Palmer). This song conjured the image of Prince with which transgender identified most closely. 'I Would Die 4 U' seems to confirm the way that transgender people have seen him: as androgynous, as gender non-conforming, as femme, as one of us, as a part of the vast, varied and fantastic transgender community. By transgender, I refer to anyone whose gender identity differs from the gender assigned at birth. Transgender is most often used as an umbrella term that includes trans women and trans men as well as non-binary, agender, genderqueer people and other gender non-normative identities and expressions. Prince fans know that 'I Would Die 4 U' is in fact one of Prince's many songs about Jesus. On the surface, this song tells us nothing about Prince's gender identity. Nonetheless, Prince provided us with a vision of gender transgression as divine and the sacred as transgender. If my friends saw this distinction, they didn't seem to care. There's something about Prince that resonates with many transgender people, that demands that we claim him as one of us. This may be especially true for non-binary trans people like me. This chapter draws upon transgender studies, Black studies and transgender history to critically interrogate that sense of connection. Engaging the affective ties between Prince and transgender communities, particularly Black trans-feminine communities, opens new ways to understand the complicated, multifaceted and often melancholic relationship between popular culture and Black and transgender subcultural expressions.

Many writers, reviewers, feminists and fans have claimed Prince as a queer icon. They have celebrated him as a supporter of Black women and an icon of non-normative gender and sexuality. In her book *Sounding Like a No-No: Queer Sounds and Eccentric*

Acts in a Post Soul Era, Black feminist and queer thinker Dr. Francesca Royster writes of her childhood experiences with Prince as a queer Black girl:

> We soon learned to turn the volume down low, singing along to those images of sex as melting sugarcane and trembling butterflies, panting along with the unnamed 'Sexy Dancer' when we were sure my mother wasn't home. Prince's appeal was tauntingly open-ended, whatever we wanted to dream up, it seemed. (Royster 1)

Royster goes on to situate her sense of connection with Prince and the possibilities he opened for her within a larger context of Black pop cultural production:

> As Mark Anthony Neal, a black feminist theorist, points out, at a time when black culture saw the emergence of strict codes of masculinity as tough and hard with the emergence of hip-hop, Prince countered with his own and very fluid ideas of black masculinity … was he woman or man? Gay or straight? he asks us. He doesn't answer directly, but offers us instead a sexual dream space. (Royster 3)

Royster beautifully reflects on the significance of Prince to Black and queer people and her analysis is essential to understanding Prince's cultural significance. The question 'Was he a woman or a man?' is not just a queer question, however. It is a trans question, too. Perhaps more trans – non-binary trans, specifically – than queer. I do not contest Prince's status as a queer icon. However, his significance to transgender communities has not been duly considered, especially as many cultural commentators and fans base their claims to Prince as a queer icon on his gender expression, rather than sexual behaviour. This particular oversight is all too common – pop culture figures, even straight ones, are often claimed as queer icons because of their gender expression, while their relevance to trans communities goes unconsidered, along with their reliance on performance styles that have their roots in subcultural spaces that trans people helped to shape. When gender transgressive artists like Prince are considered relevant only to queer people, transgender women of colour are erased from the very communities they created.

In light of this long history of reading gender non-normativity as queer to the exclusion of a transgender interpretation, I offer an alternative approach to cultural and historical analysis. I examine Prince's shifting career within the context of transgender history and consider what it means to be a trans Prince fan. I ask when, exactly, were you mine? This form of personal reflection is a transgender studies methodology; memoir and personal narrative have been central modes of inquiry for transgender studies scholars and cultural workers, including Janet Mock, Kai Green, Eli Clare and many others (Mock; Green; Clare). My analysis employs personal reflection, while also gesturing towards limitations of such an approach, especially the problems of White trans and queer people reading Prince those the prism of their desires and experiences. Specifically, I avoid drawing conclusions about Prince's gender identity, although I note where other transgender people have done so, in order to respect what C. Riley Snorton calls the opacity of Black gender non-normative historical figures (Snorton 151). The cultivation of opacity was an important part of Prince's personal, business and artistic practice; it provided a means for him to claim autonomy and supplied the magnetic mystery of his performances. Thus, I purposefully do not offer new information about Prince's gender identity or sexuality. Instead, I seek to locate Prince within US trans history and articulate why that history is relevant outside our community. I further hope that by re-contextualizing Prince in this way, scholars are inspired to consider other ways that trans history shapes broader culture.

Trans history, Prince history

Prince was born in 1958, during an era of transgender history marked by tough street queens, drag balls and jail cells. At that time, living as a transgender person made it nearly impossible to find legal work. Many transgender people, especially trans women of colour, lived on the streets. They were pursued relentlessly by police. Many were arrested for crimes related to their poverty – loitering, sex work and petty theft. They also were criminalized by local laws against cross-dressing. In response, many trans women of colour formed tight-knit communities through which they supported and defended each other (Stryker 67). Over a decade, trans women of colour across the United States formed political organizations and fought back against the police. In May 1959, a year after Prince was born, trans women, femmes and gay male hustlers in Los Angeles, many of whom were Latinx or Black, resisted when police attempted to arrest them at Cooper's Doughnuts, a popular late-night hang-out spot (Stryker 60). In 1965, Black activists in Philadelphia held sit-ins at Dewey's Lunch Counter after managers began refusing service to patrons in 'nonconformist clothing' (Stryker 62). In 1966, another riot broke out in San Francisco's Gene Compton's Cafeteria. Once again, trans women, gay men and sex workers fought back against police and private security harassment. Then in 1969 when Prince was eleven years old, the legendary Stonewall Riots erupted in New York City (Stryker 83). These riots, instigated and sustained by trans women of colour, are remembered as the beginning of the US LGBT movement. In fact, they were a continuation of a decade of trans struggle.

At the time of Stonewall, Prince was probably thinking more about school and music lessons than the burgeoning LGBT movement. Nonetheless, it is undeniable that the resistance of transgender women of colour created the context in which a Black man who did his own eyeliner could thrive. The post-soul Black cultural era into which Prince blossomed was shaped by transgender women of colour. Take Marsha 'Pay It No Mind' Johnson (*Pay It No Mind – The Life and Times of Marsha P. Johnson*). Marsha instigated the Stonewall Riots and sustained decades of transgender activism in New York City. She also performed with the Hot Peaches, a queer and trans performance group. Her work prefigured the Black Arts Movement, especially in its queer iterations. When we think of Prince, we should remember Marsha P. Johnson and the Black transgender women who birthed the LGBT rights movement.

In fact, the trans movement was particularly fierce in Prince's hometown, Minneapolis. In 1975, Minneapolis passed one of the first trans-inclusive non-discrimination ordnances in the United States. The law banned discrimination based on 'having or projecting a self-image not associated with one's biological maleness or one's biological femaleness' (Margolin). Prince was most assuredly a beneficiary of this landmark civil rights measure.

By the time, Prince released his first album, *For You*, in 1978, transgender women had been largely excluded from the LGBT communities they had helped shape. Gay activists saw them as a liability to their efforts to assimilate. Lesbian feminist refused to acknowledge that trans women were women. The 1970s and 1980s were difficult decades, to use transgender historian Susan Stryker's term. Trans women were forced to turn inwards. They took care of friends and lovers with HIV and protested in the streets with ACT UP (Stryker 90). While they struggled, there was Prince on the TV looking like he was about to sashay his way down Christopher Street pier.

There is something about Prince that calls to us as trans people. In the 1970s and 1980, he served up many images that remind me of us. A friend of mine who is an elder in the trans community recently posted on Facebook about Prince's first television performance. It was 8 January 1980. Prince played 'I Wanna Be Your Lover' wearing animal-print briefs and black thigh-highs. He flounced and whipped his hair while he told the whole world that he wanted to be like the women in our lives. In her post, my friend used the pronoun 'they' to refer to Prince (Martinez). Coming from her in this context, the pronoun 'they' signalled a respect for Prince's gender nonconformity and a desire to speak to his feminine androgyny. Her use of 'they' spoke to our desire to claim kinship with the Artist, strange as that relationship may be. Robin Power Royal, one of Prince's girlfriends from 1989 to 1991, also used 'they' pronouns for Prince throughout her interview with journalist Erica Thompson. Thompson quoted her as saying, 'I've never been around someone that was so much a boy and a girl like that in a male form' (Thompson). While these comments do not give us insight into how Prince understood himself, they do illustrate how Prince was read by others and his significance to transgender people.

In 1984, Prince incorporated into his film *Purple Rain* a symbol connected with the trans community. This sign combined the Mars and Venus symbols, representing masculinity and femininity respectively, into a signal sign. This symbol was the basis of the glyph that would become Prince's name. Likely few viewers realized that symbols like it have long been used by the trans community. LGBT publications have used the Mars and Venus signs in movement iconography since the 1960s. Circa 1993, a Minneapolis-based organization named the Gender Education Center used a symbol in its brochure that was almost identical to Prince's *Purple Rain* era sign (Davis). Today, the transgender community incorporates the same combination of Mars and Venus into our symbol. Historians may never know whether Prince was influence by the trans community or if the trans community was influenced by him. Nonetheless, evidence indicates that it is likely that Prince and transgender activists were aware of each other and were shaped by similar ideas.

Wendy Melvoin and Lisa Coleman, members of The Revolution and Prince's lesbian collaborators from the *Purple Rain* era, have talked about his status as a gay icon. In their interview with *Out Magazine*, Melvoin and Coleman beautifully express the Prince I see, someone who was not just androgynous but also femme, maybe even trans-feminine:

> Out Magazine: Did you first think Prince was gay?
> Lisa: He was little and kinda prissy and everything. But he's so not gay.
> Wendy: He's a girl, for sure, but he's not gay. He looked at me like a gay woman would look at another woman.
> Lisa: Totally. He's like a *fancy lesbian* [emphasis mine].
> Wendy: I remember being at that Sexuality video shoot and him on stage with that little black jacket and that tie thing around his neck and his black pants with white buttons on the side. And we looked at each other for the first time and I thought, Oh, I could so fall in love with that girl easy. (Walters)

Wendy and Lisa's descriptions claim Prince as queer, trans and feminine – simultaneously and inextricably. Rather than describing Prince as 'transcending' the boundaries of gender and sexuality, they locate him specifically as a 'fancy lesbian'. Because masculinity is treated as a default, feminine affect is rarely legible as androgynous. Wendy and Lisa voice this aspect of Prince's unique style: he did not redefine masculinity so much as he made space within androgyny to include femininity.

Prince's performances illustrate how his 'fancy lesbian' style could never be separated from his Blackness. Prince expressed beautifully all of these identities in 1986 through the album *Parade* and its accompanying film *Under the Cherry Moon*. The cover of 'Parade' pictures Prince with thick eyeliner ringing his wide eyes and his hands raised to frame his face. His expression mirrors the style of drag queens and trans women who participated in ball culture. Ball culture is a Black and Lantix queer and trans subculture, characterized by social networks called houses and competitions in which participants walk a runway (Bailey). The position of Prince's hands imitates the vogue dance moves created by the stars of ball culture. In *Under the Cherry Moon*, Prince engages with Black trans women's culture more directly. He portrays Christopher Tracy, a suave Black man living in Paris with his even more effeminate roommate Tricky. Prince breaks up a boring party attended by rich, White people by dancing on top of a piano in a style reminiscent of voguing. He then runs from the police, who are constantly following Tricky and Tracy, right up to the film's tragic ending. Prince vogues again as the credits roll over the song 'Mountains'(Nelson, Under). *Under the Cherry Moon* is one potent example of Prince's invocation of undeniably Black queer and trans cultural forms.

In 1987, Prince told us exactly how it would be if he were our girlfriend and damn did he make it sound good. Prince's images from the late 1980s, created while the trans community coped with mass incarceration and the AIDS crisis, are solace to me today. I can't help but see them as an expression of our beauty and potential.

The 1990s were a time of coming into our own power for both Prince and the trans community. Transgender people began to organize independent of the gay and lesbian community. We began to describe ourselves to ourselves. We developed the term 'transgender' to describe our experiences and used 'trans feminism' to describe our politics (Stryker 91). Prince created new words for himself, too. In 1993, he took the love symbol as his name. Some trans people were keenly interested in this development. The trans magazine *Cross-Talk* published a short article about his decision:

> Prince still retains his talent for puzzling [his fans]. To celebrate his 35th birthday recently, he has had his publicist announce that henceforth he is to be known only as the symbol he designed for this last album – a stylized combination of the male and female symbols. The only problem is that there is no spoken word for the name and no keyboard symbol. Nor has you-know-who revealed how it is to be pronounced. Of course, for us, the big mystery is what does this mean, genderwise? Is (s)he acknowledging androgyny or hermaphrodism? (Richards 9)

Three years later, in an interview with Oprah, Prince seemed to confirm this trans fan theory. Prince told Oprah: 'Recent analysis has proved that there's probably two people inside of me. There's a Gemini. And we haven't determined what sex that other person is yet' ('The Artist Formally Known as Prince'). This description harkened back to Prince's feminine alter ego Camille, a persona he adopted briefly in the 1980s. While Prince's statements could very reasonably be interpreted as an expression of non-binary gender identity, Prince never clarified. However, in the same interview, he did articulate his new name as a part of the tradition of Black resistance:

> 0{+> : Well, just like Muhammad Ali …
> Oprah: Mm-hmm.
> 0{+> : … and Malcolm X …
> Oprah: Mm-hmm.
> 0{+> : … people like that change their name, and some people take names that are hard to pronounce.
> Oprah: Mm-hmm.
> 0{+> : And it just so happens I picked one that you can't pronounce. ('The Artist Formally Known as Prince')

Prince's statement is another example of the way that his gender and sexuality were constructed through his Blackness. Through adopting an unspeakable symbol of gender nonconformity as his name, Prince frustrated attempts to know him, speak of him and profit from him. While Prince told Oprah that his reasons for changing his name were personal, the glyph was an effective way to protest the terms of his deal with Warner Bros. Prince understood his contract dispute as a part of Black struggle, illustrated by his decision to write 'slave' on his face (5DeCurtis). Anjali Vats writes that the love symbol 'points to and refuses slave naming practices, which attempted to deprive Black subjects of their personhood and identities. It is a new identity, one that claims the value of Black creatorship and Black entrepreneurship in ways that evoke the history of "bodies in dissent" and gesture to new futures' (24Vats 118). Prince made clear that his 'body in dissent' was both gendered and racialized simultaneously.

Prince's decision to adopt a variation on a transgender symbol as his name is an action that feels very familiar to me – and also one that highlights the differences between Prince's gender expression and that of transgender people. It is common for trans people to choose our own names to represent our sense of self and our gender. However, Prince's decision to do so was largely respected. Ours are not. Like Prince, we may yearn for what transgender activist Leslie Feinberg called 'the right to be complex' (Feinberg 70). To create space for our complexity and opacity we may practice evasion, one of Prince's primary performative strategies. Nonetheless, our names are not unpronounceable glyphs. They're simple: Marsha P. Johnson, Sylvia Rivera, Miss Major Griffin-Gracie, Laverne Cox, Janet Mock, CeCe McDonald, Chelsea Manning and many more. Still, many cisgender people can't seem to find a way to say them. Prince was respected and celebrated for a type of gender expression that gets trans people murdered. In that regard, he wasn't one of us at all.

Fast forward a little: 2014 was a landmark year for both Prince and the transgender community. Prince regained control of his masters and released two albums. At the same time, *Time* magazine declared it the year of the trans tipping point (Steinmetz). Trans people were visible in the mainstream in ways we had not been in years. That tipping point has been a space of precarity for us. Prince inadvertently illustrated that too. In 2015, Prince put on a concert in Baltimore. He played a beautiful song honouring Freddie Grey, a Black man brutally abused and murdered by the police (Case). The concert was an important part of Prince's activism and support for the Black Lives Matter movement. What Prince did not mention, however, was another police murder in Baltimore just two weeks before Grey's – the shooting of Mya Hall, a Black trans woman (Hermann). In fact, Hall was not remembered by many. The murders of Black trans women rarely are. Prince probably never even heard her name.

This is the ambiguity of the transgender tipping point. Trans people are presented as a success story, much in the same way White critics hailed Prince as transcending race while the artist made no such claim (Whiteneir 130) The media says we're the next civil rights struggle – as though the old civil rights struggles are over, as though civil rights have been enough. We are celebrated for our visibility, while Black trans women continue to be murdered for the same. Trans artists and activists Tourmaline, Eric Stanley and Johanna Burton write, 'The visual can be a trap when it is held to be the primary path toward liberation and when it's held as a teaching tool aimed at audiences outside of the trans community' (Gossett xvi). That trap can be a deadly one.

Today, we can find trans and gender non-conforming artists that are perhaps more like us than Prince. We can buy the albums of transgender musician Laura Jane Grace or watch videos featuring sissy-bounce superstar Big Freedia. Allegedly, we are liberated by becoming a niche market. Meanwhile, social safety nets shrink and there is no artist in the mainstream with a gender expression quite like Prince. It is hard to imagine such a figure would be welcomed. How are transgender people to understand our current position in neoliberal structures? What does it mean to be so visible, when that visibility can be both a means of resistance and the cause of violence? These questions are urgent, matters of life and death for the most vulnerable in the trans community. Prince's performance techniques and complicated, resistant engagement with capitalist structures can provide trans people with guidance in navigating these tensions. In an era that demands from trans people a fixed, transparent and marketable personal identity, Prince's shifts in gender expression, his commitment to his privacy and cultivation of his mystique, and his determination to own and profit from his creative labour are inspirational for me.

Conclusion

As trans people, there are so many people from whom we gather the strength to be ourselves. Our love of them tells us more about ourselves than about them. Musicians like Prince can provide us with a sense of something deep: imagination, possibility, complexity. We need harmony, rhythm and funk. Prince took the unspeakable and the opaque and he put a beat behind it. He made it irresistible. He did that for several capacious categories: Blackness, sexuality and gender. When Prince passed, I honoured his memory by learning to put on eyeliner. I wanted to celebrate his expression of a feminine androgyny. To me, he provided the sense of expanse that is missing from the limited media depictions of trans existence today. That's why here at the trans tipping point, I love Prince even more than I did when he was mine.

Works cited

'The Artist Formerly Known as Prince'. *The Oprah Winfey Show*, 1103a6ka, 21 Nov. 1996.
Bailey, Marlon M. *Butch Queens Up in Pumps: Gender, Performance, and Ballroom Culture in Detroit*. University of Michigan Press, 2013. *Project MUSE*, https://muse.jhu.edu/book/26695.
Case, Wesley. 'Prince Touched Baltimore with Concert, Song after Freddie Gray's Death, Unrest'. *Baltimore Sun*, 21 Apr. 2016, http://www.baltimoresun.com/entertainment/music/midnight-sun-blog/bs-ae-prince-baltimore-20160421-story.html.
Clare, Eli. *Brilliant Imperfection: Grappling with Cure*. Durham, NC: Duke University Press, 2017.
Davis, Debra. *Gender Education Center*. Self-Published, Circa 1993. Tretter Collection, University of Minnesota.
DeCurtis, Anthony. 'O(+> Free at Last'. *Rolling Stone*, no. 748, Nov. 1996.
Feinberg, Leslie, trans. *Liberation: Beyond Pink Or Blue*. Beacon Press, 1998.
Gossett, Che. 'Blackness and the Trouble of Trans Visibility'. *Trap Door: Trans Cultural Production and the Politics of Visibility*. Ed. Reina Gossett et al., MIT, 2017. 183–1980.
Green, Kai M. 'The Essential I/Eye in We: A Black TransFeminist Approach to Ethnographic Film'. *Black Camera* 6.2 (2015): 187–200.
Hermann, Peter. 'Baltimore's Transgender Community Mourns One of Their Own, Slain by Police'. *The Washington Post*, 3 Apr. 2015, https://www.washingtonpost.com/local/crime/baltimores-transgender-community-mourns-one-of-their-own-slain-by-police/2015/04/03/2f657da4-d88f-11e4-8103-fa84725dbf9d_story.html?utm_term=.a261c83ab173.

Margolin, Emma. 'How Minneapolis Became the First City in the Country to Pass Trans Protections'. *MSNBC*, 3 June 2016, http://www.msnbc.com/msnbc/how-minneapolis-became-the-first-city-the-country-pass-trans-protections.

Martinez, Alexis. *Don't Need to Say Anything. This Is Prince in Their First Television Appearance*. 26 Dec. 2016, https://www.facebook.com/search/str/Alexis%2BMartinez%2Bprince/keywords_blended_posts?filters_rp_author.

Mock, Janet. *Redefining Realness: My Path to Womanhood, Identity, Love & So Much More*. Reprint edn, Atria Books, 2014.

Nelson, Prince Rodgers. *Under the Cherry Moon*. Warner Home Video, 1986.

Nelson, Prince Rogers. *I Would Die 4 U*. Warner Bros. Records, 1984.

Palmer, Kim. 'Prince Fired a Revolution in Diversity in Race and Gender'. *Star Tribune*, 30 Apr. 2016, http://www.startribune.com/prince-fired-a-revolution-in-diversity-in-race-and-gender/377696181/.

'Pay It No Mind - The Life and Times of Marsha P. Johnson'. *YouTube*, 2012. https://www.youtube.com/watch?v=rjN9W2KstqE&feature=youtube_gdata_player.

Richards, Kymberleigh. 'Cross-Talk: The Gender Community's News & Information Monthly, No. 46 (August, 1993)'. *Digital Transgender Archive*. www.digitaltransgenderarchive.net, Web. 3 July 2017. https://www.digitaltransgenderarchive.net/files/8s45q876k.

Royster, Francesca T. *Sounding Like a No-No: Queer Sounds and Eccentric Acts in the Post-Soul Era*. University of Michigan Press, 2013.

Snorton, C. Riley. *Black on Both Sides: A Racial History of Trans Identity*. University of Minnesota Press, 2017. Project MUSE, https://muse.jhu.edu/book/56615.

Steinmetz, Katy. 'The Transgender Tipping Point'. *Time*, May 2014, http://time.com/135480/transgender-tipping-point/.

Stryker, Susan. *Transgender History*. Seal Press, 2008, http://www.worldcat.org/title/transgender-history/oclc/183914566.

Thompson, Erica. '"Insatiable's My Name When It Comes to U" - Interview with Robin Power Royal'. *A Purple Day in December*, 31 Aug. 2017, http://www.apurpledayindecember.com/2017/08/insatiables-my-name-when-it-comes-to-u.html.

Vats, Anjali. 'Prince of Intellectual Property: On Creatorship, Ownership, and Black Capitalism in Purple Afterworlds (Prince in/as Blackness)'. *Howard Journal of Communications* 30.2 (Mar. 2019): 114–28. Taylor and Francis+NEJM, doi:10.1080/10646175.2018.1523760.

Walters, Barry. 'The Revolution Will Be Harmonized'. *Out Magazine*, Apr. 2009, http://www.out.com/entertainment/2009/04/16/revolution-will-be-harmonized.

Whiteneir, Kevin Talmer. 'Dig If You Will the Picture: Prince's Subversion of Hegemonic Black Masculinity, and the Fallacy of Racial Transcendence'. *Howard Journal of Communications* 30.2 (May 2019): 129–43. EBSCOhost, doi:10.1080/10646175.2018.1536566.

Part Four

Politics and race

14

Prince

Introduction of a new breed leader

Kamilah Cummings

In his 1981 song 'Sexuality', Prince declared that the world needed 'new breed leaders' to marshal it into a different direction. In a career that traversed five decades, Prince emerged as one of those leaders. While countless discussions have contemplated the legacy of Prince's inimitable career, few have explored it from the perspective of leadership. However, to fully appreciate Prince's enduring impact, we must contemplate his role as a leader. When analysed within the context of recognized leadership frameworks, we can conclude that Prince was one of the most influential and successful leaders of the last half-century.

As arguably the greatest self-contained musical talent of all time, few deny Prince's artistic genius. He blurred lines, eviscerated boundaries and blended styles to create a sound that was unmistakably Prince. However, his impact extends beyond his sound. More than any music artist before or during his time, Prince was a game changer whose influence beyond music is unsurpassed. From presenting alternative depictions of Black masculinity (Cummings; Thrasher; Whiteneir Jr.) to upending staid music industry business models (Espana), Prince was 'a beacon of fluidity and rebellion' (Potts 165). He reimagined the world and courageously redefined it for many by constantly breaking new ground on and off the stage. In addition to empowering those around him, he inspired people from all walks of life to reach their highest selves by freeing themselves from the social constructs that prevented their elevation. Morris explains, 'He was being authentically himself in a way that some of us could recognize and appreciate, some of us could love and adore, and others of us tried to emulate because we understood it as an absolute reflection of the things we're all capable of' (qtd in Long). This alone qualifies Prince as a leader. However, utilizing various leadership frameworks to examine his work reveals that, as was the case with his art, Prince employed a hybridized leadership style. It was a unique fusion of thought, transformational, soulful and servant leadership. By merging these distinctive leadership styles to realize his vision of the world, Prince established himself as a new breed leader.

An overview of leadership and Prince

Regardless of the domain or style, there are some basic universal truths about leadership. Leadership is predicated more upon action than upon position or title. This is why political leaders are not the only people we think of when discussing leaders. In fact, much of the discussion of leaders in the last half-century has shifted away from those who hold political offices. For example, some of the most revered leaders of the last fifty years in the United States have included Malcolm X, Martin Luther King Jr., Steve Jobs and Bill Gates, none of whom ever held a political office. Even legendary heads of state Fidel Castro and Nelson Mandela were successful leaders long before taking office. This is because the greatest leaders gain the confidence of their followers through both their words and their actions.

Leaders make a decision to 'influence the thinking, behavior, and development of others' (Mosaic 1). In short, leaders choose to be leaders and followers choose to follow them. That is the simple equation of leadership. Of course, to lead successfully one needs to not only attract followers but gain their trust as well. In other words, leaders have to persuade followers to both accept their vision and their ability to achieve that vision. Because leadership is an evolving practice, leaders will evolve as will their relationship with their followers. However, as long as the leader has established himself as authentic, open, trustworthy and passionate about the mission, his followers will continue to believe in him (Mosaic 2).

An intentional analysis of Prince's career reveals he decided early on to be the new breed leader he summoned in 'Sexuality'. At his 2004 *Rock n Roll Hall of Fame* induction, Prince stated, 'When I first started out in this music industry, I was most concerned with freedom: Freedom to produce, freedom to play all the instruments on my records, freedom to say anything I wanted to' (Nolfi). As a result, Prince signed an unprecedented recording contract that gave a virtually unknown seventeen-year-old complete artistic control. An early indicator of Prince's leadership, his 1978 debut album *For You* introduced the world to the phrase 'Produced, Arranged, Composed and Performed by Prince' – a phrase that would inspire a future generation of self-contained artists to follow in his footsteps. With his artistic freedom, Prince established himself as a one-man musical phenomenon with his first two albums. However, on his third album, *Dirty Mind* (1980), he not only radically expanded his R&B-Funk-Rock sound to include new wave; he also overtly integrated politics into his music, signalling that politics would be integral to his art. The lead single 'Uptown' represents a utopian alternate reality that embodies Prince's vision for the world. Although Uptown is an actual neighbourhood in Prince's hometown of Minneapolis, the song suggests that it could also exist anywhere, especially in one's mind.

Prince's political beliefs undergird his work as much as sex and spirituality. He wrote about the world he lived in alongside the one he envisioned. 'Sexuality' from the *Controversy* (1981) album is significant because it both explores Prince's politics and establishes his desire to lead his listeners. It builds upon the sociocultural criticism and themes of freedom, individuality and racial harmony that he introduced in 'Uptown'. 'Sexuality' sees Prince implore his listeners to let him lead them to the place he envisions as being free from the world's pitfalls and constraints. Given that leaders 'are keenly interested in changing the world around them' (Mosaic 3), in presenting an alternate vision of society, Prince conveys his desire to change the world in 'Sexuality'. In the decades that followed, he worked to realize that change. Woodworth offers, 'It is nearly impossible to analyze his music without making reference to his statements and public actions' (39). Importantly, his leadership was not confined to his music or even his industry. As such, his impact is almost unquantifiable in its breadth and depth. It extends to areas such as poetry, film, fashion, technology and politics.

Mosaic identifies several 'truths about leadership' that are applicable to Prince. One truth is that credibility is the foundation of leadership. Prince's unrivalled talent and the sheer quality and quantity of his work earned him the utmost credibility as a master of his craft. Moreover, his work ethic, uncompromising standard of excellence and integrity in addition to his activism, philanthropy and willingness to make personal sacrifices to challenge injustices cemented his credibility. Another leadership truth is that 'values drive commitment'. Prince exhibited his values of freedom, love, equality and compassion in his work. In addition to embodying these values himself, he demonstrated his commitment to them in his inner world, which reflected his belief that neither race nor gender should dictate what one can do. Evidence of this is seen in the musicians and personnel he often employed in roles that defied race and gender stereotypes.

'Exemplary leaders – the kind of leaders people want to follow – are always associated with changing the status quo' (Mosaic 11). Prince was committed to changing the status quo. The list of ways he did so artistically and culturally is seemingly endless. For example, he shattered perceptions of what styles of music Black artists were expected to play and challenged recording industry norms regarding artists' ownership of their music. According to Mosaic, 'Leadership is an affair of the heart [and] love is the motivation that energizes leaders to give so much for others' (11). Love is a term that is inextricably linked to Prince's work. Whether it was love of music, love of God, love of self or love of mankind, love was a driving force in Prince's work. It is no coincidence that he named his charitable organization Love4OneAnother or that the unpronounceable symbol that was once his name is also known as the love symbol.

Finally, 'leaders inspire others and connect to their dreams and aspirations' (Mosaic 5). Prince led his mission to create a world of freedom, self-determination, equality, love and compassion by an example that ultimately had an intergenerational, intercultural and interdisciplinary influence. Countless fellow musicians have cited the groundbreaking trails he blazed artistically and professionally as inspirations. Singer Alicia Keys suggests, 'He is the inspiration that generations will return to until the end of time' (Nolfi). Further, musician Lenny Kravitz describes Prince as 'the one who showed me the possibilities within myself' (Bartleet). Likewise, many of Prince's followers have credited him with inspiring them to boldly approach life as he did. Gadenne reflects, 'He was unique and transgressive, and this has shown me how to be fearless ... he was creative and flamboyant, and this taught me to recognize freedom' (Potts 184).

Racial context

One must venture beyond Prince's hit songs to fully comprehend the circumstances that fuelled both his vision as a leader and his mission to realize it. Burdett argues 'of the tools of leadership none is more important than language' (8). Through his lyrics, Prince professed an unwavering belief in love, spirituality, equality, freedom and self-determination. One could argue that freedom and self-determination are chief among these tenets. From 'Uptown' (1980) to 'Free Urself' (2015), these themes recur throughout his massive catalogue. Psychoanalyst Thomas Szasz asserts that 'the law of the human kingdom is to define or be defined' (65). There is likely no better embodiment of this theory than Prince who defied pre-constructed notions of genre, race and gender to self-define his sound and image.

While self-definition may be a universal desire, it is important to acknowledge the racial context of Prince's fight to define himself. For Black people in America the need to self-define is a vital concomitant of the ongoing battle for freedom and equality. It is one that is both internal and external. Therefore, as a Black man born in America, Prince's need to 'define or be defined' was undoubtedly rooted in the continued struggle for Black people in America to be liberated from the restrictions imposed by racism. As Prince challenged limited and often distorted preconceptions of Blackness in the music industry, he confronted the reality that the constrictions of racism plague Black people collectively and individually regardless of wealth, fame, talent or physical appearance. Therefore, to properly contextualize Prince's fight for self-definition, Williams (301) argues the importance of applying Du Bois's theory of double consciousness, which posits that the 'two-ness' of being both Black and American results in Blacks seeking to reconcile these often 'warring' identities in a manner that makes it possible 'to be both [Black] and an American ... without having the doors of opportunity closed roughly in [one's] face' (Du Bois 2–3). Williams explains, 'Dubois's theory of double consciousness speaks to Prince's defying of stereotypes, power relations, and simplistic binaries' (301). Likewise, Perry applies Dubois' theory of double consciousness to Prince, drawing parallels between the life experiences of both men: 'Like DuBois, Prince's experiences of growing up in a largely [w]hite environment were still those of a [b]lack person – with race as a looming issue from childhood throughout life' (203).

Prince represented a new member of the Black freedom movement. He embodied the rebellious spirit, confidence and self-determination of the Black freedom fighters who preceded him. '[He] was that shining example of a Black person who had won his freedom on a number of levels' (Neal). However, for many Black people, particularly those who came of age in the 1980s during his meteoric rise to fame, Prince was the first real example of Black self-definition and individuality with whom they could relate. McInnis points out:

> It is this notion of individuality ... which resonates in Prince's work. It is accepting the notion that the [1980s] was a time for the struggle of the black individual – a time when he would break out and free himself of all the chains of race, class, and gender. This is why Prince's work spoke to so many of us. ... If it is true that black

music is black history, then Prince is an irrefutable part of that history. (McInnis Jr. xxiii–xxiv)

Prince used his music to communicate the ongoing struggle for Blacks in America. In doing so, he also reiterated his identity as a Black man and his connection to the Black community. From oblique references to race in songs like 'Raspberry Beret' and 'Breakfast Can Wait' to explicit commentary on topics such as slavery, systemic racism, Black love and resilience in such songs as 'Avalanche', 'Don't Play Me', 'Dear Mr. Man', 'Family Name' and 'Black Muse', Prince's catalogue includes numerous songs that depict the Black experience in America.

However, Prince's Black consciousness was not limited to his lyrics. When he wrote 'Slave' on his face during his epic battle for emancipation from his record company, he drew a profound connection between modern-day labour inequities and the past enslavement of Black people in America. 'During the dispute, Prince took his personal battle with the record company, his general ideas about the value of work, and his ideas about the work of musicians and particularized all of this within the race-specific context of the African American history of slavery and economic exploitation' (Perry 205). It was an iconic act that further endeared him to Black audiences, many of whom were his earliest and most ardent followers because of the ways he modelled Blackness. Emerson explains, 'we were proud that he was fighting the system when he was writing slave on his face and changed his name to the symbol. ... He was doing these things for other people who would come along later, not just himself"' (qtd in Italie).

As Prince's career progressed, his references to racism became increasingly more explicit, which is not unlike the trajectory of many Black leaders before him who became increasingly disillusioned and frustrated with the lack of progress in eradicating systemic racism. His philanthropic support of organizations that worked to empower Black people and to fight racial injustice bespeak his Black consciousness and commitment to his community. 'He was a reflection of us. ... He knew it would take a revolution, and through his life he tried to show us what revolution could look like' (Garza).

A widely circulated quote attributed to Prince by a former manager relates that early in his career Prince asked his record label to 'not make him Black'. Although the quote is often misinterpreted to denote a desire to disassociate from his race, it highlights that even as a young artist, Prince was keenly aware of the ways Black artists are mistreated and marginalized by the music industry. A direct correlation can be made between Prince's desire for control of his music, image and career and his experiences as a Black man in America (Woodworth 42). Given that the entertainment industry is a microcosm of society, it is clear that Prince's desire to not be made Black was actually a desire to be freed from the imposition of racism, not a desire to disassociate from his racial identity or community.

Neal notes, 'In art, business and philanthropy, [Prince] kept an investment in the Black aesthetics and communities that provided him with both his voice and vision' (Neal). Moreover, Henderson explains, 'black leadership does not simply emerge from or respond to a commonality of struggle against White supremacy, but more fundamentally it represents and reflects a commonality of culture of black people within the United States' (161). For many Black people, Prince represented the ability to explore the limitless spectrum of Black identity while still being rooted in Black culture. From his sound, dress, mannerisms and use of Black vernacular language to the people and organizations he chose to support, arguably no Black artist who achieved Prince's level of mainstream crossover success simultaneously modelled Black individuality and a connection to the Black community the way he did. Hall reflects, 'Seeing a strong, unapologetically black man direct an audience of thousands and ultimately, my heart, made it clear that being yourself could take you further than being an approximation of someone else' (Hall). Prince demonstrated that a Black person could experience cultural multiplicity while being one's authentic self – a self not prescribed by restrictive notions of Blackness. Acknowledging this aspect of Prince's legacy is essential for understanding his work and cultural impact.

The thought leader

Long before the concept of thought leadership gained traction, Prince proved himself as an innovator in his field. Llopis asserts that thought leadership 'introduce[s] new ways of thinking that will reinvent industries and significantly impact business models'. Additionally, thought leaders are identified as those who 'tend to be the most successful individuals in their fields' (Prince and Rogers). They are 'trusted sources who move and inspire people with innovative ideas [and] turn ideas into reality' (Brosseau). From his art to his business practices, Prince did not balk at thwarting convention to try what others dared not. Not surprisingly, he was often so forward thinking that it took others times to grasp his vision. Musically, Prince disregarded established musical categories to craft a distinct, highly influential signature sound. However, his innovation was not limited to his music.

Prince was a thought leader who disrupted conventional business models. Prior to the advent of compact discs, he was maverick in the ways he used the B-side single to release new music, increase sales and avoid parental advisory censorship (Sexton). He was a pioneer in adopting the internet as a medium for distributing and promoting music and concerts as well as for connecting with fans. With *Crystal Ball* (1998) he became the first major artist to independently release a full album online (Espana). Additionally, he broke new ground by brokering one-off album distribution deals with major labels, bundling albums with concert ticket sales and giving away new albums as newspaper covermounts (Espana). His creative business strategies upended traditional practices. Some of his innovations that were initially frowned upon have become commonplace.

Of Prince's numerous demonstrations of thought leadership in the music industry, perhaps none is more significant than his epic battle with Warner Bros. Records (WB) – a task he approached 'with devastating foresight' (Espana). Prior to making the unprecedented move of becoming the world's biggest independent artist, Prince released eighteen original full-length albums with WB from 1978 to 1996. However, frustrated by his lack of ownership of his master recordings and the limitations of conventional methods for distributing and promoting music, Prince waged an historic public battle in the 1990s to be released from his WB contract so he could record, release and own his music on his terms. This salient fight revolutionized the music industry and made the topic of intellectual property rights a cultural talking point. Former Prince attorney Gary Stiffelman points out, '[Prince] drew attention to the issue of artists controlling their own destiny ... and he furthered the message as much or more than anyone ... . This truly was a cause, not just "I want to make more money"' (qtd in Newman). *Rolling Stone* magazine editor Joe Levy observes, 'All of the stuff that happens in the 1990s, you look back on it and you think, this guy is a pioneer. ... Now it is not unusual to find an indie artist saying they want to remain indie to keep control of their music or to see a veteran artist suing a label for copyrights, but at [that] time Prince led the charge' (Espana).

The transformational leader

As transformational leaders seek to transform their worlds, they also seek to transform their followers. 'There is a tacit promise to followers that they will be transformed in some way, perhaps to be more like [the] amazing leader. In some respects, then, the followers are the product of the transformation' (Changing Works). Cassandra O'Neal, a former Prince keyboardist, exemplifies this aspect of Prince's leadership. 'He had this gift of being able to see things in people that they didn't see themselves. He brought out certain things that were already there, but that we hadn't discovered or hadn't tapped into' (qtd in Murray). Former drummer Cora Coleman Dunham echoes, 'He invested his time, talent, genius and energy toward my growth and evolution' (qtd in Carr). Prince not only shunned limiting social constructs to realize his potential, but also implored others to do the same.

An analysis of Prince's songs reveals that many are written as conversations with the listener. He often communicated his ongoing personal evolution through his lyrics in an attempt to inspire his followers to embark on their own journeys towards self-actualization. In his role as a transformational leader, Prince acted as the 'role model that [his] followers [sought] to emulate' (MSG Experts). Ransom reflects, 'Prince had become a part of my world. ... I was just beginning to explore my feelings, who I was, what I wanted from my relationships and from life ... exploring Prince's art through journaling, I came to identify with Prince as the consummate craftsman in self-expression' (462). Like Ransom, Prince followers from all walks of life have penned countless tributes that speak to his transformative impact on their lives.

Trust and respect are essential elements of transformational leadership. One way that these leaders gain the trust of their followers is by privileging their needs even to the sacrifice of the leader (MSG Experts). In this regard, Prince also demonstrates transformational leadership. He stated, 'All people care about nowadays is getting paid, so they try to do just what the audience wants them to do. I'd rather give people what they need rather than just what they want' (qtd in Hilburn). Prince was consistent in this throughout his career. Whether he thought his followers needed to explore their ideas about spirituality, race, gender, love, sex, war, technology, politics or even their diets, he encouraged them to be introspective and to challenge themselves as much as they challenged the status quo.

To the chagrin of audiences and industry executives, there were times when Prince sacrificed his own status and sales in his commitment to his vision. His constant change of bands, sounds and styles reflected his ongoing musical and personal transformation. In that he even challenged notions of what it meant to be Prince. His refusal to capitulate to expectation, demonstrated another aspect of freedom for his followers – the freedom to transform. He explained, 'I don't know how any of us grow if we just … tread water. The idea is that we keep growing' (*Tavis Smiley Show*).

Transformational leaders create a consistent vision that they communicate to their followers with their charm, intellect and ability to inspire. Simonton argues, 'Personality is deeply ingrained in the phenomena of creativity and leadership' (61). He adds that 'to be charismatic is to possess some mysterious attribute that provides the foundation of exceptional influence, whether that influence is exerted in intimate interpersonal contacts or before immense crowds of people' (121). Prince's charisma and personality were legendary. However, he did not rely solely on superficial charm to influence his followers. Instead, he embodied his vision. McInnis observes, 'Prince's concentration on the individual would ultimately progress to a discourse on human evolution – how does one evolve to one's highest state?' (xxiv). As a transformational leader, Prince's steadfast commitment to his own evolution inspired many of his followers to follow suit.

The soulful leader

Deepak Chopra's spiritually based leadership framework theorizes that a leader is the 'symbolic Soul of a group who acts as a catalyst for change and transformation' (6). He asserts that icons 'don't mimic popular culture, they lead it; speak with a rebel's voice; and understand and target contradictions that fuel anxieties, desires, and imagination' (22). By this definition, Prince's status as an icon is indisputable. He was, indeed, a rebel who led pop culture by confronting its contradictions.

Chopra reasons that leaders who are innovators and visionaries understand the human needs of renewal, expression and upliftment (36). Understanding that Prince's quest for individual freedom evolved into a journey towards human evolution, we can see the importance of these human needs to his work. According to Chopra, a successful visionary makes his or her vision manifest in the world. Prince manifested his vision in myriad ways. However, one of his most notable manifestations is Paisley Park – the 65,000 square-foot home, studio and 'mythical creative sanctuary' that he opened in 1987. 'In every way, Paisley Park was the fulfillment of his creative desire to live and work in a space free from limitation. … In his words, "Paisley Park is pretty much representative of everything I am musically"' (Paisley Park). Prince immortalized Paisley Park in an eponymously titled song before he even built it.

McInnis explains, '[Paisley Park] represents looking inward to find one's place, peace, and self-determination' (McInnis Jr. 36). To further manifest his vision, Prince regularly invited followers to Paisley Park for intimate parties and concerts, allowing them to experience it as a physical reality.

Another significant aspect of Chopra's theory of soulful leadership is the spiritual connection between leaders and followers. He asserts that leaders and followers 'co-create each other, [forming] an invisible spiritual bond' (26). There is no denying the spiritual bond that connected Prince and his followers. It is one of the most unique relationships between an artist and his followers. Two aspects of Chopra's model of soulful leadership that are particularly relevant to this relationship are the assertions that soulful leaders look and listen using 'the instruments of the flesh, the heart, the mind, and the soul', and that they 'establish entrainment through emotional bonding' (Chopra 51-2). Entrainment refers to the synchronization of organisms. Tools Chopra suggests soulful leaders utilize to establish entrainment include love, compassion, gestures, facial expressions, vocal tone and playing music (Chopra 52). As such, it easy to see how Prince succeeded in this aspect of soulful leadership. He allowed his fans unprecedented access to his heart, mind, soul and even flesh by employing all of these tools. Having written nearly all the songs in his vast catalogue and played most of the instruments on them, Prince forged a profound spiritual connection to and between his followers. Letteri relates, 'I love meeting people who have the same connection to him as I do. … It's this beautiful thing we all share – we just get what he was about and what he wanted us to all feel' (qtd in Earp).

Prince's unique connection to his followers is highlighted by his reference to them as 'fam', short for family. This reference provides insight into Prince's view of his relationship with his core followers who were integral to his work. It reflects the symbiotic relationship where, as the 'symbolic soul of the group', he was as driven to create as his followers were to receive his creations. 'Followers exist to fuel the Leaders' vision from inside themselves (Chopra 26). 'Prince was searching for a fan base that wanted to be challenged both by music and by subject matter' (McInnis Jr. xv). When the ephemeral fancy of mainstream audiences faded, Prince found his 'fam', and they formed a soulful connection wherein all were challenged through his art to become better versions of themselves. Describing his audience, Prince stated:

> They're so sophisticated, they almost expect me to do the unexpected, and that gives me a lot of room to challenge myself as well as them … from the beginning, as I was coming into my own persona and understanding of who I was, I never talked down to my audience. And when you don't talk down to your audience, they can grow with you, and I give them a lot of credit to be able to hang with me this long because I've gone through a lot of changes, but they've allowed me to grow, and thus we can tackle some serious subjects and try to just be better human beings, all of us. (*Tavis Smiley Show*)

One final aspect of soulful leadership is 'harmonizing the masculine and the feminine' (Chopra 72). 'Prince was not only unwilling to accept boundaries of race, he seemed unwilling to countenance societal divisions between sexuality and divinity or between masculine and feminine' (Woodworth 24). Prince harmonized the masculine and the feminine visually with his gender-fluid style aesthetic, vocally by employing his vocal range from the highest falsetto to the lowest bass and lyrically through his disregard for gendered depictions of the human experience. Singer Kimbra reveals, 'Prince, entirely changed the way I make, listen, think and feel about music. ... He rode the line between masculine and feminine, unveiling characters we recognized in ourselves' (Kimbra).

Although there are endless examples of Prince harmonizing the masculine and feminine, one of the greatest exemplars is the song 'If I Was Your Girlfriend', where his observation of the closeness that women share as friends leads him to fantasize about being his lover's girlfriend. The song, which confounded many when it was first released in 1987, depicts a man who is willing to eschew heteronormative masculine behaviour to achieve a deeper level of intimacy with his lover. In both the song and his live performance of it in the concert film *Sign o' the Times*, Prince seamlessly harmonizes masculinity and femininity in his vocals, physical movements and appearance. A further example of Prince's harmonizing of the masculine and the feminine is the symbol he adopted as his name and logo, which combines the Mars and Venus gender symbols.

The servant leader

Prince said, 'Compassion is an action word with no boundaries.' He added, 'it's obvious that the world has problems, but doing nothing about it is foolish' (Shemo 83). From *Dirty Mind* (1980) to *HITnRUN Phase Two* (2015), Prince's albums include songs that reflect his awareness of sociocultural issues and his desire to ameliorate them. Examples of this are found in such songs as 'Dolphin', 'Act of God', 'Count the Days' and 'Money Don't Matter 2 Night'. However, Prince did not stop at singing about issues. His role as a servant leader is visible in his prodigious philanthropy where he demonstrated his commitment to social justice by supporting organizations that embodied his vision to eradicate restrictions based on race, gender and socio-economic status.

Servant leadership is characterized by such traits as empathy, foresight, awareness, healing and building community. Humility is also considered an important aspect of servant leadership (Mosaic 3–4). As an effective servant leader, Prince acknowledged his limitations. His humility allowed him to call on others to help him manifest his vision. He forged relationships with important Black political activists and thought leaders such as Dick Gregory, Cornell West, Tavis Smiley and Van Jones to help address issues afflicting the Black community. Jones reveals, 'Just like [Prince] had a whole roster of musicians, he had a whole roster of intellectuals, a whole roster of political activists, a whole roster of change-makers ... . Just like he was a bandleader on the musical side, he was a bandleader on the social side' (Jones). This revelation is significant because 'servant leaders are not afraid to share their authority with others to achieve a common goal' (Mosaic 3).

Prince was seemingly as prolific in his work as a servant leader as he was in creating music. Evans points out, 'Prince left a memory that stretched far beyond his music. His generous but private giving, social activism and thoughtful philanthropic efforts touched the lives of many.' A snapshot of the organizations and individuals Prince supported financially reveals areas including the arts, education, technology and the environment. He supported people, who like himself, challenged the status quo and were innovators and visionaries in their fields. Some of his most substantial donations were to schools created by radical Black educators including Marva Collins, Eric Mahmoud and Geoffrey Canada (Cheaney; Brown; Evans; Ives); he helped fund Van Jones's Yes We Code and Green for All organizations that are aimed at increasing technology and food access to minority youth; and he was one of the first financial backers of the Black Lives Matter movement (Evans; Garza). Additionally, through his Love4OneAnother charity and other efforts he extended his charitable work worldwide. Considering his substantial philanthropic efforts, Prince meets another criterion for servant leadership – generosity. According to Minister Louis Farrakhan, whose Million Man March Prince financially supported, 'The essence of his being, in the way Prince gave to others, serviced others through his gifts and skills was a thing of beauty' (Farrakhan).

Conclusion

Simonton asserts, 'Creative geniuses can sometimes afford to be misunderstood by contemporaries … [l]eaders by contrast, must achieve greatness in their own lifetimes or else fall into permanent oblivion' (46). He expounds that this is based on the idea that unpublished or unperformed works can be discovered and appreciated after death but this is not the case for movements or battles. Prince certainly achieved greatness in his lifetime. And while it is true that for many years to come people will discover Prince's undeniable creative genius through the unparalleled body of work he created, many will also discover that Prince was, indeed, a leader. By blending leadership styles to manifest his vision of freedom, self-determination, equality, love and compassion, Prince influenced many to do the same. Beyond his impressive artistic contribution to the world, Prince led people to lead themselves and he financially supported those who led others. By virtue of these achievements, he was a leader whose influence extended beyond his art. In the song 'Pope' (1993), Prince quips that between the positions of president and pope, he'd assume the latter given the measure of influence the position carries. However, leaders are not bound by position. In the final analysis, it matters not that he was neither president nor pope because he was Prince – a new breed leader.

Works cited

Bartleet, Larry. '21 Artists That Wouldn't Be the Same Without Prince'. 22 Apr. 2016. Web. 11 May 2019. https://www.nme.com/blogs/nme-blogs/14-artists-that-wouldnt-be-the-same-without-prince-767323.

Brosseau, Denise. 'Thought Leadership Lab'. n.d. Article. 26 Jan. 2017.
Brown, Curt. 'Harvest Prep Founder Engineers School Success'. 24 Mar. 2012. Web. 27 May 2019.
Burdett, John O. 'Leadership in Change and the Wisdom of a Gentleman'. *Participation and Empowerment: An International Journal* (1999): 5–14. Article.
Carr, Keiara. 'Spotlight: Queen Cora Dunham, GearFest'. 16 June 2016. Web. 26 Feb. 2018. http://www.journalgazette.net/entertainment/music/Spotlight--Queen-Cora-Dunham--GearFest-13575014.
Changing Works. 'Transformational Leadership'. 2002–2016. Article. Web. 15 May 2017. http://changingminds.org/disciplines/leadership/styles/transformational_leadership.htm.
Cheaney, Janie B. 'Marva Collins Did It Her Way'. 6 July 2015. Web. 27 May 2019.
Chopra, Deepak. *The Soul of Leadership*. 2002. Presentation.
Cummings, Kamilah. 'One that Deserves a Copy Made: Prince & "New Black" Masculinity in 1989'. *Prince Batdance Symposium*. Atlanta, 2019. Presentation.
Du Bois, W. E. B. *The Souls of Black Folk*. New York: Dover Publications, 1903. Book.
Earp, Joseph. The Death of Prince, One Year Later: What Fan Culture Means in 2017'. 26 Apr. 2017. Web. 27 May 2019. https://thebrag.com/the-death-of-prince-one-year-later-what-fan-culture-means-in-2017/.
Evans, Kelley D. '7 Ways Prince Gave Back'. 27 July 2016. Web. 27 May 2019, 2016.
Farrakhan, Minister Louis. 'Prince—The Essence of Beauty'. 3 May 2016. Web. 11 May 2019. https://www.noi.org/prince-tribute/.
Garza, Alicia. 'Prince Rogers Nelson by Alicia Garza', 2016. http://prince.blacklivesmatter.com/prince-rogers-nelson-by-alicia-garza/.
Hall, Terryn. 'When I Saw Prince, I Saw a Vital New Black Masculinity'. 23 Apr. 2016. Article. Web. 10 May 2019. https://www.theguardian.com/commentisfree/2016/apr/24/prince-vital-new-black-masculinity.
Henderson, Errol. 'Still Walters Runs Deep: Synthesizing Ronald Walters' Theses on Black Leadership and Black Nationalism'. *What Has This Got to Do with the Liberation of Black People?: The Impact of Ronald W. Walters on African American Thought and Leadership*. Ed. Robert C. Smith, Cedric Johnson, and Robert G. New. New York: State University of New York Press, 2014. 159–85.
Hilburn, Robert. 'The Renegade Prince'. *LA Times*, 21 Nov. 1982. Web.
Italie, Leanne. 'Nearly 6 Months Later, Prince Superfans Are Still Mourning'. 12 Oct. 2016. Oct. 2016. https://www.bostonglobe.com/arts/music/2016/10/12/nearly-months-later-prince-superfans-are-still-mourning/1X10g8q4Mnapqi3ZLFgNUN/story.html.
Ives, Brian. 'Prince's Secret Charitable Efforts Highlighted in New Mini-Doc'. 13 Nov. 2016. http://news.radio.com/2016/11/13/prince-secret-charitable-efforts-mini-doc/.
Jones, Van. 'Prince, the Secret Philanthropist: "His Cause Was Humanity"'. 25 Apr. 2016. Article. Web. 7 May 2017. http://www.rollingstone.com/music/news/prince-the-secret-philanthropist-his-cause-was-humanity-20160425.
Kimbra. 'Reflections on Prince (The Beautiful One)'. 22 Apr. 2016. Web. 12 May 2019. https://kimbramusic.tumblr.com/post/143251121609/reflections-on-prince-the-beautiful-one.

Llopis, Greg. 'Thought Leadership Is the New Strategy for Corporate Growth'. 18 Aug. 2014. Article. Web. 14 May 2017. https://www.forbes.com/sites/glennllopis/2014/08/18/thought-leadership-is-the-new-strategy-for-corporate-growth/2/#be9d3126f4de.

Long, Stephanie. 'Purple Reign: How the World's First Academic Conference Devoted to Prince Reclaimed His Blackness'. 7 June 2017. Web. 12 May 2019. https://cassiuslife.com/6211/prince-academic-conference-england/.

McInnis Jr., and C. Leigh. *The Lyrics of Prince Rogers Nelson*. Jackson: Psychadelic Literature, 2000 [1995]. Book.

Mosaic. 'Leadership'. n.d. *Mosaic Projects*. White Paper. 13 May 2017. http://www.mosaicprojects.com.au/WhitePapers/WP1014_Leadership.pdf.

MSG Experts. 'Transformational Leadership Theory'. n.d. Article. 15 May 2017. http://www.managementstudyguide.com/transformational-leadership.htm.

Murray, Nick. 'The Wisdom of Prince, as Told by His Collaborators'. 27 Apr. 2016. Web. 6 Aug. 2017.

Neal, Mark Anthony. 'When a Race Man's Color Is Purple'. 23 May 2016. https://www.ebony.com/entertainment/prince-philanthropy-causes/.

New Power Generation. 'Count the Days'. *Exodus*. By Prince Rogers Nelson. Chanhassen, 1995. mp3.

Newman, Melinda. 'Inside Prince's Career-Long Battle to Master His Artistic Destiny'. 28 Apr. 2016. Web. 24 May 2019. https://www.billboard.com/articles/news/cover-story/7348551/prince-battle-to-control-career-artist-rights.

Nolfi, Joey. 'Prince Dead: Relive Singer's 2004 Rock and Roll Hall of Fame Induction'. 21 Apr. 2016. Web. 26 May 2019.

Paisley Park. 'About Paisley Park Studios'. 2019. Web. 27 May 2019.

Perry, Twila. 'Prince: double-consciousness in expressing the value of work'. *Howard Journal of Communications* (2019): 202–210. Journal article.

Potts, Annie K. 'The Intersectional Influences of Prince: A Human-Animal Tribute'. *Animal Studies Journal* (2016): 152–186. Journal Article.

Prince. 'Act of God'. *20Ten*. By Prince Rogers Nelson. Chanhassen, 2010. mp3.

Prince. 'Avalanche'. *One Nite Alone*. By Prince Rogers Nelson. Minneapolis, 2001. Compact Disc.

Prince. 'Black Muse'. *HITnRUN Phase Two*. By Prince Rogers Nelson. Chanhassen, 2015. mps.

Prince. 'Breakfast Can Wait'. *Art Official Age*. By Prince Rogers Nelson. Chanhassen, 2013. mp3.

Prince. 'Controversy'. *Controversy*. By Prince Rogers Nelson. Minneapolis, 1981. mp3.

Prince. 'Days of Wild'. *Crystal Ball*. By Prince Rogers Nelson. Chanhassen, 1998. mp3.

Prince. 'Dear Mr. Man'. *Musicology*. By Prince Rogers Nelson. Chanhassen, 2004. mp3.

Prince. 'Dolphin'. *The Gold Experience*. By Prince Rogers Nelson. Chanhassen, 1995. mp3.

Prince. 'Don't Play Me'. *The Truth*. By Prince Rogers Nelson. Chanhassen, 1995. mp3.

Prince. 'Family Name'. *The Rainbow Children*. By Prince Rogers Nelson. Chanhassen, 2001. mp3.

Prince. 'Free Urself'. By Prince Rogers Nelson. Chanhassen, 2015. mp3.

Prince. 'I Will'. *Chaos and Disorder*. By Prince Rogers Nelson. Chanhassen, 1996. mp3.

Prince. 'If I Was Your Girlfriend'. *Sign o' the Times*. By Prince Rogers Nelson. Minneapolis, 1987. mp3.

Prince. 'Money Don't Matter 2 Night'. *Diamonds and Pearls*. By Prince Rogers Nelson. Chanhassen, 1991. mp3.
Prince. 'Paisley Park'. *Around the World in a Day*. By Prince Rogers Nelson. Minneapolis, 1985. mp3.
Prince. 'Pope'. *The Hits / The B-Sides*. By Prince Rogers Nelson. Chanhassen, 1993. mp3.
Prince. 'Sexuality'. *Controversy*. By Prince Rogers Nelson. Minneapolis, 1981. mp3.
Prince. 'Slave'. *Emancipation*. By Prince Rogers Nelson. Chanhassen, 1995. mp3.
Prince. 'Tavis Smiley Show'. *Tavis Smiley*, 2004. Transcript.
Prince. 'Uptown'. *Dirty Mind*. By Prince Rogers Nelson. Minneapolis, 1980. mp3.
Prince, Russ Alan, and Bruce Rogers. 'What Is a Thought Leader'. 16 Mar. 2012. Article. 14 May 2017. https://www.forbes.com/sites/russprince/2012/03/16/what-is-a-thought-leader/#591dfb897da0.
Ransom, Kimberly C. 'A Conceptual Falsetto: Re-imagining Black Childhood Via One Girl's Exploration of Prince'. *Journal of African American Studies* (2017): 461–99. Journal.
Sexton, Adam. 'Cool As the Other Side of the Record: The B-Sides...and Beyond'. *Prince Batdance Symposium*. Atlanta, 2019. Presentation.
Shemo, Catherine Censor. 'A Prince of a Guy'. *Vegetarian Times*, October 1997: 79–83. Article.
Simonton, Dean Keith. *Geniuses, Creativity, and Leadership*. Cambridge: Harvard University Press, 1984. Book.
Slave Trade: How Prince Re-Made The Music Business. Directed by Elio Espana, 2014. DVD.
Szasz, Thomas Stephen. *Words to the Wise: A Medical-Philosophical Dictionary*. Piscataway: Transaction, 2004. Book.
Thrasher, Steven W. 'Prince Broke All the Rules about What Black American Men Should Be'. 21 Apr. 2016. Web. 10 May 2019.
Whiteneir Jr., Kevin Talmer. 'Dig If You Will the Picture: Prince's Subversion of Hegemonic Black Masculinity, and the Fallacy of Racial Transcendence'. *Howard Journal of Communications* (2019): 1–15. Journal article.
Williams, James Gordon. 'Black Muse 4 U: Liminality, Self-Determination, and Racial Uplift in the Music of Prince'. *Journal of African American Studies* (2017): 296–319. Journal article.
Woodworth, Griffin Mead. *'Just Another One of God's Gifts': Prince, African-American Masculinity, and the Sonic Legacy of the Eighties*. Los Angeles: UMI Dissertation Publishing, 2008. Book.

15

'Microchip in your neck'

Prince's 'War'

Zack Stiegler

In July of 1998, Prince unceremoniously released the twenty-six-minute track 'The War'. Edited down from a forty-five-minute performance at Paisley Park a month earlier, Prince first posted the song to his Love4OneAnother website as a RealAudio file. In the following weeks, a cassette of the recording was issued as a mea culpa for fans following the botched rollout of the *Crystal Ball* CD set by Prince's 1-800-NEW-FUNK mail order service (Nilsen et al. 224, 226).[1] The track arrived without fanfare, and remained little more than a curiosity among the most ardent collectors of Prince's musical output. Yet 'The War' is singular in the context of Prince's oeuvre, a lengthy, abstract exegesis reflective of junctures both in Prince's personal and professional lives, as well as in the larger cultural moment. 'The War' is also one of Prince's most topical lyrics, taking aim at HIV/AIDS, the 1997–8 Asian financial crisis, the horrific June 1998 dragging murder of James Byrd Jr. in Texas, racial injustice and an overall diminishing faith in government. This litany of social, cultural and political ills paints a dire picture of America at the end of the millennium, a stark contrast to the dance-in-the-face-of-apocalypse attitude of '1999'.

In this chapter, I consider 'The War' through the lens of these coinciding moments: In relation to Prince's personal and artistic transition of the late 1990s, as well as the cultural anxieties that emerged as we inched towards the twenty-first century. More importantly, I also read 'The War' through its racial dimensions, with close attention paid to the ways in which the piece plays utopic and dystopic strains of Afrofuturism against each other to stage a broader social commentary.

Background

Reflecting on the song six years after its release, the editors of *Uptown* magazine described 'The War' as a piece that 'contains little melody, [but] is in many respects more risky and adventurous than just about anything else Prince released during the '90s' (Nilsen et al. 41). Indeed, 'The War' is one of the more challenging recordings in

Prince's catalogue, with lyrics that are among his most straightforwardly political and evangelical.

Throughout its twenty-six minutes, 'The War' centres around a repeated crowd chant of 'One, two / the evolution will be colorized', a refrain of sorts that provides the foundation for Prince's appraisal of American culture at the close of the twentieth century. The phrase itself is a modified referent to Gil Scott-Heron's 'The Revolution Will Not Be Televised' (1970/1971),[2] an allusion that provides an initial indication that 'The War' operates through a racial framework. In Heron's piece, the titular refrain serves as a commentary on popular media, politics and conspicuous consumption as distractions from and limiters of agency, citizen action, protest and social movement towards racial justice. 'The War' makes similar references to mass media (lyrically represented by 'Saturday morning cartoons') as distractions from our social and political surroundings, a point to which I will return. The use of 'colorized' accentuates the chant's racial implications, a point made explicit via an inscription on the back cover of a limited promotional CD of 'The War'. The stanza reiterates that 'the evolution will be colorized', and is offset by a final line of text printed in mirror image that when reversed to right reading, adds, 'Why do u think they call it race?'

Also worth noting here is that throughout his career, Prince intentionally assembled bands comprised of diverse gender and ethnic identities (Touré 98–101). The incarnation of Prince's New Power Generation (NPG) band featured on 'The War' is comprised entirely of Black musicians: Kirk Johnson (drums), Marva King (vocals), Morris Hayes (keyboards), Mike Scott (guitar) and Rhonda Smith (bass). As I have argued elsewhere, Prince occupied multiple sites of racial identity throughout his career, though for much of the 1990s, his performed racial identity is best described as strategic, allowing Prince to 'exercise agency by utilizing essentialism at a particular moment, for a particular purpose' (Stiegler 215). This remains true in 'The War', providing Prince with a platform from which to articulate his Afrofuturist critique.

Afrofuturism, technology and 'The War'

Although Mark Dery coined the term 'Afrofuturism' in 1994, he was giving name to themes expressed across a body of work that stretched back nearly half a century. Dery defines Afrofuturism as 'speculative fiction that treats African-American themes and addresses African-American concerns in the context of twentieth-century technoculture – and, more generally, African American signification that appropriates images of technology and a prosthetically enhanced future' (180). Womack supplements this concept to note that Afrofuturism often entails 'a total reenvisioning of the past and speculation about the future rife with cultural critiques' (209; see also A. Nelson 36).

Lynn Spigel skilfully articulates mid-century Afrofuturist work with dominant cultural narratives of the period. Most compellingly, Spigel discusses rampant discrimination and displacement of African Americans via housing policies, transportation discrimination, urban renewal and privileging of White mobility throughout mid-twentieth-century America. In contrast, Spigel argues that intergalactic Afrofuturist works including those of Sun Ra, Parliament Funkadelic and Lee 'Scratch' Perry served as counter-narratives that provided a shared diasporic identity, a sense of racial pride, a vision of progress in race relations and laying claim to outer space in light of what she refers to as the 'struggle over access to the spaces of everyday life' (Spigel 143, 145, 168–9, 173–4; see also Eshun 288).[3]

Afrofuturism typically manifests in its utopic strain, envisioning science and technology as means to a redemptive or emancipatory future for the historically oppressed.[4] The dystopic strain of Afrofuturism takes a more critical stance, however. For example, Eshun cautions us that 'Afrofuturism is by no means naively celebratory', while emphasizing that envisioning dystopic futures provides an equally valuable counterpoint to current social realities (297). Womack further argues that Afrofuturism engages an awareness that 'new technologies have emerged with a double-edged sword, deepening as many divides as they build social bridges' (36).

'The War' incorporates both utopic and dystopic strains of Afrofuturism, although it is the latter that dominates. While the lyrics cover an array of topics, the central theme describes a crumbling, resource-deficient dystopia in the not-too-distant future. Here, citizens are given opportunity escape to an underground metropolis paradise, at a cost: willing citizens must allow the government to implant a microchip into their neck to access the underground metropolis (New Power Generation).

'The War' takes up both technology and displacement; however, Prince subverts the Afrofuturist counter-narrative of space and technology as liberating. Instead, technology produces a false consciousness in 'The War'. Echoing critical theorists of the Frankfurt School, 'The War' depicts mass media as mere distractions from our social and political surroundings, and importantly, the larger project – the 'evolution' in question. Put another way, 'The War' presents a dystopic strain of Afrofuturism masquerading as utopic; the song offers a clear path to a seemingly better future via the resource-rich underground metropolis, but this paradise is merely a cover-up for the further exploitation and subjugation of Black identity via the 'microchip in your neck'.

The microchip serves as the state's price of admission to the underground metropolis, and draws on the futurist concept of transhumanism. Transhumanism considers the possibilities of merging technologies with the human body to extend life, perhaps indefinitely into what Womack calls 'a post-human life' (29). Some transhumanists explore how such convergence of the biological and the technological could enhance human life, though in the case of 'The War', Prince suggests that transhumanism could be used to exploit its subjects. To submit to the microchip is to surrender agency, privacy and, indeed, one's very identity. Importantly, at one point Prince specifically refers to a '*chocolate* microchip for your neck', again underscoring the song's racial perspective (emphasis added). 'The War' is thus at odds with the perceived benefits of technological advancement, and with typical Afrofuturist narratives of technology as emancipatory. Instead, technology and mass media blockade that progress and reaffirm existing power structures. In this view, media and technology reduce 'culture to technological capacity' and 'overlook the human body in favor of the machines they sit behind' (DeIuliis and Lohr 167, 170). Recalling Neil Postman's (1993) critique of a technopolistic culture, 'The War' cautions against an uncritical acceptance of technological innovation, noting that such developments may simply be used to reinforce rather than break down existing structures of domination.

However, 'The War' is not absent redemptive potential. While Afrofuturist works typically consider technology as 'tools capable for intervention within the current political dispensation', the intervention offered by 'The War' is divine rather than technological (Eshun 301). Prince in effect constructs a divide between God and country, favouring religion as the true redemptive path. Those who want access to the resource-rich utopia of the underground metropolis prioritize the state over God, or at the very least are indifferent to the state's usurpation of their identity and free will. Those who prioritize their faith in God over the state entrust their fate to him/her/it. In 'The War', this deference to God operates as an act of sociopolitical resistance, the means by which individuals can stand against and be liberated from groupthink, governmental exploitation and the false consciousness of technology and mass media.

Moreover, prioritizing God over country underscores where Prince was in his own spiritual journey at the time he recorded 'The War'. For much of the preceding year, Prince traversed the country on his Jam of the Year tour, joined by Larry Graham and Graham Central Station. One of Prince's major musical influences since childhood, Graham also became something of a spiritual mentor to Prince, engaging in Bible study, discussion and tutelage of the Jehovah's Witness faith, of which Graham was an adherent, and to which Prince eventually converted in 2001 (Hahn 220–22, 243; Greenman 138). As the tour progressed, elements of this spiritual awakening shaped Prince's performance, from eliminating or modifying his most salacious material to incorporating teachings of the Jehovah's Witness faith into his concerts. In a particularly noteworthy example, Prince reworked 1987's 'The Cross' as 'The Christ', as in a performance at the Essence Awards in 1998. In front of a screen reading 'STAUROS: A WOODEN STAKE OR POLE', Prince addressed the theatre and the televised audience: 'Stauros. By definition a wooden stake driven into the ground used to cause torture or death. Stauros. Perhaps someone lied about the way someone died' ('The Christ'). Prince and the NPG then launched into a revamped version of 'The Cross/Christ', refashioned as a duet between Graham and Prince.[5] 'The War' stands as Prince's first recorded output to express this newfound shift in spirituality, a sentiment that would be expressed more directly and more confidently in 2001's *The Rainbow Children*.

Prince's treatment of technology in 'The War' is complicated, contentious and even contradictory. As others have noted, Prince's relationship with technology was somewhat tumultuous (Shah; Thomas; Zarucky). He was quick to embrace and make innovative use of new technologies in the studio, a disposition that facilitated his commercial and creative emergence in the 1980s. For example, Prince's mastery in programming and playing of electronic instrumentation such as the Linn LM-1 drum machine, and his fluency on the Yamaha DX7, Oberheim OB8 and Fairlight synthesizers helped to form his signature sound, as well as what came to be known as 'the Minneapolis Sound' more generally. From the 1990s onward, Prince was often ahead of the curve in utilizing technology to engage with his audience while also circumventing traditional channels of music distribution. He was among the first pop artists to embrace the CD-ROM format with 1994's *Interactive* game; 1998's *Crystal Ball* collection employed the internet and mail order as an early means of direct distribution; from 2001 through 2006, his NPGMusicClub was among the first artist websites to provide streaming audio of new and archival music; and at least early on, he made use of websites and chatrooms as platforms to communicate with and engage his audience.

Despite his early embrace of the internet, however, Prince had a notoriously inconsistent web presence over the years, an ambivalence that culminated in his 2010 declaration that the internet is 'completely over' (Willis). Moreover, while he was quick to pursue the opportunities afforded by internet technology, he was also sceptical of the ways that these same technologies diminished his control over how his image and work were utilized.

Acting on these concerns, Prince became especially litigious from the 1990s onward. In 1999, Prince took legal action against Swedish fanzine *Uptown* for alleged copyright violations. In similar fashion, in 2007 he issued cease and desist letters to a series of fan-operated websites, seeking cessation of 'all use of photographs, images, lyrics, album covers and anything linked to Prince's likeness' (Prince Fans United 2007). Also in 2007, Prince and the Universal Music Group famously sued Stephanie Lenz, who posted a twenty-nine-second video of her infant son dancing to 'Let's Go Crazy'. Seven years later, Prince filed suit against twenty-two individual web users for $1 million each in damages for 'massive infringement and bootlegging' of audio and video recordings of his live performances dating back to 1983 (*Prince v Chodera* 2014). Prince withdrew this complaint twelve days after filing it, while the 1999 *Uptown* suit and the 2007 actions were ultimately settled out of court (Baym 2018, 114; Ellin 1999; Hahn 2003, 224–5). The Lenz suit did go to trial, with both the federal district and appellate courts ruling in favour of Lenz on the grounds of fair use (*Lenz v. Universal Music Corp* 2008; *Lenz v. Universal Music Corp* 2015).[6]

Throughout his career then, Prince's relationship with technology was fraught with tension. On the one hand, he was an enthusiastic early adopter, deploying new technologies to innovate in the studio, circumvent established norms of the music industry and to build a stronger sense of community with fans. At the same time, he often struggled to harness the internet's capabilities. This duality is present within and surrounding 'The War', embodying Prince's love–hate relationship with technology.

Within the text of 'The War', there's a distrust, and perhaps even a phobia, of new technology, as expressed via the surveillance microchip and the soporific effects of mass media. Yet in distributing the song, Prince utilized the accessibility and immediacy of the internet and streaming audio. In fact, 'The War' is in many ways indicative of Prince's positioning within the music industry in 1998, when digital audio on the web was in its nascency. A number of established artists, including the Beastie Boys, Billy Idol and Tom Petty, were reprimanded by their respective labels for posting MP3s of their then-current singles in 1998 and 1999 (C. Nelson 'Beastie Boys'; C. Nelson 'Downloadable'). Having recently severed ties with Warner Bros. Records after a very public dispute with the label, Prince was able to freely experiment with alternate methods of distribution. While not major commercial successes, Prince's early forays into online music distribution, including *Crystal Ball* and 'The War', earned him accolades as a pioneer. To that end, in 1999, 'The War' yielded Prince a *Yahoo Internet Life* award for 'Best Internet-Only Single'. In accepting the award, Prince cautioned against the internet: 'The one thing I want to say is, don't be fooled by the internet. It's cool to get on the computer, but don't let the computer get on you. It's cool to use the computer, but don't let the computer use you. You've all seen *The Matrix*. There's a war going on. The battlefield's in the mind. The prize is the soul' (qtd in Greenman 7). Alongside his newfound industry freedom and spiritual awakening, then, 'The War' is reflective of Prince's ambivalence towards technology, which he continued to grapple with until his death in 2016.

Conclusion

'The War' is one the most under-discussed compositions in Prince's catalogue. Book-length treatments of his life and work at best give the song a brief mention, although more often they ignore it completely. 'The War' also received little attention in the many commemorative magazines published after Prince's passing. Otherwise complete discographies in tribute issues including those from *Newsweek*, *Time*, *The Source* and Condé Nast make no mention of 'The War', even where they noted similarly limited releases such as *One Night Alone* (2002), *Xpectation* (2003), *The Slaughterhouse* (2004) and *The Chocolate Invasion* (2004). This journalistic neglect of 'The War' could be due to the song's relative obscurity, its limited availability on streaming platforms,[7] its twenty-six-minute runtime, the free-form experimentation of its music or the esoteric narrative of its lyrics. Despite this paucity of attention, however, 'The War' is a rich and fascinating text, even as it is challenging in content and form. It is Prince at his most political, his most evangelical and, in an abstract way, his most personal. Collectively, Prince's religious reawakening, his break from the corporate music industry and his relationship with a rapidly changing technological environment underscore that the late 1990s was a time of significant transition for Prince both personally and professionally.

The year 1998 found us at a cultural juncture as well. Technology was evolving at an unprecedented pace, the breadth and depth of its impact not immediately apparent. Cultural anxiety about the new online technological frontier reached fever pitch in 1998–9, when the impending Y2K glitch threatened the stability and security of digital networks as the date rolled over into the year 2000. Thus, 'The War' is certainly a product of its time, a direct response to, and commentary upon, the social, cultural and political moment, in addition to reflecting Prince's contemporaneous personal and professional dispositions.

At the same time, much of the song's lyrical content anticipates the cultural impact of technology in the early twenty-first century. 'The War' may not have been flawlessly prescient, but there's certainly something to be said for Prince's discussion of technological distraction, government surveillance and transhumanism well before the Fear of Missing Out (FOMO), the revelations of widespread NSA surveillance of US citizens and the development of medical nanotechnologies became part of the cultural discourse. Despite its dystopic outlook, 'The War' in this sense brings to mind Marshall McLuhan's claim that artists 'pick up the message of cultural and technological challenge decades before its transforming impact occurs', and that their art in turn is charged with helping to 'face the change that is at hand' (70).

Yet with Afrofuturism emerging as a coherent framework for understanding and analysing themes across disparate works, we are able to better situate 'The War' within an ongoing chronology of Black cultural expression. With its focus on media-as-distraction, new technological forms and their attendant false consciousness, the song extends the argument of 'The Revolution Will Not Be Televised', updating it for the then-bourgeoning digital age. This critique is uniquely emboldened by Prince's subversion of typical Afrofuturist narratives in popular music, presenting a utopic vision of the future only to confront it with a dystopic alternative as a warning about the perils of godless blind faith in government, mass media and technology. 'The War' clearly presents religious faith as an intervention in the cultural moment; along with that, however, the song advocates the exercise of a hyper-critical consciousness as the key to exercising agency and dismantling oppressive power structures, an argument that remains salient two decades later.

Notes

1. Advertised as a limited-edition release available only through Prince's mail order service, *Crystal Ball* met with several production and shipping delays. When the album was finally issued in early 1998, some fans were overcharged, received multiple copies or failed to have their orders filled. In addition, Prince struck a retail distribution deal for the set, diminishing *Crystal Ball*'s status as an exclusive release (Hahn 223).
2. Scott-Heron released alternate versions of 'The Revolution Will Not Be Televised' on each of his first two LPs, 1970's *Small Talk at 125th and Lenox* and 1971's *Pieces of Man*.
3. For a further discussion on the influence of Afrofuturism on Prince's work, see Chapter 3 in Hawkins and Niblock.
4. See for example Hazel 2012 and Womack.
5. Prince also alludes to this notion of stauros in 'The War' through the line, 'Claimin' God was backin' U on a cross, what a fool.'
6. The fair use statute is a provision of US copyright law that permits certain uses of copyrighted works without penalty (United States Code).
7. At press time, Tidal is the only platform to host a sanctioned stream of the song.

Works cited

Baym, Nancy. *Playing to the Crowd: Musicians, Audiences, and the Intimate Work of Connection*. New York, NYU Press, 2018.

'The Christ'. *The 1998 Essence Awards*, performance by Prince and the New Power Generation, Essence Television Production and Bob Bain Productions, 1998.

DeIuliis, David, and Jeff Lohr. 'Rewriting the Narrative: Communicology and the Speculative Discourse of Afrofuturism'. *Afrofuturism 2.0: The Rise of Astro-Blackness*. Ed. Reynaldo Anderson and Charles E. Jones, Lanham, Lexington Books, 2017. 167–84.

Dery, Mark. 'Black to the Future: Interviews with Samuel R. Delany, Greg Tate, and Tricia Rose'. *Flame Wars: The Discourse of Cyberculture*. Ed. Mark Dery, Durham, Duke University Press, 1994. 179–222.

Ellin, Abby. 'They're King-Size Issues, Whatever You Call Him'. *New York Times*, 21 Mar. 1999: 97.

Eshun, Kodwo. 'Further Considerations on Afrofuturism'. *CR: The New Centennial Review* 3.2 (2003): 287–302.

Greenman, Ben. *Dig If U Will the Picture: Funk, Sex, God, and Genius in the Music of Prince*. New York, Henry Holt Publishing, 2017.

Hahn, Alex. *Possessed: The Rise and Fall of Prince*. New York, Billboard Books, 2003.

Hawkins, Stan, and Sarah Niblock. *Prince: The Making of a Pop Music Phenomenon*. Farnham Surrey, Ashgate Publishing, 2011.

Hazel, Tempestt. 'Black to the Future Series: An Interview with D. Denenge Akpem'. *Sixty Inches from Center*, 23 July 2012. Web. 21 Apr. 2017. http://sixtyinchesfromcenter.org/archive/?p=16638.

Lenz v. Universal Music Corp. '572 F. Supp. 2d 1150'. *Northern District of California*, 2008.

Lenz v. Universal Music Corp. '801 F.3d 1126'. *Ninth Circuit Court of Appeals*, 2015.

McLuhan, Marshall. *Understanding Media: The Extensions of Man*. New York, McGraw-Hill, 1964.

Nelson, Alondra. 'Introduction'. *Future Texts* 20 (2002) 1–15.

Nelson, Chris. 'Beastie Boys, Billy Idol Mp3s Pulled from Web'. *Mtv.com*, 23 Dec. 1998. 17 July 2017. http://www.mtv.com/news/510420/beastie-boys-billy-idol-mp3s-pulled-from-web/.

Nelson, Chris. 'Downloadable Tom Petty Single Pulled from "mp3.com" site'. *MTV.com*, 11 March 1999. Web. 16 May 2017. http://www.mtv.com/news/512759/best-of-99-downloadable-tom-petty-single-pulled-from-mp3com-site/.

New Power Generation. 'The War'. [Audio cassette]. *NPG Records*, 1998.

Nilsen, Per, J. Mattheij, and Uptown Staff. *The Vault: The Definitive Guide to the Musical World of Prince*. Linghem, Uptown, 2004.

Postman, Neil. *Technopoly: The Surrender of Culture to Technology*. New York, Vintage Books, 1993.

'Prince Fans Fight Back against Attacks'. *Archive.org*, 5 Nov. 2007. Web. 23 May 2019. web.archive.org/web/20080509073719/http://www.princefansunited.com/pfu_press_release.pdf.

Prince v. Chodera. 'No. 14-273-EDL'. *Northern District of California*, 2014.

Scott-Heron, Gil. 'The Revolution Will Not Be Televised'. *Small Talk at 125th and Lenox*, Flying Dutchman/RCA, 1970.

Scott-Heron, Gil. 'The Revolution Will Not Be Televised'. *Pieces of a Man*, Flying Dutchman/RCA, 1971.

Shah, Hasit. 'Poor Lonely Computer: Prince's Misunderstood Relationship with the Internet'. *NPR.com*, 8 Mar. 2016. Web. 17 July 2017. http://www.npr.org/sections/therecord/2016/03/08/469627962/poor-lonely-computer-princes-misunderstood-relationship-with-the-internet.

Spigel, Lynn. *Welcome to the Dreamhouse: Popular Media and Postwar Suburbs.* Durham, Duke University Press, 2001.
Stiegler, Zack. 'Slave 2 the System: Prince and the Strategic Performance of Slavery'. *Journal of Popular Music Studies* 21.2 (2009): 213–239.
Thomas, Matt. 'From Counterculture 2 Cyberculture and Back Again'. *IASPM-US Annual Conference*, 24 Mar. 2012, NYU, New York, NY.
Touré. *I Would Die 4 U: Why Prince Became an Icon.* New York, Atria Books, 2013.
United States Code. Title 17, U.S. Government Publishing Office, 2017. Web. 23 May 2019. https://www.govinfo.gov/content/pkg/USCODE-2017-title17/html/USCODE-2017-title17.htm.
Willis, Peter. 'Prince: World Exclusive Interview'. *Daily Mirror*, 5 July 2010. Web 5 May 2017. http://www.mirror.co.uk/celebs/news/2010/07/05/prince-world-exclusive-interview-peter-willis-goes-inside-the-star-s-secret-world-115875-22382552/.
Womack, Ytasha. *Afrofuturism: The World of Black Sci-Fi and Fantasy Culture.* Chicago, Chicago Review Press, 2013.
Zarucky, James. 'Strange Relationship: Prince's Love/Hate Approach Towards Digital Technology and the Internet'. *Purple Reign: An Interdisciplinary Conference on the Life and Legacy of Prince*, 26 May 2017, University of Salford, Salford, UK.

16

Prince

Conscious and strategic representations of race

Twila L. Perry

Introduction

While many articles in the media have described Prince as an artist who traversed boundaries of music genre, gender and race, there has been little in-depth exploration of Prince's relationship to the issue of race. Indeed, media treatment of Prince has often suggested that race was not important to him or that somehow he had 'transcended' race.

This chapter argues that rather than being 'transcended', race was a factor of central importance throughout Prince's life and career. At important junctures in his life and career, Prince made conscious and strategic choices in his representation of race that reflected issues and dilemmas of both historical and contemporary relevance in the lives of many African Americans. The same issues continue to be reflected in ongoing discussions in academic discourses about race in the law and in other disciplines.

While there are many situations and incidents in Prince's life and career that offer insight into the ways that he consciously and strategically made choices about the representation of race, this chapter will examine Prince's actions at two major junctures in his career. In the earliest years of his rising fame, the early 1980s, the media often celebrated Prince as a kind of 'post-racial' icon, sometimes describing him as biracial. Prince himself contributed to the confusion about his racial identity – a conscious and strategic response to the racialized structure of the recording industry of that time. The chapter will then discuss Prince's extended dispute in the 1990s with Warner Bros. over his record contract. Again, Prince engaged in conscious and strategic representations of race, although in a way that was very different from his public approach to race in the prior decade. During the dispute with Warner Bros., Prince compared record contracts to slavery, changed his name to an unpronounceable symbol and began to perform with the word 'SLAVE' written across his face.

Prince's actions in representing race as he did, while not always consistent, can be viewed as reactions, both practical and emotional, to the treatment of African Americans and as a conscious decision to connect with issues relevant to the past and the present of that group. Racial identity, the relevance of slavery, the political significance of naming, and symbolic and practical representations of the Black body are issues underlying Prince's actions and continue to be subjects of active debate in scholarship addressing the intersection of race and the law with issues of hierarchy, economic exploitation and cultural power in American society.

Transcending race

During his career, and after his death, the view has often been expressed that Prince was an artist who transcended race. For example, at the time of his death, the *New York Times* stated that Prince was 'a unifier of dualities – racial, sexual, musical and cultural ... transcending them in his career' (Pareles, 'Prince: An Artist'). A popular Minneapolis news site stated that 'Prince transcended race and taught fans that their lives could be more than what they thought' (CNN Wire). Such statements are representative of the many articles over the years that have expressed the opinion that Prince transcended race.

An important initial question is: What does it mean to 'transcend' race? Definitions of 'transcend' tend to employ words and phrases such as 'to rise above' or 'to exceed the limits of' or 'to be greater than' or 'to be stronger than' or 'to surpass' (*Merriam-Webster Dictionary*; *Merriam-Webster Thesaurus*). It is likely that not all writers who have used the word 'transcend' have had the exact same definition in mind. However, there does seem to be a common understanding that the word suggests that to transcend a status is positive rather than negative and that the context the individual has transcended is inferior to the new context. Thus, statements that Prince transcended race seem to reflect the view that transcending race is superior to having a specific racial identity. The suggestion seems to be that it is somehow better for Prince to have transcended race than for him to have viewed himself and to have been viewed by others as an African American.

Prince and critical scholarship about race

Prince's actions in relationship to race reflect a number of themes that are often addressed in the recent legal scholarship movement known as critical race theory. While there is probably no one definition of critical race theory with which everyone would agree, there is likely general agreement that it is an approach that seeks to address issues at the intersection of race and the law in ways that delve behind formal legal rules and doctrines. Critical race theory has been described as a movement that 'challenges the ways in which race and power are constructed and represented in American legal culture and, more generally, in American society as a whole' (Crenshaw, at xiii, xiii).

Critical race scholarship often asks questions about the limitations of the law to deal with the realities of the Black experience and the realities of racism. For example, formal analysis of civil rights law might address critical issues such as voting, employment, housing discrimination or educational opportunity in terms of the need for changes in legislation or changes in the ways judges have interpreted legislation or legal concepts. A critical race analysis would go beyond analysis of the formal legal rules to examine ways in which even formal legal equality is insufficient to address more subtle issues of cultural hegemony, subordination and power relationships.

Thus, issues concerning Prince's racial identity reflect ongoing issues in critical race scholarship about legal and social definitions of race, about the political and societal consequences of individuals choosing their own racial identification, as well as issues of hierarchy based on racial features of people of colour. Prince's analogy between record contracts and slavery resonates with critical race scholarship addressing the limitations of contract law to address issues of economic exploitation. Prince's name change resonates with critical race legal scholarship concerning the relationship of names to questions of power and cultural hierarchy. Finally, Prince's performing and appearing in public with 'SLAVE' scrawled across his face resonates with the history of legally sanctioned abuses of the bodies of African Americans during slavery as well as discussions about the Black body today – as both an object of oppression and a space for expressions of liberation.

Conscious and strategic representations of race

Prince as a post-racial icon?

It is probably accurate to say that Prince's music transcended genre and racial lines. He was equally at home with rhythm and blues as with rock. It is clear from reported discussions that it was important to Prince from the earliest times in his career to have a band that was racially integrated (Dickerson 20). It has often been noted that Prince's concerts had some of the most racially diverse audiences. During the concerts, he often spoke about the need for all people to find common ground (Johnson). The lyrics to some of Prince's songs could certainly be read as expressing the belief that he wished that race did not matter. The fact that Prince became so closely associated with the colour purple could be argued to be further evidence that race was not important to him – perhaps purple could be a colour that unites us all.

In the early 1980s, when Prince first started to gain major acceptance in the White music world, numerous articles in the media celebrated him as a kind of post-racial icon. In a 1981 article, *New York Times* critic Robert Palmer stated, 'Prince himself transcends racial stereotyping because, as he once put it, "I never grew up in one particular culture"' (Palmer).The same article optimistically goes on to state, 'One suspects that as time goes on, more and more American pop will reflect a similar biracial orientation. If that's so, Prince's black-white synthesis isn't just a picture of what could be, it's a prophecy' (Palmer). After Prince's death, an obituary in the *Los Angeles Times* stated that Prince 'was our first post-everything pop star, defying categories of race, gender and commercial appeal' (Brown and Rotterberg).

During the early 1980s, articles in the media sometimes stated that Prince was biracial. In his 1984 review of *Purple Rain*, noted *New York Times* movie critic Vincent Canby wrote, 'Prince's background is ... mixed' (Canby). In the semi-autobiographical film, *Purple Rain*, Prince is depicted as being the child of an interracial marriage, with a White mother and a Black father.

There are statements Prince himself made in the early 1980s that contributed to the perception that he was biracial and that added to confusion about his racial identity. For example, there are reports of Prince describing himself as part Italian (Light 24). There are also reports that early in his career, Prince told those who had responsibility for promoting him not to state that he was Black (Wall 31).

In some of his early songs, there are lines that certainly suggest that Prince did not view race as important. In 'Controversy' there is the oft-quoted line: 'Am I Black or White?' (Prince). In another part of the same song, he sings, 'people call me rude, I wish we all were nude, I wish there was no Black and White, I wish there were no rules' (Prince).

An important point that is not in dispute, but needs clarification, is the fact that both of Prince's parents were Black (Toure 103). Although Prince was a person who would probably be described by most people as a light-skinned Black person, he was not someone who, in the current common understanding of the term 'biracial' in America, would be considered to be biracial, as that term is commonly understood to be an individual having parents of two different races (Perry 56–87). Realistically, an individual, no matter how light-skinned, with two Black parents, growing up in America in the 1970s, would not have self-identified as biracial and would not have been considered to be biracial by the larger society. Prince grew up in the north area of Minneapolis where many of the city's small populations of African Americans lived. Neither he nor any of the people in his community would have considered him to be anything other than an African American.

The question, then, is what motivated Prince to encourage confusion about his racial identity. The answer seems clear. Prince made conscious and strategic decisions about representing his racial identity as a response to his understanding of the reality of racism in the structure of the music industry at the time he was beginning his career.

In the late 1970s and early 1980s, the recording industry in the United States was very much structured along racial lines (Thorne 63–4). It would not be an exaggeration to describe the administration of the industry as essentially segregated. In record companies, Black artists were handled by a separate division and their music was not promoted to wider racial audiences. In the early 1980s, MTV, founded in 1981, was well known for not airing the videos of Black artists (Light 195). African American scholar Marc Anthony Neal has been widely quoted as stating that prior to Michael Jackson's iconic 'Thriller' video in 1982, MTV was 'the best example of cultural apartheid in the United States' (Alban). Prince, as a young, aspiring Black artist, was well aware of the racialized structure of the music industry. It is very likely that Prince generated confusion about his racial identity for practical reasons – in the hope of escaping having his music and his career pigeonholed in a racially segregated system. Prince sought to blur his racial identity in the early 1980s because he understood the realities of race in America.

Racial definitions in the United States

Prince's actions in the 1980s with respect to the issue of racial identity must be examined within the context of the long history of the significance of racial definitions in the United States. The issues raised by his actions in seeking to blur his racial identity at that time are still being explored and debated today in society and in academia.

Although both of his parents were African American, from his appearance it is clear that there is some racial mixture in Prince's background. But then again, there is some racial mixture in the past of many, if not most African Americans (Higginbotham 41). Most African Americans who have some racial mixture in their past still consider themselves simply to be African Americans rather than biracial individuals.

The United States is a country with a history of racial definitions embedded in the law (Haney Lopez), and those racial definitions have not only past but also present relevance. During slavery, under state laws, the status of a Black child was passed down through the mother in order to avoid children born of enslaved Black women and their White owners from being born free (Higginbotham 44, 128). Part of the troubling racial history of the United States is what is known as 'the one drop rule', which meant that any person whose biological heritage included African ancestry was considered to be Black. Black blood was considered to be a taint (Davis 5–6). Even long after slavery, racial definitions legally permeated many aspects of life, restricting, for example, the choice of marriage partners, where one could sit in a bus and which bathroom could be used in public places.

This kind of racial discrimination gave rise to the tactic of racial passing. Some Black people who believed that they could not be recognized as Black simply slipped over into the White world for the purpose of avoiding the burdens of being Black (Kennedy 281–338).

Prince did not attempt to 'pass' as a White person. Although he was light-skinned, he was not someone who Americans would look at and assume was White. What Prince sought to do in leading the press to believe that he was biracial was to 'pass' as biracial rather than 'pass' as White. This was a conscious and strategic choice to escape the pigeonholing of the segregated recording industry. In essence, Prince attempted to access what he probably considered to be the cultural power of a biracial identity – which he understood, in the American racial hierarchy, to have more cachet with White audiences than a monoracial identity, that is, simply being deemed to be Black. And, as troubling as the thought may be, his understanding did reflect what many researchers have demonstrated to be a reality of race in America – that many Whites do prefer African Americans who are biracial, or who appear to be biracial, to those who are not (Baynes 160).

In taking this action, Prince was responding to the racial context as it existed in the early years of his career. However, today, debates about the definition of race and the claiming of racial identity continue. Many scholars view race as a social construct rather than a biological reality. There is now a debate as to whether people who traditionally had been considered to be African Americans should and/or should be able to claim a biracial or a multiracial identity. Some view it as an inherent right of any individual to claim and define his or her own racial identity. They see the question of claiming a racial identity as simply a matter of personal choice. Others see the claiming of a biracial identity as potentially problematic in the struggle for racial equality because it separates African Americans into two different groups. Such a separation has implications for the ability to keep track of racial progress and has the potential for the groups to be pitted against each other. Today, even the much maligned 'one drop rule' is not without controversy. It has been argued that despite its racist origin, the 'one drop rule' kept African Americans as a unified group as they fought against racial discrimination and fought for racial equality in the civil rights era.

Prince's willingness to blur the line of racial identity in the early days of his career reflects long-standing issues in African American life. Both Black people in everyday life and academics continue to debate these concerns.

Representations of race in the Warner Bros. dispute

Even much later in his career, the themes of unity and people cooperating and caring for each other across racial lines were often present in Prince's songs and commentary during his concerts. His 2010 song, 'Compassion', contains the lyrics, 'Whatever skin you're in, we need to be friends, black, white and yellow, we can all be friends' (Prince). In a concert performance on 2 May 2015, he ended the performance of a song by stating, 'Take care of each other. Don't matter the color. We're all family' (Minsker).

Such recent pronouncements might seem to suggest that even later in his life, Prince did not think race mattered or believed that it should not matter. However, an examination of Prince's music as well as some of his actions in the 1990s and the early 2000s makes it clear that Prince took a very different public approach to race than he had in the early 1980s.

Prince signed his first recording contract with Warner Bros. in 1978, Prince remained with Warner for the next fourteen years, and in 1992, the parties entered into a new, major contract (Phillips, 'A King's Ransom'). Within a short time, however, the deal turned sour, primarily over differing views concerning the timing of record releases. Eventually, the disagreement escalated into a long and bitter battle ('Slave Trade'). During the course of the dispute, Prince engaged in a number of actions which some people viewed as bizarre, self-indulgent publicity stunts that hurt his career. Prince compared record contracts to slavery, he changed his name to an unpronounceable symbol and he began performing with the word 'SLAVE' written on his face. Rather than viewing these actions in a negative light, this chapter argues that in engaging in these actions, Prince was again addressing the issue of race in a manner that was both conscious and strategic. Again, the issues he raised concerning race are relevant to the past and present of African Americans and continue to be addressed by scholars, legal academics and others who write about race.

The contract

Many articles have sought to describe the terms of the 1992 contract between Prince and Warner Bros. While not all of the reports were completely consistent, a general picture of the contract terms did emerge.

While articles broadly described the contract as a deal for $100 million dollars, it seems that the contract was only potentially worth that amount. Prince was to receive a $10 million dollar advance per record and a royalty rate that has been reported variously as either 20 per cent or 25 per cent. However, this royalty rate would be received only if the previous album sold at least five million copies. It has been said that the reason for this royalty structure was to encourage Prince to devote more time and effort to each album and to promote those albums through videos, touring and the gradual release of singles, rather than releasing albums so frequently (Phillips, 'Just How Princely').

Prince soon became dissatisfied with the contract. It is undisputed that the controversy was not over the financial aspects of the contract. An incredibly prolific songwriter, Prince wanted to be able to release albums whenever he chose to, rather on a schedule determined by the record company (Pareles, 'A Re-Inventor'). Prince was also unhappy that the contract gave Warner Bros. ownership of his master tapes (Pareles, 'A Re-Inventor'). Master tapes are the original recordings of a piece of music and can have great economic value for the owner (Christman). Prince's battle with Warner Bros. was well publicized, controversial and financially costly to him (Ro). And in the end, he had to fulfil the contract – which he did, for the most part, by giving Warner songs he had written earlier but had never released.

Record contracts as slavery

At the time he signed the contract with Warner Bros. in 1992, Prince was a wealthy, successful entertainer. He had no shortage of bargaining power and was in a position to be represented by the best attorneys available. But independent of his personal situation, Prince's battle with Warner Bros. was significant because it drew a great deal of public attention to the issue of fairness in the contracts entered into by recording artists not in a similarly advantaged position. The battle also focused particular attention of the historical and contemporary exploitation of Black musicians. Prince focused on the issue of exploitation in these contexts by publicly comparing contracts between recording artists and record companies to slavery.

Contract negotiations in the recording industry are often between two parties who are not in the same structural position. Typically, the record company has a great deal of power, whereas the aspiring artist or any artist who is struggling to survive does not. Not surprisingly, this can result in a contract in which the artist is, or at least feels, disadvantaged.

Traditional principles of contract law do not account for many of the complexities in real-life contract transactions. Contract law generally does not recognize economic and social inequalities but instead assumes autonomous choice and self-sufficiency of the parties to the contract (Morant). Inequality and disparities in bargaining power between parties to a contract have long troubled some scholars of contract law who believe that the law needs to develop more sophisticated and realistic analyses of the importance of these factors. However, as of the present, a contract between a struggling artist and a company in the recording industry in which such disparities exist has little chance of being voided on the basis of such differences.

While it is likely true that many artists have been exploited by the music industry, there is a particularly grim history of exploitation and discrimination in the case of Black musicians (Kelley 6–23). It has been observed that 'the appropriation of the creative output of black creators for a long period of U.S. history parallels the pervasive subordination of blacks generally under color of law' (Greene 1183). Numerous scholars have explored the role of both contract law and copyright law in the subordination of Black musicians throughout American history in the contexts of blues, jazz, rock 'n' roll and other Black music traditions (Greene 1182; Chase; Kofsky 87; Tate).

Prince was aware of the history of the exploitation of Black recording artists by the record industry. It would not be unreasonable to assume that his knowledge of this particular history as well as that of slavery and discrimination and his own life experiences as a Black person inspired his slavery analogy.

Prince's determination to link recording contracts to slavery was also expressed through the name he chose for the first album he released after the end of the Warner Bros. contract. The album was a three-CD compilation, released in 1996, entitled 'Emancipation' (Prince). In the title song of the album, the refrain repeated is 'Break the chain! Break the chain!' In a performance at the 28th Annual NAACP Image Awards, Prince performed a dance number that visually expressed the idea of emancipation. He performed with a large group of Black men and women as backup dancers. At the start of the dance, Prince and the dancers are all in chains. They then break the chains and dance to a medley of the song 'Emancipation' and another race-conscious Prince song, 'We March' (NAACP; Prince).

Decades after his contract with Warner Bros. had ended, Prince continued to invoke the comparison between record contracts and slavery. In his 2002 song 'Avalanche', he references both to slavery and to the economic exploitation of struggling recording artists (Prince). In a meeting at his Paisley Park Studios in 2015, he told a group of reporters from the National Association of Black Journalists, 'Record contracts are just like – I'm gonna say it – slavery' (Krebs).

Prince's use of the slavery analogy during his dispute with Warner Bros. may have reflected a combination of factors – the hope that publicly comparing his contract to slavery might embarrass Warner Bros. enough for them to release him from his contract, and/or pure anger expressed in the way a creative artist might express it. But Prince was also a Black man who grew up in America with the experiences that status entails. It is reasonable to conclude that his actions during the dispute with Warner Bros. reflected his own feelings about slavery and past and present discrimination against African Americans, especially in the context of the music industry.

The name change

When Prince first changed his name to the unpronounceable glyph, neither those charged with announcing his performances nor those who interviewed him for the media were sure how to address, describe or announce him. Eventually, he was often called 'The Artist Formerly Known as Prince' or sometimes, simply, 'The Artist'. Some referred to him as 'TAFKAP'.

Prince's former long-time attorney, Londell McMillan, once explained that Prince thought that by changing his name to a symbol, he could rescind and void the contract with Warner Bros., but clearly, that was not the case (Kim). In the end, Prince was not able to get out of the contract – it terminated after he had fulfilled his obligations under it. He later resumed the use of his own name.

Rolling Stone magazine has called Prince's name change the fourth boldest career move in rock history (Rolling Stone). While Prince's name change did not gain him release from his contract and is widely regarded as having damaged his career, it offers another illustration of a way in which Prince exercised a conscious and strategic choice about representing race.

Names have both practical and legal significance. A name allows a person to be identified and differentiated from other individuals. The common law rule is that any person has a right to change his or her name at will, as long as the name change is not for the purpose of fraud. The right to name oneself has been considered to be one of privacy and personal autonomy, and some have argued that naming oneself has an element of constitutional dimension.

For many people, names also have tremendous symbolic value. Names can function as a connection to ancestors and to ethnicity. Names, thus, can have personal and cultural/political as well as legal significance.

Names can have a particular symbolic value to people who have been oppressed, subordinated and forcibly stripped of their names. In recent years, for example, legal scholars have discussed the importance of names in the context of societal hierarchies. Feminist legal scholars have analysed the way in which the formerly common practice of women changing their names to their husbands' names after marriage is a reflection of the gender hierarchy in society, and have interpreted women maintaining their birth names after marriage as an assertion of gender equality (Emens).

A group for which names have long had a symbolic political value are African Americans.

During slavery, a legally sanctioned institution in America for hundreds of years, Black people were stripped of their African names and renamed by those who held them in bondage. When slavery ended, many freed slaves took on the names of their former owners out of a practical legal need to have a last name – and there have long been deep feelings among African Americans about this historical aspect of their last names.

There are many examples in recent times of African Americans taking steps that demonstrate the cultural and political importance of names. Muhammad Ali dropped his birth name of Cassius Clay, Malcolm X and others in the Nation of Islam dropped the last names they were given at birth and adopted 'X' for their last names as an acknowledgement of the fact that as a result of slavery, their African names are unknown. Beginning with the Black Power movement in the 1960s, many Black Americans began to give their children African first names as a way of connecting to their African heritage

At the time he took the step of changing his name, Prince issued the following statement in which he connected the importance of a person's name to the ideas of slavery and exploitation:

> The first step I have taken toward the ultimate goal of emancipation from the chains that bind me to Warner Bros. was to change my name from Prince to The Love Symbol. Prince is the name that my mother gave me at birth. Warner Bros. took the name, trademarked it, and used it as the main marketing tool to promote all of the music that I wrote. The company owns the name Prince and all related music marketed under Prince. I became merely a pawn used to produce more money for Warner Bros. (Guerrascio)

Of course, Prince's statement that he was changing his name to the love symbol, does not sound terribly political. However, in the same statement, Prince made it clear that he did connect his name change to his own feelings of exploitation as well as with the history of Black musicians. He said,

> By my 35th birthday, June 7, 1993, I was beyond frustrated with my lack of control over my career and music. It seems reminiscent of much that had been experienced by other African-Americans over the last couple of hundred years. They had turned me into a slave and I wanted no more of it. The dilemma had only one clear solution. I was born Prince and did not want to adopt another conventional name. The only acceptable replacement for my name , and my identity was ... a symbol with no pronunciation that is a representation of me and what my music is about. This symbol is present in my work over the years, it is a concept that has evolved from my frustration. It is who I am. (Guerrascio)

Years later, after Prince was no longer under contract to Warner Bros., the song 'Family Name' on his album *The Rainbow Children* contained the lyrics, 'You might say "What you mad about?" But you still got your family name' (Prince).

Writing 'SLAVE' on his face

In light of the important role of the visual and the physical in his performances, it should not be surprising that Prince incorporated aspects of physicality and performance into his battle with Warner Bros. He did this by performing with the word 'SLAVE' written across his cheek during the record contract dispute.

In a 1996 *Rolling Stone* interview, Prince said, 'People think I'm a crazy fool for wiring slave on my face, but if I can't do what I want to do, what am I? When you stop a man from dreaming, he becomes a slave, That's where I was. I don't own Prince's music. If you don't own your masters, your master owns you' (Pareles, 'A Re-Inventor').

Indeed, many in the media did ridicule Prince, a rich, famous entertainer for performing with 'SLAVE' written on his face (Segal). Prince was clear about this possible reaction and in an interview he made it clear that he was not seeking to compare his situation to that of people who had been actually enslaved (BET Interview).

It seems clear that writing 'SLAVE' on his face, like changing his name, was a tool in Prince's campaign to pressure Warner Bros. to release him from his contract and return his master tapes to him. Thus, he had a specific goal in using this tactic. However, that action can also be viewed as one that constituted a conscious and strategic representation of race. By that act, Prince once again took his fight beyond the context of the law – linking his personal battle with Warner Bros. to the history of slavery and the use of the Black body as a symbol and a physical tool in African American history. The Black body, past and present, is the subject of a great deal of discourse in writings about race, both inside and outside of academia (Coates; Roberts).

During slavery, the Black body was exploited – the unpaid labour of the slave benefited the slave owner, not the slave. The bodies of slaves were abused in other ways as well. Laws in many jurisdictions permitted slaves to be branded (Blassingame 165 n.19, 280,339, 632). The mark burned onto the body identified that individual as a slave and was a symbol that demonstrated that someone else owned and controlled that person's body and owned the fruits of his or her labour. Branding was also one of the forms of punishment visited upon the Black body (Blassingame 262-3). Slaves could be branded for being absent from the plantation without permission, running away or encouraging others to run away (Higginbotham 177-83).

The Black body is still a powerful symbol in America and is a continuing subject of controversy. It is a frequent subject of discussion by African Americans in the media and by legal scholars and other academics who write about race. The recent bestselling book by Ta-Nehisi Coates, *Between the World and Me* is, in many ways, a book-length meditation on the Black body, the constant threats to it and the violence that is often visited upon it (Coates).

When Prince performed with 'SLAVE' written on his face, he used his own Black body to send a message that linked his struggle to that of past and present African Americans. He, and not anyone else, was in control of his Black body and he had the power to use his body as he chose. He demonstrated the way in which the Black body is not only a site of oppression but can also be a site of resistance. African Americans have long demonstrated this in many ways, from sit-ins for integration during the civil rights era of the 1950s and 1960s to African American athletes wearing shirts with 'I Can't Breathe' on the front as a reminder of Eric Garner dying at the hands of the police in New York City for the 'offence' of selling loose cigarettes on a street.

Prince chose to use his body to send a message about the relationship between Black labour, economic exploitation and the record industry. By performing with 'SLAVE' on his face, Prince chose to make a conscious and strategic representation of race – he used the power he had over his own body to employ it as a site to send a powerful message that African Americans have been exploited, continue to be exploited and that he identified with the struggles of the race.

Conclusion

Because his music crossed lines of genre and often expressed the view that people must learn to care for each other regardless of race, it is not difficult to see why Prince would be described by some as an artist who transcended race or to whom race was not important.

However, this view represents wishful thinking more than reality. Throughout his career, Prince was very aware of the role of race in American society and responded to it in his work in ways that were both conscious and strategic. This does not mean that Prince believed that race should matter – he dealt with the reality that it did matter and dealt with that fact in ways that reflected his own personality and creativity. It is also clear that as the years passed, while Prince continued to promote a message of racial peace and cooperation, he became increasingly public in his identification with and support for issues affecting the African American community. As scholars continue to study Prince in the future, it is important that his relationship to issues of race and to the African American community be recognized as an important part of his life, his career and his legacy.

Works cited

Alban, Debra. 'Michael Jackson Broke Down Racial Barriers'. 29 June 2009, www.cnn.com/2009/showbiz/music/michael.

Baynes, Leonard M. 'It's Not Just Black and White Anymore, Why Does Darkness Cast a Longer Discriminatory Shadow Than Lightness?' An Investigation and Analysis of the Color Hierarchy'. *Denver University Law Review* 75.1 (1997): 131–5.

BET Interview: Prince, 23 Apr. 2016. www.youtube.com/watch?v=pqyjwhFiQqg.

Blassingame, John W. *The Slave Community*. New York: Oxford UP, 1972.

Blassingame, John W. *Slave Testimony: Two Centuries of Letters, Speeches, Interviews and Autobiographies*. Baton Rouge: LSU Press, 1977.

Brown, August, and Rotterberg, Josh, 'Prince, Master of Rock, Soul, Pop and Funk dies at 57'. *The Los Angeles Times*, 21 Apr. 2016, www.latimes.com/local/obituaries/la-me-prince-20160421-story.html.

Canby, Vincent. '"Purple Rain" with Prince'. *The New York Times*, 7 July 1984. www.nytimes.com/movie/review?res=950CE4D9143AF93.

Chase, Anthony R., 'Race, Culture and Contract Law: From the Cottonfield to the Courtroom'. *Connecticut Law Review* 28.1 (1995): 1–66.

Christman, Ed. 'Prince Gets Masters Back, Which Labels Say "Scares Us Silly"'. *Billboard*, 25 Apr. 2014. www.billboard.com/biz/articles.news.legal-and-management/60.

CNN Wire. 'Our Northern Star: Minneapolis and Prince-A Love Story'. 24 Apr. 2016, www.wktr.com/mcPCh.

Coates, Ta-Nehisi. *Between The World and Me*. New York: Spiegel & Grau, 2015.

Crenshaw, Kimberly et al., eds, *Introduction to Critical Race Theory: The Key Writings That Formed the Movement*. New York: The New Press, 1996.

Davis, F. James. *Who Is Black?: One Nation's Definition*. University Park: Penn State UP, 1991.

Dickerson, Dez. *My Time With Prince: Confessions of a Former Revolutionary*. Nashville: Pavilion Press, 2003.
Emens, Elizabeth. 'Changing Name Changing: Framing Rules and the Future of Marital Names', *University of Chicago Law Review* 74.3 (2007): 761–864.
Greene, K. J. 'Copynorms, Black Cultural Production, and the Debate over African-American Reparations'. *Cardozo Arts and Entertainment Journal* 25.3 (2008): 1179–228.
Guerrascio, Jason. 'A Secret Letter Prince Wrote to His Fans Explains Why He Changed His Name to a Symbol in the 1990's'. *Business Insider*, 18 May 2016, www.businessinsider.com/prince-secret-letter-2016-5.
Haney Lopez, Ian. *White By Law*. New York: NYU Press, 2006.
Higginbotham, A. Leon. *In the Matter of Color: Race and the American Legal Process: The Colonial Period*. Oxford: Oxford UP, 1978.
Johnson, Kenneth. 'Prince in Charlotte 1997: Loose, Funky and Energized'. *The Charlotte Observer*, 4 Aug. 1997, reprinted, 21 Apr. 2016. www.charlotteobserver.com/entertainment/article7.
Kelley, Norman. 'Notes on the Political Economy of Black Music'. *Rhythm and Business: The Political Economy of Black Music*. Ed. Kelley, Norman. New York: Akashic Books, 2005.
Kennedy, Randall. *Interracial Intimacies*. New York: Vintage Books, 2003.
Kim, Susannah. 'What It Was Like to be Prince's Lawyer When He Changed His Name to a Symbol'. abcnews.go.cm/Business/princes-lawyer-changed-symbol/story?id=38606016.
Kofsky, Frank. *Black Music and White Business: Illuminating the History and the Political Economy of Jazz*. Atlanta: Pathfinder, 1997.
Krebs, Daniel. 'Prince Warns Young Artists: Record Contracts are Slavery'. *Rolling Stone*, 10 Aug. 2015. www.rollingstone.com/music/news/prince-wa.
Light, Alan. *Let's Go Crazy*. New York: Atria Books, 2014.
Minsker, Evan. 'Prince Shares Full "Dance Rally 4 Peace" at Paisley Park Audio'. *Pitchfork*, 13 May 2015. https://pitchfork.com/news/59557-prince-shares-full-dance-rally-4-peace-at-paisley-park-audio/.
Morant, Blake. 'The Relevance of Race and Disparity in Discussions of Contract Law'. *31 New England Law Review* 31.3 (1997): 889–940.
NAACP. '28th Annual NAACP Image Awards, 1997, Part 1'. www.youtube.com/watch?v=3OPLAzMAJZ4.
Palmer, Robert. 'Pop Life: Is Prince Leading music to a True Biracialism'. *The New York Times*, 2 Dec. 1981. www.nytimes.com/1981/12/02/arts/the-pop-life-is-princ.
Pareles, Jon. 'Prince, An Artist Who Defied Genre Is Dead at 57'. *The New York Times*, 22 Apr. 2016. www.nytimes.com/2016/04/22/arts/music/prince-death.
Pareles, Jon. 'A Reinventor of the World and of Himself'. *The New York Times*, 17 Nov. 1996. www.nytimes.com/199611/17/arts/a-re-inventor-of-his-world-a....
Perry, Twila. 'Race, Color and the Adoption of Biracial Children'. *17 Journal of Gender Race and Justice* 17.1 (2014): 73–104.
Phillips, Chuck. 'Just How Princely is Prince's Warner Bros. Deal?' *The Los Angeles Times*, 5 Sept. 1992. www.latimes.com.entertainment/music/la-et-ms-prince-warner-bros-deal-1992090s-story.html.
Phillips, Chuck. 'A King's Ransom for Prince: Artist Signs $100 Million Contract with Warner'. *Los Angeles Times*, 4 Sept. 1992. www. latimes.com/1992-09-04/business/fi-6479_1_warner-bros.

Prince. 'Avalanche'. *One Nite Alone*, NPG Records, 2002.
Prince. 'Compassion'. *20TEN*, NPG Records, 2010.
Prince. 'Controversy'. *Controversy*, Warner Bros. Records, 1981.
Prince. 'Emancipation'. *Emancipation*, NPG Records/ EMI Records, 1996.
Prince. 'Family Name'. *The Rainbow Children*, NPG Records, 2001.
Ro, Rohin. 'A Prince by Any Other Name'. *Vanity Fair*, 19 Oct. 2011. www.vanityfair.com/cultural/2011/prin.
Roberts, Dorothy. *Killing the Black Body: Race, Reproduction and the Meaning of Liberty*. New York: Pantheon Books, 1997.
Rolling Stone. 'The 25 Boldest Career Moves in Rock History'. *Rolling Stone*, 18 Mar. 2011. www.rollingstone.com/music/lists/the-25.
Segal, David. 'Purple Reign, Prince Is Back in the Building and Ready to Rattle the Rafters'. *The Washington Post*, 12 Aug. 2004. www.washingtonpost.com/wp-dyn/articles/A 58135-2004Aug11.html.
Slave Trade: How Prince Re-Made the Music Business. Pride, 2014, DVD.
Tate, Greg. *Everything But the Burden: What White People Are Taking from Black Culture*. New York: Broadway Books, 2003.
Thorne, Matt. *Prince, the Man and His Music*. Chicago: Bolden Books, 2016.
Toure. *I Would Die For You: How Prince Became an Icon*. New York: Atria Books, 2013.
'Transcend'. *Merriam-Webster Dictionary*. Merriam-Webster, 2019. http://www.merriam-webster.com/dictionary/transcend.
'Transcend'. *Merriam-Webster Thesaurus*. Merriam-Webster, 2019. www.merriam-webster.com/thesaurus/transcend.
Wall, Mick. *Purple Reign*. London: Orion Books, 2016.

17

It's all about what's in your mind
The origins of Prince's political consciousness

Crystal N. Wise

Throughout his career Prince has written songs that include social and political commentary. His initial lyrical expressions of political consciousness are featured on his critically acclaimed third studio album, *Dirty Mind* – released 8 October 1980. This album presented a pivotal turn in Prince's music and lyrics. While Prince had become known for his romantic and sexually suggestive songs, such as 'Soft and Wet' (1978) and 'I Wanna Be Your Lover' (1979), on the *Dirty Mind* album Prince broadened, deepened and expanded his musical style and lyrical content. *Dirty Mind* was a departure from Prince's previous albums in that the original demo recordings of the tracks recorded in his home studio, were 'more stripped down and raw' (Hawkins and Niblock 2011: 20) and for the most part left as first recorded on the album release (Ro 2011). Prince had also changed his appearance to match the edgy content of *Dirty Mind*'s music and lyrics. During this era, he pushed boundaries brazenly, wearing a trench coat over briefs, thigh-highs and a bandana tied around his neck. Additionally, the lyrical content is a mixed bag of songs that ranged from sex to failed relationships to societal ills. To some these choices may seem pornographic or solely in service of commercial success; however, I would argue that Prince aspired to generate real social change through his artistry.

It is important to note that although Prince waited until his third album to explicitly express his political consciousness; his self-determination and resistance is evident on his first two albums in that he produced, arranged, composed and performed the majority of the music on these albums. In addition, on the album covers, Prince introduced himself to the world baring his naked Black body, first crowned with an afro and then underneath pressed out shoulder-length curls. He also featured a dove on the inner sleeve of the first album and then himself atop a Pegasus on the back of the second album – symbols that are commonly associated with peace, love, purity and freedom, and counter stereotypical views of Black males. These artistic choices are not only reflective of Prince as an individual but aligned to and an extension of his familial and musical heritage. As explicated by Baraka (1963), the quest for freedom, citizenship, social and political change is inscribed into the core of African American music given its origins reside in the music of enslaved African Americans and the blues music of their freed descendants. Therefore, Prince's first albums are political as he is in direct lineage of African American musicians and thus his business and artistic choices from the first two albums would also provide insight into his political consciousness. However, this chapter is primarily concerned with Prince's lyrical expressions of his political consciousness given his verbal expressions are an unmistakable declaration to represent himself as having a political identity.

'Partyup' in 'Uptown'

I identified 'Uptown' and 'Partyup' from the *Dirty Mind* album as Prince's earliest lyrical articulations of his political consciousness through a process of carefully reading the lyrics of each song, starting with his first commercially released studio album. A song is considered to contain political commentary if it 'explicitly or implicitly describes the social, economic, and political conditions of people and the forces that create these conditions' (Stewart 2005: 196). 'Uptown' and 'Partyup' both feature Prince sharing his discontent with social and political issues.

The fact that Prince used both of these songs to promote the *Dirty Mind* album makes it clear that he was interested in sharing his political beliefs as widely as possible. Prince selected 'Uptown', a song in which he expresses his discontent for 'narrow-minded' beliefs that attempt to constrain him, as the first released single from the album. He describes Uptown as what I have concluded as a place where he is 'free to be'. He carries this sentiment on to the last track of the album, 'Partyup', which he chose to perform during his first appearance on *Saturday Night Live*. 'Partyup' is an anti-war song, in which Prince tells his listeners that he is going Uptown to party instead of killing or dying in a war. The repetitive use of Uptown as a place of refuge in an oppressive society signifies that this place plays an important role in Prince's political consciousness. Uptown is also a neighbourhood in Minneapolis, Minnesota, Prince's hometown.

Prince is known for his love of his birthplace and life-long hometown of Minneapolis, Minnesota. He maintained close ties to the city even after becoming a world-renowned music icon. Always showing pride for his beloved hometown, when asked about growing up in Uptown on a radio interview via telephone in 1986 with the Detroit disc jockey, The Electrifying Mojo, he describes how he turned Minneapolis into his Uptown by changing the music scene and engineering the party. He said, 'We put together a few bands and turned it into Uptown. That consisted of a lot of bike riding nude, but ya know it worked. We had fun.' Here Prince is indicating that Uptown was a real place for him. Not just a mythic or utopian place as one might initially infer when listening to 'Uptown' and 'Partyup'. Akin to other African American artists and more generally to the African American experience, Prince created a physical and psychological space that was counterculture as a means to be free from and resist the oppressive dominant society (Iton 2010). For Prince, Uptown is at least in part the inspiration of the song 'Uptown' and thus can be considered the lyrical birthplace of Prince political consciousness.

Given that Prince chooses to speak his political consciousness for the first time using his lived experience in Uptown as inspiration, the songs 'Uptown' and 'Partyup' are worthy of study as they are Black popular culture texts that go beyond the mythic – which Hall (1993) contends is not typically the case with commodified and stereotyped artefacts of popular culture. It is understandable why utopian or alternative representations of life for African Americans in popular culture can be viewed as mythical given the continued economic, social and political struggles we see in present day. It is even ironic that during the *Dirty Mind* era as Prince debuted his political beliefs, he was again met with similar prejudiced views he and other Black musicians experienced in mainstream Minneapolis, when he performed in 1981, as an opening act for the Rolling Stones at the Coliseum in Los Angeles, California. During the performance, Prince and his band were verbally and physically assaulted. The predominantly White audience yelled racial and homophobic slurs and threw food and other objects at Prince and his band (Wawzenek 2016). This assault suggests that Prince's 'Uptown' is also in part mythic, 'in the mind'. The Rolling Stones' intolerant crowd reflected the mindset of mainstream America. It is inspiring that despite Prince not finding his utopian Uptown on a Los Angeles stage, he continued to express his 'freedom to be' over a career that spanned five decades. An exploration of Prince's early political views provides insight into how an artist who represents a multitude of identities demanded and maintained his vision of freedom throughout his career.

Methodology

To better understand the origins of Prince's political consciousness I used the theories of conceptual metaphor and systemic functional linguistics (SFL) to analyse the literal and figurative meanings that Prince associates with 'Uptown' on the songs, 'Uptown' and 'Partyup'. I also employed Greenwood and Christian's (2008) definition of political consciousness that explains it as the political beliefs that are shaped and formed by an individual's experiences as a result of their multiple social identities. To consider Prince's individual experiences in my analysis, I drew upon Prince's personal, historical, social and cultural experiences as an African American in Minneapolis, Minnesota. I combined these perspectives to analyse Prince's literal and figurative use of 'Uptown' to reveal his early political views in relation to who and what Prince names as oppressive forces and liberating actions.

Conceptual metaphor

Conceptual metaphor refers to how we structure concepts in relation to one another to express our thoughts. These structures are based on our experience with the concepts in our physiological and cultural worlds. Kovecses (2015) describes conceptual metaphor as how we understand one domain of experiences relative to another domain of experiences. Lakoff and Johnson (2008) theorized that our system of conceptual metaphors is structured in a way that places the target domain (the more abstract concept) in relation to a source domain (typically a more concrete concept). Scholars have presented a variety of ways to categorize metaphors. For example, for orientational metaphors, specifically 'up', which I use to analyse the lyrics in 'Uptown' and 'Partyup', Lakoff and Johnson explain that in English we refer to happiness as 'up', because within our human bodies we perceive feelings of happiness as spatially up.

To locate and establish an understanding of Prince's use of the 'up' orientational metaphor in the two songs, I employed the Prazzlejaz Group's metaphor identification process (MIP) (2007). The Prazzlejaz Group is a collective of international scholars who developed the MIP as a tool to identify how metaphors are used in written and oral discourse. The MIP is a four-step process that includes reading the entire text for meaning, breaking the text into individual words or phrases, then considering the contextual meaning, the basic meaning (e.g. the meaning that may be found in the dictionary) and comparing the contextual meaning to the basic meaning to decide whether there is a difference in the two meanings and whether the two meanings can be understood in comparison to one another, and finally decide whether the word or phrase is metaphorical based on the comparison of the two meanings. After identifying the metaphorical words and phrases in the lyrics, I then considered whether and how they represented the source or target domains for 'up'. (For a more enlightening and enjoyable read of this analysis, access the printed lyrics of 'Partyup' and 'Uptown'.)

To illustrate using the song 'Partyup', I carefully read the lyrics while also listening to the song and found that Prince is generally expressing discontent with the US government's military drafting policies and participation in war. After breaking up the lyrics into words and phrases I analysed and compared the contextual meaning of the words and phrases to their basic meaning. In the first line of the song, Prince expresses discontent in a combination of three words and phrases. The first two words, 'we' and 'don't', were not metaphorical. The word, 'give', however, before 'a damn', is metaphorical. The basic meaning of give is to present or offer something whereas the contextual meaning of 'give a damn' signifies a level of care about something. We can see that there is a contrast in the two meanings, but in comparing the two meanings, we can understand an abstraction of presenting or offering care in relation to physically presenting or offering care. In other words, Prince is stating that he is not offering any amount of sentiment or care for a war.

After applying MIP to the rest of the lyrics, I considered Prince's metaphorical statements in terms of the target and source domains for 'up' (and 'down'). With 'up' as the source domain, scholars have identified happiness, rationality, positivity, more, health, control, status, virtue or good as target domains that are culturally and physically constructed as upwards because they are perceived in relation to a vertical path (e.g. 'climbing the corporate ladder' or 'cheer up'). I hypothesized Prince would refer to 'up' and its target domains to realize liberation and oppression in his lyrics. For example, Prince's use of the metaphor 'don't give a damn', to express his feelings about the war, indicates that he perceives war as negative and also that he has no feelings about it. Negative and no are in opposition of the target domains of 'up', and therefore can be understood as in conflict with Prince's literal and figurative conceptions of his Uptown.

In addition, I analysed the lyrics of 'Uptown' and 'Partyup' line by line to identify realizations of the liberating aspects of Uptown and the oppressive aspects of the social and political issues Prince names and tracked them using SFL's cohesion analysis methods.

Systemic functional linguistics

SFL is Halliday's (2014) framework of language that views language as a social meaning making-process, in which the communicator draws upon language resources that relate to the social context to construct their message. I use this framework as a discourse analysis tool to explore Prince's lyrics to reveal his views of society. SFL allows us to see how language is used to establish a social world. I use the framework to analyse how Prince structures the lyrics in 'Uptown' and 'Partyup' to communicate his social and political views. The structure of our language choices is shaped by three main functions, which include ideational (what experience is being described and how the language is structured to convey these experiences), interpersonal (using language to enact social relationships) and textual (the language choices that construct the coherent messages). In this study, I used this framework to identify whom, and what, Prince names as actors and track the ways he refers to them through a cohesion analysis. In song lyrics, songwriters often use creative and figurative language to refer to the same referent for artistic and entertainment purposes. Therefore, this analysis is instrumental in uncovering such choices.

In SFL the language a communicator chooses to refer to participants can be analysed through a cohesion analysis. Relative to this study, the participants refer to the people, places and things that Prince describes as oppressive forces or as liberation. With artistic texts such as song lyrics, writers often name participants using figurative language or with varying degrees of ambiguity. To identify the participants in 'Uptown' and 'Partyup', I first listed the participants that related to oppression or liberation using Eggins's (2004) method of developing chains of reference that identify the same participant. For example, on 'Uptown', Prince meets a female who questions his sexuality based on his appearance while he is 'downtown'. In the first verse of the song, Prince refers to oppressive actors as, 'your fine city', 'she', 'stranger', 'little girl', 'her', 'baby', 'her eyes', 'a crazy little mixed up dame' and 'a victim of society'. I continued to develop reference chains related to oppression and liberation in 'Uptown' and 'Partyup' to reveal how Prince conceptualized the physical and utopian states of Uptown. Using these example, you can see how 'downtown' is negatively associated with the source domain, 'up' and the target domains, 'little', 'crazy' and 'victim' refer to oppositional concepts of more, rationale and control indicating Prince's views of 'downtown' or mainstream society as oppressive. I discuss this analysis further in the following section.

On the tracks 'Uptown' and 'Partyup', Prince indeed provides a clear picture of his perceptions of oppression, his ideas of liberation and his construction of Uptown as his utopian society. The conceptual metaphor analysis of 'up' in relation to oppression and liberation reveals that Prince was conscious of the social and political elements that threatened his freedom and the freedom of others. Prince used both embodied and cultural conceptions of the spatial orientations 'up' and 'down' to express his views of society, his physical Uptown and his utopian Uptown. In the following discussion, I demonstrate how Prince utilized conceptual metaphors for 'up' and 'down' to reveal his political consciousness and his ideas of freedom.

The streets of your fine city

On 'Uptown' Prince meets an attractive woman while walking down the streets of 'your fine city'. This stranger, this 'mixed up dame', asks Prince if he is gay. Prince narrates this interaction in the first verse. The cohesion analysis revealed that this woman and society are the same actors of oppression. This is not only shown by tracking the references for the woman to the line that references her as a 'victim of society' but also revealed in how Prince uses metaphors that suggest *down* is less, bad, inferior and not rational. For example, when Prince is in the city (participating in society) he is walking 'down' the streets of a place that is later referred to in the song as 'downtown'. The attractive woman is referred to as 'little' and 'crazy' and 'mixed up'. Prince uses 'little' to show less, and 'crazy' and 'mixed up' to indicate not rational. In Prince's view, these are the qualities that manifests within individuals who are 'victims' (under the influence) of society. Later in the song he refers to 'downtown' as 'narrow-minded' indicating a relationship to the metaphor that expresses high-minded as a virtue or a desirable quality. In 'Downtown', as in our existing society, people's sexuality is determined based on their clothes and hair, which Prince views as 'narrow-minded' – meaning 'less'. We see here Prince shows a consistency with 'downtown' and mainstream society related to down and, therefore, oppressive.

Prince's lyrical choices of 'victim', 'games' and 'lose' imply that mainstream society is like a competition where there are winners and losers, those who are superior and inferior. The competition points to the power structure of the oppressive society where when Prince and others like him operate within it, they lose. They are relegated to a lower status because they do not possess the same virtue. We see this in the lyrics that indicate Prince's reaction when he is asked whether he is gay. He sings lyrics to express that he is surprised and flustered, yet confident in who he is. As Prince sees it, dressing as he does, is not an indication of his sexual orientation so he enters a confused state when he interacts with the 'narrow-minded' people downtown (an oppressive society), where it is rational and acceptable to prejudge others based on appearance.

Prince is consistent with his portrayal of societal oppression as down on 'Partyup'. At the end of the song, he chants in favour of partying and in opposition of the draft and war. Prince associates the war and the government with negativity and being in a low position. For example, he names an army bag as a 'drag'. Drag signifies both an unpleasant state as well as a downward motion. He uses the 'life is up' metaphor to show why the government's decision to draft young people and fight war is oppressive as it not only 'kills' the youth but makes them murderer people who have not directly wronged them. Here Prince associates war and the oppressive nature of the draft as forcing death on others, which is in opposition to life. In the lyrics, 'because of their *half-baked* mistakes/ we get ice cream, *no* cake/ all lies, *no* truth' we can see that Prince views the government as providing the people with *less* than what they deserve (no cake) and governing in an unethical manner as they withhold the truth.

Prince as a young man, who wishes to express himself in any way he chooses, shows that societal prejudices and the draft are oppressive forces that challenge his freedom. He distinctly utilizes the system of conceptual metaphors that relate down as negative to indicate he believes that mainstream society and the government promote negative stereotypes, divide and cause harm to innocent people. Prince protests by sharing with his audience his personal beliefs and experiences that defy these oppressive forces.

We don't give a damn

Prince commits to partying and freeing the mind as a means to realize his personal liberation in response to the maltreatment he experiences in mainstream society. Prince uses his real experiences of living in Uptown as inspiration for these songs. In a 1981 interview in Amsterdam (this was Prince's first time performing outside of the United States) with Mick Boskamp, Prince describes Uptown as a place where individuality was praised and the standard. He stated, 'You were ridiculed often for copying people and picking up trends and wearing what everybody else had on and saying what everybody else said and playing the same music as everybody else.' For Prince, what is upright, superior, good and positive is based on his Uptown in Minneapolis where he experienced a freedom to be, a freedom to be your own self.

On the two tracks, Prince responds to prejudices and war with a carefree attitude because to care would be to fall to an emotional response, which is not rational as in high level. Instead of adhering to society's notions of what is 'good' or 'virtuous', he describes himself and his group as railing against societal norms as he sings on 'Uptown' that he and those who are free-minded refuse the rules of society and do as they please. On 'Partyup' he reinforces his protest with chants that tell the government to fight their own wars. These sentiments suggest that Prince learned early on to be guided by another set of rules beyond societal norms as he views them as oppressive in that they support death and destruction.

For Prince, control and power operates differently in Uptown than it does in mainstream society. Prince, ironically, shows that in Uptown it is not only about reclaiming control but also about 'losing' control to achieve euphoria. He urges his listeners to 'get down' to keep the partying going. Such actions will put you in a 'hot' condition where you'll lose control and not want the party to stop. 'Get down' in the literal sense indicates 'down' as a negative state in the system of conceptual metaphor used so far. However, 'get down' refers to dancing, having a good time. To be able to understand this contradiction, the origins of 'get down' must be considered. 'Get down' comes from African American music and dance, which is rooted in African tradition that shows power and intensity is perceived to come from closeness with the earth (Welsh-Asante 1996). As an African American and a musician largely influenced by African American musical styles and genres, Prince's use of 'get down' is based in his culture and therefore 'get down' (similar to how he used 'got to party down' in 'Partyup') works in his system of conceptual metaphors to signal spirituality, positivity and euphoria. Hot is also used to show intensity and increased energy. These metaphors serve as vehicles for reaching a euphoric state through free-minded partying. As described in the next section, this is a liberating practice not only for Prince but for his oppressors as well. Prince brings the 'narrow-minded' female to Uptown who 'loses' control and thus liberates herself which intensifies the party for others too. In the following lines, Prince expresses that this stranger's liberation in Uptown inspired an intensification in his already liberated state.

Prince also contrasts his Uptown with the mainstream society by stating that people of various racial and ethnic backgrounds party together. He sings about people from various racial and ethnic backgrounds having a good time partying together in Uptown. In these lyrics, he is apt to name this as positive with the word 'good' and he also tells how diverse groups of people are in accord, in a happy place. Growing up in Minneapolis, Prince experienced a racially segregated but diverse city. Prince had a wide range of musical influences, including a father who was a jazz musician, and he also grew up in close proximity to White American culture (Hawkins and Niblock 2011). These experiences influenced not only his musical style but also his choices for forming his band (Ro 2011; Thorne 2012). On the inner sleeve of the *Dirty Mind* album, we see a band that is racially diverse. Prince was sure to reflect that as he experienced Uptown, people of different backgrounds get together and have a good time. During this decade (though in some ways it still is today) when music categories were segregated by race (Starr and Waterman 2006), Prince singing about everybody being happy and actually playing music together is a direct challenge of the existing power structure. This same concept is part of the concept of 'Partyup' when he protests, 'Revolutionary rock and roll'. Prince shows that he is hopeful that the way he lives his life and creates music can combat and transform mainstream society. He is advocating for his listeners to lose control not to their government but to a higher power that is achieved when everyone is 'partying' together. In a sense, Prince is convinced he can funk society or at least his listening audience into freedom.

It's all about being free

Within the lyrics of 'Uptown' and 'Partyup' Prince also expresses his vision of utopia. Though 'Uptown' is based on Prince's experiences in the Uptown neighbourhood of Minneapolis, Minnesota, Prince reiterates on both songs that 'Uptown' is also about freeing your mind. Prince uses his female character, the attractive woman that he meets in the city to illustrate this. In the first verse of 'Uptown' Prince describes how the attractive woman prejudges him based on his appearance (see the section, 'The streets of your fine city'). The woman is representative of the biased and intolerant views that the larger society holds. Despite her rude behaviour, Prince is still open to the woman and invites her to Uptown.

At first glance or first listen, Prince's appearance and the song's lyrics may be construed as pornographic. However, as Lorde (2007) astutely clarifies in *Sister Outsider*, there is a difference between pornographic and the use of the erotic. In the second verse of 'Uptown' it becomes clear that Prince's intention is not lewd, but he is using the erotic to liberate himself, the woman from downtown, and his listeners. Lorde explains the erotic as

> a resource within each of us that lies in a deeply female and spiritual plane, firmly rooted in the power of our unexpressed or unrecognized feeling. In order to perpetuate itself, every oppression must corrupt or distort those various sources of power within the culture of the oppressed that can provide energy for change. (53)

Throughout his career, Prince did not shy away from expressing his spirituality and his feminine energy. It is clear on 'Uptown' that Prince empowers himself by invoking the erotic to seek a better existence for himself and society. Using the woman as a metaphor for mainstream society, Prince shows liberation is possible by embracing other perspectives, fully experiencing another's way to be and know, and sharing power to be in harmony with others. The metaphors of 'control is up' and 'euphoria is up' in the second verse show that when the rules of 'Uptown' govern, people can reach a higher level. Prince signals this by lyrically painting the picture of freedom and joy with people dancing in the streets, 'mak[ing] love' to strangers, and having a never-ending good time. Prince croons about the state of madness that the woman from 'downtown' achieves at the party in Uptown. Contrary to the irrational crazy that she is in in the first verse, the 'mad' she experiences in the second verse is equivalent to a high euphoric state, spiritual. The woman is symbolic of the higher state of mind that society needs to aspire to in order to realize true freedom by allowing others 'freedom to be'. Prince similarly expresses a desire for mainstream society to look more like his utopia on 'Partyup'. He repeats that liberation starts in the mind and that Uptown is a place for the liberated and those with a desire to become liberated. In these lyrics, just as he imagines mainstream society (via the attractive woman) 'going Uptown', he also calls for the government to be 'high-minded' and go Uptown by choosing life and freedom over death and destruction for its citizens. Through erotic imagery and lyrics, Prince provides a path to liberation to his listeners.

Conclusion

> Uptown is more or less a state of mind and it has nothing to do with financial status. It all has to do with how free you are inside and how good you feel about yourself and how strongly you feel about yourself and what you stand for and your beliefs. (Prince 1981)

Prince uttered these words in the same 1981 interview with Mick Boskamp, in which he also spoke of individuality. Prince was disputing Boskamp's misconception that 'Uptown' was about Prince's aspirations to live the financial 'good life'. As a young 22-year-old musician outside of United States for the first time, Prince stood firm in his freedom to be. He made it clear that his mind, his consciousness, was focused on his freedom and the freedom of others. He revealed that it is his early experiences of exerting his freedom in the multicultural setting of Minneapolis that shaped the beginnings of his political consciousness. From exploring Prince's earliest expressions of his political consciousness, it becomes apparent that Prince was not just selling a utopian fairytale – in his world, Uptown was where he and his peers resisted being stereotyped, limited or placed inside a box. Prince's freedom was not mythic, as he more recently reminded us in his five-word acceptance speech for his Lifetime Achievement Award at the Webby Awards in 2006 for again exercising a 'freedom to be' as he was the first major artist to use the internet to distribute music directly to fans. He poetically stated, 'Everything U think is true.'

Prince truly believed that freedom is born in the mind. He graciously shared his vision for a freer and more just society, by urging us to dance and party together, to reach for a free and elevated mindset. He projected his multifaceted identities to invite us to his Uptown, with the smallest hope that at least for the length of a song, he could funk you into letting go of society's biased and oppressive notions, but also with the greater ambition to help us free our minds. By the end of 'Uptown', Prince implores that everybody has got to go Uptown. Let's go, go, go.

Works cited

Eggins, Suzanne. *An Introduction to Systemic Functional Linguistics*. 2nd edn. London: Bloomsbury, 2004.

Greenwood, Ronni Michelle, and Aidan Christian. 'What Happens When We Unpack the Invisible Knapsack? Intersectional Political Consciousness and Inter-Group Appraisals'. *Sex Roles* 59.5–6 (2008): 404–17. doi:10.1007/s11199-008-9439-x.

Hall, Stuart. 'What Is This "Black" in Black Popular Culture?' *Social Justice* 20.1–2 (1993): 104–14. JSTOR, www.jstor.org/stable/29766735.

Halliday, Michael Alexander Kirkwood, and Christian M. I. M Matthiessen. *Halliday's Introduction to Functional Grammar*. New York: Routledge, 2014.

Hawkins, Stan, and Sarah Niblock. *Prince: The Making of a Pop Music Phenomenon*. Surrey: Ashgate Publishing Group, 2011.

Iton, Richard. *In Search of the Black fantastic: Politics and Popular Culture in the Post-Civil Rights Era*. Oxford: Oxford University Press, 2010.

Baraka, Amiri (Jones, Leroi). *Blues People: Negro Music in White America*. New York: William Morrow and Company, 1963.

Kövecses, Zoltán. *Where Metaphors Come From: Reconsidering Context in Metaphor*. Oxford: Oxford University Press, 2015.

Lakoff, George, and Mark Johnson. *Metaphors We Live By*. Chicago: University of Chicago Press, 2008.

Lorde, Audre. *Sister Outsider*. Berkeley: Crossing Press, 2007.
Nelson, Prince Rogers. Interview by the Electrifying Mojo. 'Listen to Prince's Interview with Detroit's Legendary Electrifying Mojo'. *Daily Detroit*, Daily Detroit Staff, 7 June 1986. Web. 13 July 2017. http://www.dailydetroit.com/2016/04/21/listen-princes-interview-legendary-electrifying-mojo/.
Nelson, Prince Rogers. Interview by Mick Boskamp. 'Prince Interview with Mick Boskamp...Amsterdam 1981'. MixCloud, Ernand, 9 May 1981. Web. 13 July 2017. https://www.mixcloud.com/Kierienos/prince-interview-with-mick-boskampamsterdam-1981/.
Nelson, Prince Rogers, speaker. *Honoring the Best of the Internet*, The Webby Awards, 2006. Web. Accessed 9 June 2019. https://www.webbyawards.com/winners/2006/special-achievement/special-achievement/lifetime-achievement/prince/?/.
Prazzlejaz Group. 'MIP: A Method for Identifying Metaphorically Used Words in Discourse'. *Metaphor and Symbol* 22.1 (2007): 1–39. doi:10.1207/s15327868ms2201_1.
Prince. *Dirty Mind*, Warner Brothers Records, 1980.
Prince. 'I Wanna Be Your Lover'. *Prince*, Warner Brothers Records, 1979.
Prince. 'Partyup'. *Dirty Mind*, Warner Brothers Records, 1980.
Prince. 'Soft and Wet'. *For You*, Warner Brothers Records, 1978.
Prince. 'Uptown'. *Dirty Mind*, Warner Brothers Records, 1980.
Ro, Ronin. *Prince: Inside the Music and the Masks*. New York: St. Martin's Press, 2011.
Starr, Larry, and Christopher Waterman. *American Popular Music: The Rock Years*. New York: Oxford University Press, 2006.
Stewart, James B. 'Message in the Music: Political Commentary in Black Popular Music from Rhythm and Blues to Early Hip Hop'. *The Journal of African American History* 90.3 (2005): 196–225. doi:10.1086/jaahv90n3p196.
Thorne, Matt. *Prince*. London: Faber & Faber, 2012.
Wawzenek, Bryan. 'That Time Prince Got Booed Off the Rolling Stones' Stage'. *Ultimate Classic Rock*, 8 Oct. 2016. Web. 9 June 2019. https://ultimateclassicrock.com/prince-booed-rolling-stones.
Welsh-Asante, Kariamu. *African Dance: An Artistic, Historical, and Philosophical Inquiry*. Trenton: Africa World Press, 1996.

Index

Academy Awards of 1985   12–13
Across 110th Street (Shear)   92
Adams, Stacy   52
affirmative theory of desire   143
African American Film Critics
        Association   22
African Americans
  community   195
  music   94, 198–9
    and dance   204
  in popular culture   200
Afrofuturism   176–81
Age of Innocence, The (Scorsese)   21
Aledakoba, Celestina   141
Ali, Muhammad   192
Allen, Woody   19
Alphaville (Godard)   9
America
  Black people in   164
  music history   56–7
  pop   186
American Bandstand   59
'Anna Stesia' (*Lovesexy*)   142
Annis, Francesca   21
Annual NAACP Image Awards   191
Ant, Adam   138
Anzaldúa, Gloria   118
Apollonia 6   62
Apted, Michael   10
Are You Experienced (Prince)   95
Around the World in a Day (Prince)   20, 23, 71, 74
Artist/ Rebel/ Dandy: Men of Fashion (Irvin)   46
Art Official Age (Prince)   34
Attanasio, Paul   18
August, Bonnie   36

Bad Timing (Garfunkel)   10
Baker, Heyward   132
Baker, Houston J.   88

Bakersfield Sound   56, 59
Baker v. Nelson   50
Baldwin, James   88, 118
'Ballad of Dorothy Parker, The'   140
ball culture   153
Ballhaus, Michael   19, 21
Baltake, Joe   19
de Balzac, Honoré   46
Baraka, Amiri   88, 198
Barry Lyndon   21
Barthes, Roland   47
Batman (Burton)   11
Baton Rouge Morning Advocate, The   24
Baudelaire, Charles   45, 46, 52
Beatles, The   9, 39, 56, 71
Beatty, Warren   21
Beaulieu, Allen   37
Beautiful Ones, The (Prince)   3, 53, 133
Beethoven's Fifth Symphony   109
'Beggin' Woman Blues'   88
Belafonte, Harry   9
Bell, Thomas L.   58
Bentley, Fonzworth   48
Benton, Jerome   13, 16, 18, 21, 25, 26, 29, 52
Berkoff, Steven   21
Between the World and Me (Coates)   194
Beverly Hills Cop   21
Bey, Yasmin   10
Billboard   6 n.4
Billboard's Catalog Albums Chart   2
Billy Budd   21
biracial identity   188, 189
Birth of Venus, The (Botticelli)   120
Black Album, The (Prince)   69, 73, 74
Black American community, misogyny and acceptance in   129–31
Black community   48, 49, 60, 129, 130, 165, 166, 170
Black dandy   48
Black dandyism   48

Black entertainers   49
Black feminists   119, 150
Black Lives Matter movement   122, 126, 155, 171
Black masculinity   130, 139
  depictions of   161
Black men   22, 52, 120, 125, 191
Black Moon (Malle)   21
Black people, in America   164
Black Population by Regional Counties   60
Black Power movement   192
Black recording artists   191
'Black Sweat' (*3121*)(Prince)   141
Black trans-feminine communities   149
Bland, Michael   34
Blaxploitation films   92, 130
Blinn, William   12
Bliss, Atlanta   21
Blitz   22
Bloom, Howard   20
BlueNose Coffee   104–5
blues
  aesthetic   88–9
  definitions   85–6
'Blues in C (If I Had a Harem)'   86–8
blues-influenced songs   92
bluesmen   90
'Blues Queens'   85
Bobby Z   21, 37, 39, 111
Body of Evidence (Edel)   10
Boggs, Grace Lee   118
Boskamp, Mick   204, 207
Bowie, David   10, 11, 138, 146
Boxill, George Ian   3
Boyz n' the Hood (Singleton)   11
Bradley, Lee Conley   90
'Breakfast Can Wait'   165
Bremer Trust   3
Bride Wore Black, The (Truffaut)   21
Brooks, Greg   21
Broonzy, Big Bill   90
Bros, Warner   12, 35, 36
Brown, James   35
Brownmark   21
Brummell, George 'Beau'   46, 48
Bundt, Nancy   51
Burdett, John O.   164

Burton, Johanna   155
Byrd, James, Jr.   175

Calloway, Cab   48
Cammell, Donald   10
Canada, Geoffrey   171
Cardiff, Jack   10
Casablanca   39
Castro, Fidel   162
Cat Glover   86–8
Cavallo, Bob   26
Chamblis, Charles   49
Chappelle, Dave   45
Cher   10
Chicago Blues   56, 59
Chinatown   21
Chocolate Invasion, The (Prince)   180
Chopra, Deepak   168, 169
choreography   5
civil rights law   186
Clare, Eli   150
Clark, Dick   49, 59, 60
Clay, Cassius   192
Cliff, Jimmy   11
Clockwork Orange, A   21
'Cloreen Bacon Skin'   25
Coates, Ta-Nehisi   194
Coco, Joey   18
Cohen, Sara   103
Coleman, Lisa   21, 28, 37, 40, 79, 152, 153
Cole, Shaun   38
Collins, Marva   171
Coloring Party (Sunday, 23 April 2017)   105
ColorWheel   105
Come (Prince)   36
common law rule   192
conceptual metaphor   200–2
contract
  negotiations in recording industry   190
  between Prince and Warner Bros   189–90
contract law   190
Controversy (Prince)   38, 40, 51, 70, 78, 79, 93, 141, 162

Coppola, Francis Ford   21
Corrigan, Dan   110
Cotton Club, The   21
countless fellow musicians   163
Cox, Laverne   155
Crenshaw, Kimberlé   119
critical race
  analysis   186
  scholarship   185
  theory   185
criticism, sociocultural   162
Cross-Talk   154
Crystal Ball (Prince)   166
culture, technopolistic   178
Cymone, André   37, 40, 132

'dandyfied urban cowboy'   37
dandyism   46–50, 52, 53 n.4
  Black   48
  duelling approaches to   52
  evolution of   49
  legacy of   53
  modern   46
'Darling Nikki' (Prince)   140
d'Aurevilly, Barbey   48
Dave Clark Five, The   9
Davis, Angela   118
Day For Night (Truffaut)   21
Day, Morris   13, 15, 16, 25, 52, 130
Dean, Michael   18–19
Deleuze, Gilles   142, 143, 145
Deleuzian theory   143
Deleuzo-Guattarian idiom   146
Denver Sound   59
Departed, The (Scorsese)   21
Dery, Mark   176
desiring-machines   143
Desperately Seeking Susan (Seidelman),   10
Dessau, Bruce   22
Detroit Techno   59
Diamonds and Pearls (Prince)   36
Dickerson, Dez   1, 36–8, 40, 62, 79, 141
Dirty Mind (Prince)   9, 34, 35, 37, 40, 57, 70, 72, 78, 162, 170, 198, 199, 205

Dirty Mind era   39, 51, 200
disagreement   17, 189
discrimination   50, 189, 191
  housing   186
  law banned   152
  non-discrimination   50, 151–2
  racial   91, 188, 189
  transportation   176–7
Dixon, Willie   87
Doyle, Sean   21
Du Bois's theory   164
Dune   21
Dunham, Cora Coleman   167
Dylan, Bob   10, 107

Eggins, Suzanne   202
Electra, Carmen   133, 134
Electric Ladyland (Hendrix)   93
Electric Mud (Hendrix)   91
Ellington, Duke   23
Ellington, Mercer   86
Ellison, Joy   50, 51
Ellison, Ralph   88
emotional response   204
Essence Awards   178
Essence Music Festival   26
Essex, David   10
Exodus (Preminger)   21

Faenza, Roberto   10
'Faith' and 'I Want Your Sex' (Michael), 73–4
Faithful, Marianne   10
'fancy lesbian' style   153
Farrakhan, Louis   171
Fassbinder, Rainer Werner   21
Fear of Missing Out (FOMO)   181
Feinberg, Leslie   155
Felder, Don   77
feminism, misogyny and   131–5
Fink, Matt   21, 37, 38
Fire Within, The (Malle)   21
'5 Women' (Prince)   84, 92
Foil, David   24
FOMO, *see* Fear of Missing Out (FOMO)
For You LP (Prince)   77
France, Marie   40

Index

Francis L. 12
Freedia, Big 155
'Free Urself' 164
French Riviera 18
Freud's theory 132
Fuchs, Cynthia J. 146 n.1

Gadenne 163
Gallen, Joel 80, 81
Gangs of New York (Scorsese) 21
Garcia, Mayte 41, 53, 133, 134
Gardner, Emma 140
Garelick, Rhonda 53 n.2
Garfunkel, Art 10
Garner, Eric 194
Gates, Bill 162
Gay and Lesbian Alliance against Defamation (GLAAD) 121
gay community 153
Gaye, Marvin 142
gender
  expression 117–18, 156
  and sexuality 121
Gender Education Center 152
'Genderfuck' (Reich) 146 n.1
Generation Z 121–5
'Gett Off' 137
Girl 6 (Lee) 11
Girl on a Motorcycle, The (Cardiff) 10
GLAAD, *see* Gay and Lesbian Alliance against Defamation (GLAAD)
Glick, Elisa 48
Goble, Blake 22
Godard, Jean-Luc 9
Goldstein, Patrick 18
Goodchild, P. 143
Goodfellas (Scorsese) 21
Got to Be Something Here: The Rise of the Minneapolis Sound (Swensson) 49
Grace, Laura Jane 155
Graduate, The 21
Graffiti Bridge (Prince) 4, 11, 13, 17, 27, 36
Graham, Larry 178
Granley, Chris 81, 82
Grantis, Donna 80

Grateful Dead band 58
Great Depression 47
Green, Al 142
Green, Kai 150
Gregory, Dick 170
Griffin-Gracie 155
Guardian, The 139
Guattari, Felix 142, 143, 145
Guitar Player 80
Guitar World 76, 82
Gumbel, Bryant 26
Guy, Buddy 88

Halliday, Michael 202
Hall, Stuart 200
Hall, Terryn 139
Harder They Come, The (Henzell) 11
Hardy 25
Harlem Renaissance 48
Harrison, George 47, 80
Harry, Deborah 10
Hawkins, Roy 91
Hawkins, Stan 48, 70, 142
Hayes, Morris 176
Haze, Angel 122–3
Head (Rafelson) 9
Headrick, George 25
Hear My Train A-Comin (Hendrix) 84
Hebdige, Dick 47
hegemonic masculinity 4
Heilbrun, Carolyn 36
Henders, Doug 71
Hendrix, Jimi 39, 84, 91–6
Hensen, Kristin D. 104, 105
Hicks, Dylan 60, 61
hip hop music 130
Hitchcockian phallic symbol 95
HITnRUN Phase Two (Prince) 170
Hoberman, J. 19, 20, 22–5
Hoffs, Susanna 134
Holland, Nancy J. 4, 68, 90, 134
'Holy River, The' (*Emancipation*) (Prince) 142
House, Son 89, 90
Howe, Michael 3
How Minneapolis Made Prince (Hicks) 60

Hughes, Langston   88
'Human Body, The' (*Emancipation*)
    (Prince)   141
human identity   50
Human Rights Campaign   124
human sexual response cycle   143, 146
humility   170
humour   138, 141, 144
    forms of   137
Hüsker Dü   61
Husney, Owen   39
Hutchence, Michael   10
hyper-masculinity   130
hypersexual buck   89

Ice Cube   11, 25
identity
    biracial   188, 189
    monoracial   188
    multiracial   188–9
    racial   5, 16, 165, 176, 184–9
'If I Had a Harem'   86–8
'If I Was Your Girlfriend'   140
'International Lover'   137, 144–6
Irvin, Kate   46
'I Wanna Be Your Lover'   36, 78, 198
'I Would Die 4 U'   149

Jackson, Michael   142, 187
'Jack U Off'   141
Jagger, Mick   10–11
James, Rick   120
Janzen, Sullivan   106
jazz musicians   12
Jefferson Airplane band   58
Jelks, Vaughn Terry   40
Jenkins, Andrea   149
Jensen, Joli   111
Jobs, Steve   162
Joe, Cousin   88
Johansson, Ola   58
Johnson, Kirk   176
Johnson, Mark   200
Johnson, Marsha P.   155
Johnson, Robert   89, 90
Johnson, Virginia E.   143
Johnston, Becky   13, 25
Jones, Grace   10

Jones, Jill   16, 19, 21, 27, 79, 133
Jones, Robert J.   105
Jones, Van   170
Journal of Popular Culture (Plasse)   17
Juice (Dickerson)   11

Kalogerakis, George   45
Karlen, Neal   16, 17, 28
keyboard rhythm   78
Keys, Alicia   163
Kid's wardrobe   40
Kid, The   15, 16, 27
    in *Purple Rain* (Prince)   90
Kimbra   170
King, B. B.   84, 91
King, Marva   176
Kodak Ektachrome film   73
Kotero, Apollonia   135
Kövecses, Zoltán   200
Krantz, Nate   108, 109
Kravitz, Lenny   163
Kreps, Daniel   82
Krull   21

La Bohème (Puccini)   46
Lacey, Rubin   90
'Lady Cab Driver' (Prince)   79
Lakoff, George   200
Lambert, Mary   19
Land of 10,000 Loves: A History of Queer Minnesota (Van Cleve)   50
Lange, Greg   107
Lang, Stacia   53 n.1
language transforms   117
Last Temptation of Christ, The (Scorsese)   21
Laurel   25
law
    civil rights   186
    contract   190
    rule   192
leader
    servant   170–1
    soulful   168–70
    thought   166–7
    transformational   167–8

leadership and Prince   162–3
Ledbetter, Huddie   90
Leeds, Alan   2, 74
Leeds, Eric   21
Lee, Spike   11
Lenz, Stephanie   179
lesbian community   153
'Let's Go Crazy'   12, 93
Let's Pretend We're Married (Gowers)   40, 141
Lewis, Jerry   25
literary arts event   106
Live at the Regal (King)   92
Loft Literary Center   106
Lomax, John   90
Lorde, Audre   119, 206
Los Angeles Times   18
Love4OneAnother   163, 175
Lovesexy (Prince)   34, 38, 67, 120, 142
    and postmodernism   69–74
Love Symbol (Prince)   36
Low   11
Luther King, Martin, Jr.   162
Lydon, John   10
Lynne, Jeff   80
Lynskey, Dorian   45
Lyotard, Jean-Francois   68

McCraney, Tarell Alvin   126
McDonald, CeCe   155
McGrath, Judy   41
McInnis, Jr.   164, 168
McLuhan, Marshall   181
McMillan, Londell   192
Madonna   10, 11
'Madonna-whore complex'   132
Magnoli, Albert   12, 16, 52
Mahmoud, Eric   171
Malcolm X   162, 192
Malle, Louis   21
Mandela, Nelson   162
Mandingo   96 n.2
Manning, Chelsea   155
Mann, Mark   80
Man Who Fell to Earth, The (Bowie)   10, 11
Marchese, Angela   42

Marchese, Angie   108
Mars, Bruno   27
Martin, Dean   25
Marxism   68
masculinity   118, 119
    Black   130, 139, 161
    hegemonic   4
    hyper-masculinity   130
    'peacock strutting'   137
    and self-parody   144
Masters, William   143
master tapes   190, 194
Melvoin, Susannah   21, 25, 133
Melvoin, Wendy   16, 21, 28, 152, 153
Memphis Sound   56, 59
Mendelsohn, John   41
Mercury, Freddy   138
metaphor
    conceptual   200–2
    orientational   201
metaphor identification process (MIP)   201
Michael, George, 73
Mickey One (Penn)   21
microchip   177
Miller, Janice   38
Minneapolis
    2016 May Day parade   106
    visiting   110
Minneapolis Sound   57–9, 61–3, 79, 93, 178
Minneapolis Star Tribune   24, 37, 126
Minnesota
    artists on Prince   105–7
    Prince from   107
    professional sports teams   109
Minnesotan, Prince as   108–9
MIP, *see* metaphor identification process (MIP)
misogyny, and feminism   131–5
Mock, Janet   150, 155
modern dandyism   46
modernism   68
Mod Squad   17
Moers, Ellen   46, 47
Monáe, Janelle   122
Mondino, Jean-Baptiste   21, 71, 73

monoracial identity 188
Moonlight 125
Morris Day of the Time 12
Morrison, Toni 88
Mosaic 163
Most Beautiful: My Life with Prince, The
    (Garcia) 53, 133
mourning, methodologically 102–3
'Movie Star' 25
Mpls St Paul 111
MTV's Video Music Awards 137
multiracial identity 188–9
Murger, Henry 46
Murphy, Charlie 45
Murray, Charles Shaar 94
musical ensemble technique 96 n.3
music Black artists 163

name change 191–3
Nashville Sound 59, 63
Neal, Mark Anthony 150, 165, 187
Ned Kelly (Richardson) 10–11
Nelson, Jimmy 77
Nelson, John L. 12, 15, 17, 23–4, 35, 76, 131
Nelson, Rogers 9, 42, 76, 102, 129, 137
New Orleans Jazz 56, 59
New Power Generation (NPG) 3
    band 176
New Romanticism 51
Niblock, Sarah 48, 70
1999 (Prince) 38, 71
Noblick, Sarah 142
'Nothing Compares 2 U' 133
NPG, *see* New Power Generation (NPG)

Obama, Barack 5
Ocean, Frank 122, 130
Octopussy 21
Of Dandyism and of George Brummell
    (D'Aurevilly) 46
Ohmes, Jeremy 61
Oldham, Will 10
Olson Memorial Highway 49
O'Neal, Cassandra 167
One Night Alone (Prince) 180

optimistic faith in the triumph of justice in
    the form of karma, An 88
Order of Death (Faenza) 10
orientational metaphors 201
Ortegón, Tammy 105, 106

Painter of Modern Life, The
    (Baudelaire) 46
Palm Desert Sound 58
Palmer, Robert 186
Parade (Prince) 72
Parents, Families and Friends of Lesbians
    and Gays (PFLAG) 129–30
Parker, Charlie 86
Parke, Steve 73
'Partyup' 199–201, 203, 205, 206
    in 'Uptown' 199–200
Pat Garrett and Billy the Kid
    (Peckinpah) 10
Patton, Charlie 89
Peacock Revolution 36
'peacock strutting' masculinity 137
Peckinpah, Sam 10
Penn, Arthur 21
Performance (Cammell and Roeg) 10
Persons of Color as a Percent of Total
    Population 60
Peterson, Paul 25
Petit, Chris 10
Petty, Tom 80
PFLAG, *see* Parents, Families and Friends
    of Lesbians and Gays (PFLAG)
Philadelphia Daily News 19
Philadelphia Soul 59
'Pilot Prince' 144–6
pluralism 68
political consciousness 200
polyrhythmic drums 78
'pop dandy' 45
'Pope' 171
Pop, Iggy 10
popular culture
    African Americans in 200
    Prince's impact on 34
Postman, Neil 177
postmodernism 67–9
    Lovesexy (Prince) and 69–74

postmodernity   89–91
post-racial icon, prince as   186–7
Pound, Ezra   68
Powell, Aubrey   72
Power of Soul: A Tribute to Jimi Hendrix   95
Prazzlejaz Group   201
Preminger, Otto   21
Presley, Elvis   9
Prince
  album   1, 3
  artistic boldness   2
  boundary-breaking self-expression   121
  career   1
  choreography   5
  and critical scholarship about race   185–6
  cultural impact of   34
  culture   1–2
  death   1, 3
  evolution   3
  fans   1
  history   151–6
  impact on the global cultural landscape   2
  leadership and   162–3
  life and legacy   1
  from Minnesota   107
  Minnesota Artists on   105–7
  as Minnesotan   108–9
  performance and costuming   4–5
  as post-racial icon   186–7
Prince (1977)   36
Prince (1979)   70, 72, 78
Prince and Warner Bros, contract between   189–90
'Prince as Queer Poststructuralist' (Walser)   138
Prince: The Man and His Music (Thorne)   24
prodigy   76
psychedelic rock   58
psychoanalysis   142, 143
Purcell, Steve   26
Purple House (Prince)   84, 95–6

Purple Rain (Prince)   2, 4, 9–12, 15–17, 20, 27, 29, 34, 40, 51, 62, 79, 110, 119, 152, 187
  'The Kid' in   90
Purple rain coats   40–2
Purple Rain Deluxe Edition (Prince)   3
Purple Reign conference   1
Purple Snow   60
'Pussy Control' (*The Gold Experience*)   138

Queen Latifah   11
queerness, in Black American community   129–31
Question of U, The (Prince)   84
Quicksilver Messenger Service band   58

race; *see also* racism
  analysis, critical   186
  conscious and strategic representations of   186–94
  Prince and critical scholarship about   185–6
  transcending   155, 185
  in Warner Bros dispute   189–94
racial context   164–6
racial definitions, in United States   188–9
racial discrimination   91, 188, 189
racial identity   5, 16, 165, 176, 184–9
racism   11, 60, 164; *see also* race
  imposition of   165
  lethal combination of   124
  reality of   187
  systemic   165
Radio On   10
Rainbow Children, The (Prince)   178, 193
Rainey, Ma   85
'Rally 4 Peace'   92
Ramone, Johnny   76, 82
'Raspberry Beret'   27, 47, 165
'Rated P 4 Funky' (Ortegón)   105
R&B-Funk-Rock sound   162
R&B music   130
Reagan era   139–40
Reagan, Ronald   5
record contracts, as slavery   190–1
recording industry, contract negotiations in   190

Redding, Noel 95
Red House (Hendrix) 84, 95–6
Reich, June 146 n.1
Revolution, The 1, 3, 12, 16, 28, 51, 52, 79
Rhode Island School of Design exhibition 46
Richard, Cliff 9
Richard, Little 35, 36, 48, 120
Rising Star: Dandyism, Gender, and Performance in the Fin de Siècle (Garelick) 53 n.2
Ritchie, Casci 51
Rivera, Sylvia 155
Robbins, Ronnie 25
Rock n Roll Hall of Fame (Prince) 162
Rodgers, Nile 92
Roeg, Nicolas 10
Rogers, Susan 25
Rolling Stone 16, 17, 28, 82, 132, 192
Roma culture 46
romantic discourse 146
Romantic dressing 38
Rose, Cynthia 11
Rosemary's Baby 21
Rothkopf, Joshua 78, 82
Royal, Robin Power 152
Royster, Francesca, Dr. 51, 150
Rushin, Steve 111

Sabathani Community Center 105
Safford, Wally 21
Salewicz, Chris 40
Sallet, Emmanuelle 28
San Francisco Sound 56, 58, 63
Santana 35
'Satisfied' (*3121*)(Prince)2006) 141
Satriani, Joe 80
Saturday Night Live 199
Scenes of Bohemian Life (Murger) 46
Scorsese, Martin 21
Scott, Mike 176'Seduction 747' 144
self-aggrandizement 141, 144
self-determination 94, 117, 125, 163, 164, 169, 198
self-expression 36, 117, 119, 121, 123, 125
  Prince's boundary-breaking 121

self-parody, masculinity and 144
sensationalism, visual 39
servant leader 170–1
Set It Off (Gray) 11
sex and spirituality 162
'Sexuality' 161–3
sexuality, gender and 121
sexual response mechanism 146
SFL, *see* systemic functional linguistics (SFL)
Sgt. Pepper 74 n.1
Sgt. Pepper's Lonely Hearts Club Band 71
Shabazz, Rashad 49
Shaft (Parks) 92
Shakur, Tupac 11
Sharon, Mary 21, 23, 24
Shaw, Mattie 17, 76, 131
Sheila E. 133, 134
Sights, Sounds, Soul: The Twin Cities through the Lens of Charles Chamblis (Davu) 49
Sign o' the Times (Prince) 13, 17, 67, 69, 74, 88, 131, 170
Simonton, Dean Keith 168, 171
Sims, Josh 39
Sinatra, Frank 9
Sister Outsider (Lorde), 206
Sites of Popular Music Heritage (Cohen) 103
Slade in Flame (Richard Loncraine) 9
Slaughterhouse, The (Prince) 180
small-scale events 103–4
Smiley, Tavis 170
Smith, Bessie 85
Smith, Chazz 35
Smith, Mamie 85
Smith, Rhonda 176
Snorton, C. Riley 150–1
Sobczynski, Peter 13, 20
social realities 177
societal oppression 203
sociocultural criticism 162
'Soft and Wet' 198
soulful leader 168–70
soulful leadership, Chopra's model/theory of 169

Sounding Like a No-No: Queer Sounds and Eccentric Acts in a Post Soul Era (Royster)   149–50
Spice Girls, The   9
Spigel, Lynn   176
spirituality, sex and   162
'Spooky Electric' (the Devil)   69
Stamp, Terence   21
Stanley, Eric   155
Stardust (Apted)   10
Star Spangled Banner, The (Hendrix)   94
Star Tribune   17
Station to Station (Bowie)   11
Stewart, Alexandra   21
Stiffelman, Gary   167
Strickler, Jeff   18, 24
stylization of process   88, 90
Subculture: The Meaning of Style (Hebdige)   47
Sub Pop   58
Superman   21
Superman II   21
Swanson, Jackie   27
Swensson, Andrea   49
Sylbert, Richard   21
systemic functional linguistics (SFL)   200, 202–3
systemic racism   165
Szasz, Thomas   164
Szymczyk, Bill   91

'TAFKAP'   192
Taylor, James   10
T-Bone Walker-style melodic phrase   87
Teaching to Transgress: Education as the Practice of Freedom (Hooks)   118
technopolistic culture   178
'Temptation' (*Emancipation*) (Prince)   142
Testolini, Manuela   134
That'll Be the Day (Whatham)   10
'Thrill Is Gone, The' (King)   92
Thomas, Kristen Scott   18
Thompson, Erica   152
Thorgerson, Storm   72
Thorne, Matt   24
thought leader   166–7

Thrasher, Steven W.   139
3 Nites in Miami Glam Slam 94 (Prince)   95
Thrill Is Gone, The (King)   80, 91
Timberlake, Justin   10
Titon, Jeff Todd   91
Tracy, Christopher   18, 22–9
transcending race   155, 185
transformational leader   167–8
transgender   149
  ambiguity of   155
  community   51, 149, 150, 152
  people   150–3
  symbol   155
  women of colour   151
trans history   151–6
transhumanism   177, 180
Treatise on Elegant Living (Balzac)   46
trench coat, revolutionizing   39–40
'Tricky'   18, 23–8, 153
Trio, Rogers   23, 131
Truffaut, François   21
Trump administration   5
truths about leadership   163
Truth, The (Prince)   84
Tucker, Chris   25
Twin Cities Funk & Soul   60
Two-Lane Blacktop (Hellman)   10

'undecidedly intellectual sex'   48
Under the Cherry Moon (Prince)   4, 11, 13, 15, 17, 18, 21, 22, 24–9, 71, 153
United States, racial definitions in   188–9
Universal Music Group   179
'Uptown'   164, 205, 206
  'Partyup' in   199–200
Uptown   175
urban Blaxploitation films   92
Urban Research and Outreach-Engagement Center (UROC) partners   105

Vai, Steve   80
'values drive commitment'   163
Van Cleve, Stewart   50

Vanity 6 62
Vats, Anjali 154
Vaughan, Stevie Ray 88
Vert, Lil Uzi 131
Very Best of Prince, The (Prince) 2
Vidovic, Ana 82
visual sensationalism 39
Vogue (Kalogerakis) 45

Waits, Tom 10
Walser, Robert 138
Walsh, Joe 77
Warner Bros 184, 193
    dispute, race in 189–94
Waronker, Lenny 16
'War, The' (Prince) 175–81
Waters, John 21
Waters, Muddy 84, 87, 89, 92
Weaver, Miko 21
Webby Awards (2006) 207
Wells, Louis 40
West, Cornell 170
Whatham, Claude 10

When Doves Cry (Prince) 11, 12
White Album, The 71
Who's Afraid of Virginia Woolf? 21
Williams III, Clarence 12, 17
Williams, James Gordon 164
Williamson, Lori 108
Wilmington, Michael 19, 21
Wilson, Dennis 10
Winwood, Steve 80
Womack, Ytasha 176, 177

Xpectation (Prince) 180

Ya Salaam, Kalamu 88
Young, M.A 131
Young, Neil 82
Young, Vershawn Dr. 130
Your Average Nigga: Performing Race, Literacy and Masculinity (Young) 130

Zacharek, Stephanie 15
Zannalee (Prince) 84, 89, 107

www.ingramcontent.com/pod-product-compliance
Lightning Source LLC
Chambersburg PA
CBHW072232290426
44111CB00012B/2058